Other Septembers, Many

Other Septembers, Many Americas

Selected Provocations

1980–2004

ARIEL DORFMAN

SEVEN STORIES PRESS

New York • London • Toronto • Melbourne

Seven Stories Press
140 Watts Street
New York, NY 10013
www.sevenstories.com

IN CANADA
Publishers Group Canada, 250A Carlton Street, Toronto, ON M5A 2L1

IN AUSTRALIA
Palgrave Macmillan, 627 Chapel Street, South Yarra VIC 3141

LIBRARY OF CONGRESS CATALOGING-IN-PUBLICATION DATA
Dorfman, Ariel.
  Other Septembers, many Americas : selected provocations,
  1980–2004 / Ariel Dorfman.— A Seven Stories Press 1st ed.
    p. cm.
  Includes index.
  ISBN 1-58322-632-X (pbk. : alk. paper)
  I. Title.
PQ8098.14.O7A6 2004
864'.64—dc22
                    2004007935

College professors may order examination copies of
Seven Stories Press titles for a free six-month trial period.
To order, visit www.sevenstories.com/textbook/
or fax on school letterhead to 212.226.1411.

Book design by India Amos

Printed in Canada

9 8 7 6 5 4 3 2 1

Contents

Foreword

At Home Among the Cyclops

He was an E. T. who couldn't go home. And yet when he swept into our offices in the spring of 1980, pushing his younger son in a stroller, tall and exuberant, with a booming voice that embraced you, not just you but the editor in the neighboring office and her colleague next door and the assistant down the hall and the copyeditor in the far office, and when, despite the busyness of the work day, he had somehow gathered us all in the office of yet another colleague and was telling us stories about how the world worked and why Babar the elephant was a neocolonialist and the Lone Ranger was never alone, this exile via Paris from Augusto Pinochet's Chile, born in Argentina, schooled in New York before his diplomat father was ejected from a U.S. gripped by McCarthyite fervor, looked for all the world at home. He looked more relaxed, more at home than any of us. He looked like he owned us all.

In the years to come, he would finally return to a democratic Chile, travel from Japan to England as his works were read and his plays staged, and settle in Durham, North Carolina, where he teaches at Duke University; he would write cultural criticism, political essays, op-ed pieces, plays, poetry, screenplays, children's books, and novels. He would write alone and with his

TOM ENGELHARDT is consulting editor for Metropolitan Books, co-editor of Metropolitan's American Empire Project, creator of the Nation Institute's Tomdispatch weblog (www.tomdispatch.com), and author of a novel, *The Last Days of Publishing*, and a history of the Cold War, *The End of Victory Culture*. He was formerly an editor at Pantheon Books.

sons. He would write again and again about torture, the over-throw of governments, U.S. foreign policy, and especially about the disappeared—the subject of his second novel, *Widows*, about those who were disappeared first and foremost in his own country, Chile, under the Pinochet onslaught, and later by the thousands in Argentina, Ethiopia, Iraq, Rwanda, and in other places around the world—and he would write about those who were disappeared in harder-to-describe ways, those who were disappeared, for instance, by never making it into our worldview at all here in bunkered North America.

Ariel's deepest subject is certainly what we miss and what goes missing in our world. It's a subject that life prepared for him as he prepared for it, unknowingly, in Santiago (where, as he tells us in one of his essays, he once took to the streets with other Chilean demonstrators, crying out, "It can't happen here!"). After the terror of postcoup Chile and years of flight, resistance, and exile, he came to the country whose government had been so intent on overthrowing his, the country he had lived in as a boy and again briefly after college, arriving this time as a messenger from another planet. His job, it seemed—and you can see this in many of the essays that follow—was to remind us amnesiacs of the memories we don't seem to have, the memories we refuse to entertain.

For we "Americans" (who immediately sweep so many other Americans from sight just by appropriating that term), Ariel is like another eye. Of course, we have no idea that we are a Cyclops of nations. But a warning: Be careful as you plunge into these essays; as with new prescription glasses, you can find yourself a bit unsteady as you adjust to focusing both eyes at once.

In the months after the September 11th assaults on New York and Washington, one of the strangest spectacles (for me at least) was the way in which we appropriated all the roles on the global stage—greatest victim, greatest survivor, greatest dominator—leaving to the rest of humanity but a single role, that of Evil One. Though September 11th might have opened us to much of the horror and suffering that the rest of the world considers the terrible norm, for months our rites—whether in the White House, Washington's National Cathedral, or sports stadiums and arenas around the country—were intent on reaffirming our aloneness in suffering, in power, in the world. Even allies, as the Bush administration soon made clear, were largely unwelcome visitors to our shores.

With gentleness, grace, and firmness, Ariel Dorfman reminds us in this book, as he did in the months after the attacks, that ours was the second September 11th, not the first, and in many ways not—terrible as it was—the worst. On September 11, 2001, the planes in the skies over Washington and New York were commandeered by Islamist terrorists intent on destroying three symbols (financial, political, and military) of our global power, no matter who died in the process. (Let's skip the fact here that, once upon a time and in the context of a war against the Soviets in Afghanistan, our CIA had been all too happy to arm and support the very jihadists who would plan these assaults.)

On September 11, 1973, the terrorizing planes in the skies over Santiago about to attack the presidential palace, though manned by Chilean pilots, were backed by American power. This reflected the desire of President Richard Nixon and National Security Adviser Henry Kissinger (whose face now looks like a Greek tragedy mask even though the tragedies he caused were all suffered by others), to crush an elected government in Latin America that called itself socialist.

The world, of course, gains depth and dimensionality when there are two images of the same thing—as with those old stereopticon shows that used two projectors. Double vision. September 11th, September 11th. Two of them and Ariel Dorfman saw them both, while we managed to ignore the first and want no competitors, nor any history, to go with the second. The casualties from the Chilean September 11th, from the military coup that overthrew Salvador Allende and plunged Chile into dictatorship, occurred not in a few split seconds of horror but over years in which Chileans, one by one, were disappeared by Pinochet's regime, but the toll was no less horrifying for that.

Moving from the global to the personal, let me offer a little story about Ariel's vision of our world and how it should work. In 1980, when he first came to visit me, I was an editor at Pantheon Books and knew his name only because it sat next to that of a man named Armand Mattelart in an account—both Marxist and amusing—the two had written for the Allende government on the impact of

Disney comics in the Third World (*How to Read Donald Duck*). When he launched into his critique of Babar, the French elephant whose adventures were chronicled by Jean de Brunhoff, I was particularly interested because de Brunhoff's books had been icons of my childhood. Ariel described vividly the way de Brunhoff in children's picture books had tortured history into the shape of a colonial tale that fit well with the French imperial *mission civilatrice*. He was dazzling and convincing. And yet, as I listened, I felt a certain sadness. Who, after all, could look at de Brunhoff's monkey village with its shops and restaurants hanging like little submarines from the trees, or the mermaids who inhabited his offshore islands, or those vast painted elephant butts, which unforgettably sent a whole army of terrified Rhinos into flight, without mourning the fact that these might now be exiled from the child's world?

Finally, I asked hesitantly, "So what do you do with your sons and Babar?" He looked at me with astonishment—because Ariel is a bit larger than life, he did a genuine double take—and then responded, as if this were the only conceivable answer in our world or any other, "I read Babar to them."

Believe me, you recognize sanity when it stares you in the face; you recognize the kind of impurity that makes a decent world possible, that makes life worth the bother, that makes Ariel a writer filled with surprises, that makes collected essays—including those that redefine Latin American culture in light of his North American experience and those that explore the artistic imagination as a special form of hope—an adventure for any reader, and that made me decide during that first meeting to publish his work sight unseen, including his essay on Babar.

This book reprints a wonderful essay, written two decades ago, about the movie *E. T.* and its strange novelization by William Kotzwinkle. It's an appreciation of the charm of the Steven Spielberg film that nonetheless reveals the distinct limits of how alien any alien we welcome to our shores could possibly be: A lone extraterrestrial of unfathomable age and wisdom lands in California, visibly a close relative of Yoda, a cousin to Miss Piggy, ugly, alone, despite his considerable intellectual capacities incapable to the end of speaking anything but broken English, "more like a small savage from the third world or the backlands than a Milky Way wizard," a childlike creature who might indeed be "enticed out of the foliage by a string of Reese's Pieces, almost as if he were a famished waif in an Asian or African alley." This is a description that only an E. T. in our culture could provide. The movie, Ariel tells us, is an assimilationist masterpiece about an alien capable of hiding in plain sight in a suburban closet filled with various commercial dolls. But Ariel wonders, "Does every stranger have to first be infantilized and Americanized in order to gain acceptance [here]?" It's a question that seems, if anything, even more pertinent now in our new age of gated communities, closed-down borders, Patriot Acts, and Homeland Security. It's the sort of question only an Ariel Dorfman could raise.

Read these essays, poems, and commentaries. What you'll discover, I suspect, is that *we* are the extraterrestrials, and that it was our good luck that Ariel Dorfman never went home.

Tom Engelhardt
March 2004

By Way of Introduction

In August of 1980, accompanied by a growing family and forty-seven peripatetic boxes of books, I arrived in the United States after seven years of European exile. I had the firm intention of rapidly departing a year later for Mexico: my wife, Angélica, and I wanted our two sons to grow up speaking the Spanish that was their heritage, one of the few legacies from our scorched Chilean homeland that had survived our wanderings. We would wait out there, we thought, the rest of our banishment, using our *séjour* South of the Border as a first step back to the Chile that someday would surely be able to rid itself of Pinochet.

That plan fell through when the Mexican government of López Portillo decided, in 1981, not to grant me a visa.

My relationship with the gringo country where I was stranded—no exaggeration, we really had no other place to go—was not exactly an ordinary one. This was the land that had received me when I was a child of two and a half fleeing the Argentine military, that had given me the language in which I write this introduction, and given me as well the smuggled wonders of its literature, this was the America that had tendered my first movies, my first comics, my first radio shows, my first seductive encounter with the popular culture that was on the brink of conquering the world. The America of my pals on the corner and my baseball glove and my candy bars. And, someday, jazz and Fitzgerald and Emily Dickinson.

But also the America that had persecuted my father in the early fifties and forced us to leave the United States for Chile. The same America that would, furthermore, many years later (after I had become a Chilean citizen and returned to the Spanish of my birth and to the struggle for liberation that had marked the history of Latin America), be instrumental in destroying democracy in my adopted homeland, helping to overthrow the Allende government in 1973 and bolstering the dictatorship that kept me homeless and adrift, and my countrymen shadowed by death and destruction. The America that had during most of my life monstrously intervened on the side of tyranny and misery in so many other sorry lands.

I did not have much time, however, to dwell upon this contradiction between the country I had loved as a child and the imperial America that demolished democracy elsewhere even while it guarded that democracy so carefully for its own citizens. Instead, I turned that contradiction—and so many others—into a source of creative tension. I was being offered a chance, even if I had not sought it, to see this democratic Empire up close, to watch it with my now Chilean eyes, to burrow into the English language I had made my own as a child from a perspective and vocabulary and field of feeling that I had perfected during my Latin American adulthood.

A chance, I gradually realized, to be a bridge between continents, cultures, languages. And a bridge that could only explain the two antagonistic shores coupled together through hate and love by looking at its own self, by asking myself what separated me from this America that was once again mine to inhabit. A stranger here and yet a native, I was perfectly positioned to be of service or to go mad.

It took me a while, I must confess, to understand how much I still belonged to that society that was providing me with refuge from the storm, it took time before I allowed the old affection to emerge from underneath the renewed anger.

The United States was not doing much to help. By the time I arrived in this country, the part played by the American administration in the overthrow of Allende had been amply documented by journalists and by an official investigative committee headed by Senator Frank Church. From my European banishment, I had watched how the news of this scandalous intervention had, albeit briefly, occupied the front-page headlines, but my disembarkation in the United States coincided with the moment when the story was again fading from view. It is a sobering experience to watch the history of one's country erased. And of course, along with my history, it was the history of the United States, the victimizer, that was being conveniently expunged: the same pattern of intervention, overthrow, and then oblivion, inflicted on elected governments across the globe, Guatemala and the Congo, Iran and Indonesia.

And Nicaragua. A few months after we came to the United States, Ronald Reagan was elected president. I watched with amazement how a contra war against the Sandinista government was waged in the name of freedom and democracy by Americans who seemed not to know that for more than a century their nation had done its utmost to destroy those very ideals in Nicaragua.

It seemed to me that this systematic forgetting of history was rooted in the deepest needs of the United States populace, their desire for innocence, their urge to suppress the messy, violent, bothersome version of what had been done in their name. That story, were it to be remembered, would violate the smooth surface of everyday life here. An ongoing process, because the past, as I knew and I saw, does not die easily. Some part of it keeps resurfacing, sticking out its tongue, refusing to behave, stepping out of the parentheses, dancing back into consciousness. Even in those margins of consciousness, they are there, the men and women whose lives and experiences cannot be totally obscured. And so, as if on a mission, armed with the English language the Americans themselves had so generously furnished me, I took it upon myself to present the sub-versions, the versions that lurk underneath, that refuse to be tamed, that keep demanding that we confront the pain of history, the pain of memory.

My exiled condition provided me with a perch from which to analyze my place of exile. Latin America was the source of my critical view of the United States, fed it, murmured its exasperation, kept me trenchant and often outraged, and made me an outsider. Latin America was also a place that my now distant eyes, my suddenly strange eyes, were forcing me to look at anew from a fresh perspective.

I could speak to the United States where I lived with the voice of a Latin American and to the Latin America that I inhabited only in my mind from the remoteness of living in North America.

It was this double life, of belonging and longing, that has stimulated, for almost a quarter of a century, the publication in both languages of a series of . . . what can I call them? Visions, I guess, though I prefer Provocations. Using my double homelessness to examine these two Americas where I was condemned to dwell, their demeanor and misdemeanors, their desires and frustrations, always attempting to connect what I saw to the problems of the wider world. And all the while searching for a home, a foundation, a stable border of my own, demanding of myself what role critical inquiry and storytelling can play in resolving the crises and cruelty of our times, interrogating the compassionate imagination for answers both aesthetic and political, wondering how hope and trust can persist, wanting to believe that there had to be alternatives to the way the world was organized, stubbornly predicting that the world could, indeed, would be different. Seen in retrospect, I was also probably working out for myself, in journalism, speeches and essays, many of the themes and obsessions that I was hunting down during this period in my fiction, poems and plays. Many of these pieces can therefore be read concurrently as windows onto my literary landscape and how it intersects with my moral and social concerns.

Had it not been for the events of September 11, 2001, these interventions of mine in the public arena might well have remained uncollected, floating in the vague vastness of newspaper archives and the limitless and intangible fields of cyberspace, one piece anthologized here, another reprinted there. But as I tried to make sense of that 2001 explosion in the heart of America, as I observed the reaction of its citizens to the pain and fear, as I started to measure the consequences that all of us on this planet would pay for that terror, I also felt that much of what I had insolently created in the previous twenty-one years (yes, that is how long I had been in the United States since that arrival in 1980) had taken on a new significance, and perhaps might be worth gathering in the more permanent form of a book.

It is too soon, I believe, to really understand what happened to America on September 11 and the days that followed, but I would tentatively venture that we Americans received that day the curse and the blessing of being able to look at ourselves in a way that had been denied to most of us our whole lives, of experiencing the terror and victimhood that so many other inhabitants of this scarred planet have had to wade through day after day since birth. Never before had Americans been asked to imagine themselves so deeply and distressingly a part of the rest of humanity. Never before had the future of the planet depended on how Americans met that challenge. Never before had they been faced with the unresolved dilemmas of their own past in such a dramatic fashion. Never before had they been ripped apart, to this degree, by the ravages of guilt and rage, the difficulties of memory and forgiveness, the uses and abuses of power, the true meaning of freedom and responsibility. And consequently, never were Americans more tempted to apply amnesia to their yesterdays and innocence to their tomorrows, and sweetly and malignantly rid themselves of the complexity and contradictions of their newly naked predicament.

Many of the dilemmas the men and women of the United States are facing are the very ones I have been struggling to understand for the last decades. Each one of these texts—including the most recent, which deal with the many traumatic aftermaths of the two September 11s, the one in Chile in 1973 and the one in New York in 2001—can be understood as an attempt to break down the barriers that separate Americans and foreigners, to employ the many Americas I carry inside to envision a different dialogue, another sort of relationship.

The world has recently become even more divided, even more dangerously divided, than when I first arrived in the United States in 1980 with my family and my books, my ghosts and my hopes. And the country that welcomed us has become even more powerful than before, struggling anew with the demons of its imperial ambitions and its democratic fears, trying to establish and maybe avoid with the rest of the world the sort of dominance it exercised over its Latin American neighbors for the last century and a half to our mutual detriment. No better time, therefore, to consider the intricate, almost intimate, questions of power and resistance I posed these last two decades. Perhaps my deliberations yesterday and today can contribute to the collective imagining we desperately and urgently need in these perilous times, if we are to find our way out of the blindness that threatens to engulf all the inhabitants of a planet that deserves something better.

PART ONE

I Have Been Through This Before

Globalizing Compassion

Photography and the Challenge of Terror

We have grown strangely used to them over the last twenty-five years, the women with the small photo of a man pinned to their dark dresses, the extended tribe of those whose loved ones, from Chile to Kurdistan, from Argentina to Ethiopia, from Guatemala to Guinea, have been abducted in the night and never heard of again. Mothers and daughters, wives and sisters, demanding to know the true fate of their men, demanding that they be returned to their families alive. They have become a habitual presence, these faraway women on the television screen asking at least for a body to bury, asking that they be allowed to start mourning their dead. A widespread, almost epidemic, image of tragedy and defiance that is just as much a part of our planetary imagination as the brands and logos that pervade us with an opposite sort of message: the Golden Arches of McDonalds, the red glistening cans of Coca-Cola, the Nike symbols of acceleration, the United Colors of Benetton that promise life everlasting through incessant consumption.

The misfortune of women who search for information about their missing husbands, sons, fathers, brothers, lovers, is as haplessly old as the wars and slaughterhouses with which we humans have disgraced ourselves throughout our history. What is specifically new about the iconic representation of woe which anyone who owns a television can now recognize and identify, is not the repression or

---

The present expanded version was delivered as the Amnesty Lecture at the Edinburgh Book Festival, August 2003, and published in the *Chronicle of Higher Education* (Washington, D.C.) the same month. An extract of this piece was published as "Dark Blizzard of Photos Connect Those Left Behind" in the *Los Angeles Times*, December 24, 2001.

the pain, but rather the form of spectacle that these demonstrations have taken, how the performance of that pain is only conceivable in the context of present-day globalization. Indeed, those marching women brandishing a black-and-white photo have become so natural to our eyes, so much a part of the mythical landscape of our time, that we tend to forget that there was a time, not very long ago, when photographs did not constitute an automatic ingredient of that sort of protest.

As far as I can tell the first time photos were displayed as a means of responding to the state terror that uses disappearance as a form of control and punishment was in June 1977 when a group of Chilean women whose relatives had been arrested by General Pinochet's secret police in the years after the 1973 coup decided to go on a hunger strike to force the military and judicial authorities to acknowledge those detentions. That they chose to do so in the regional offices of the United Nations in Santiago may have initially been due to the relative safety that an international organization provided under a dictatorship but, more crucially, suggests that their targeted audience was potentially the wide world beyond the country's frontiers rather than their own countrymen, most of whom had no way of being informed about even the existence of this rally. I am not sure if the organizers of that protest immediately realized how influential and far-reaching the image they had created was to become in their own struggle and they certainly could not have anticipated the ways in which it would be adopted by people with similar dilemmas all over the globe, from Cyprus to Mexico. What probably mattered most to them was that the exhibition of those photos fiercely expressed the core of their tragedy. The central drama of those women was, after all, that they had no body to oppose to the denial of responsibility by the authorities, no way of countering the refusal of the judges to accept writs of habeas corpus because, to put it bluntly, there was no corpus. No body. Dead or alive. The photo became a substitute for the body that the government officials contended had never been arrested, a way of bringing into visibility someone who was at that very moment being hidden from view, whose corpse, if indeed the detainee had been killed, was being denied the right to denounce the crime committed against it, the only vocabulary left to the dead. When the relatives showed bystanders that replica in celluloid, they were making present and material and lifelike what had been phantasmagorically removed from their hands, they were calling attention to a moment that had existed in the past when that loved one had been alive and a finger had clicked on a camera, they were demanding a moment in the future when that loved one could once again stand in front of them, could step out of the photo and into life, could climb out of their memory and into life. It was only in the months and years that followed, as the relatives took their protest into the streets, that they discovered that, beyond telling the essence of their predicament with extreme efficiency and extraordinary poetry, those stark semblances of the missing also answered the needs of the contemporary media, its time constraints, its hunger for visually striking imagery, its audiences with their short attention spans. And when the police attacked the women, jailed them, ripped the photos from their dresses or kicked the placards upon which the photos had been reproduced, these scenes were then also transmitted over and over again to the world. In the violence done to the relatives because they dared to remember and to bring their memories into communal spaces, the regime was being forced to publicly reenact the secret, covert outrage done to the original bodies in the dank privacy of jails and basements and concentration camps.

Making that violence globally visible was a particularly apt response to disappearance because that extreme form of repression originated, in fact, in a strategy of a dictatorship that had a global component from the start. The new rulers of Chile were determined to integrate their country into the worldwide market and join what they called the "civilized concert of nations." A membership that entailed two contradictory requirements. On the one hand, the need to terrorize a restless and recalcitrant populace into submission and make it economically and politically pliant for the experiment of what was, quite blatantly, called "shock therapy." This was coupled, on the other hand, with the need to present an immaculate face to the international community and therefore distance officials from any acts of barbarism. And disappearances fit this bill perfectly: dissidents and revolutionaries could be conveniently tortured to death without any of their executioners ever being held accountable; terror could reign in the whispers of the mind without the government having to openly admit to being the source of those whispers, of that terror.

It is this perverse tactic of invisibility that the bodies of the women and the photos pinned to their clothes fracture, that the photos of their resistance and repression further perturb and disrupt, a cycle of visual transgressions that were to grow amazingly into a worldwide movement. It is incredible, after all, that one small gesture by one solitary woman in a violated Chilean home, a woman who looks at the faded image of her absent loved one and comes to understand that its public exposure can keep him alive inside her and in the world, so encouraging that merely that one modest, unpretentious image can speak louder than all the machinery of the State, and can finally spread and extend its reach until it is imitated all over the world. The ferocity with which the masters of these many misdeveloped nations have dragged their societies, quite literally kicking and screaming, into modernity is answered by a denunciation of the consequences of that process of forced development, using none other than the central invention of modernity, photography, shrewdly appropriated by the victims. Two possibilities of globalization face to face: the high technology of systematic fear employed by tyrants, their scientific use of torture and censorship and propaganda and, of course, of spying through cameras, confronted by the cunning and defiance of multitudes of humiliated women with their low-tech performances, their snapshots of bodies that refuse to be silenced. The technology of dictators, which tries to turn the lives of their subjects into fictions, confronting the technology of the rebels, who use what is, after all, no more substantial and material than a replica, a trace on a piece of paper, a representation of existence, to shove denied reality back into the dictator's face. Two ways of using and abusing science: one that is secretive and affirms the right to exist only for those who have monopolized science's knowledge and chained that knowledge to destruction, and another, more democratic form of science that puts in the hands of people everywhere the means to re-create and multiply their own existence.

At a time in history when it is all too easy to feel defenseless and passive and irrelevant in the face of a global profiteering disorder that often seems to be beyond the control of even its most dominant elites, a planetary network that acts according to scarcely comprehensible laws, it is heartening to see how some of the least powerful people on this Earth can score a victory of the imagination against their enemies, can prove that it is possible for the modernity of human rights to defeat the modernity of inhuman authoritarianism. Indeed, I would venture to suggest that the relatives of the disappeared are handing us a model for how other humans can make use of the forces of globalization to make this world a less threatening home for us all.

And yet, a note of caution.

If you go through a little booklet published many years ago by the Association of Relatives of Arrested and Disappeared Persons in Chile, which lists and seeks to portray some of the peasants abducted by the authorities since 1973, you will notice, on the very first page, six names with respective spaces for their photos. Two of these spaces are blank—those meant for Antonio Aninao Morales and Juan Salinas Salinas. Of these two, not even a photograph remains. They are men who lived their twentieth-century lives without once being photographed. Let me repeat this: they were never captured by the process invented by Louis Daguerre more than a hundred years before their birth. It is only the kidnapping of Salinas and Aninao that, paradoxically, calls them at all to our attention among the millions who are too poor or marginalized to have been captured by a camera, who are outside the eyes of modernity. And if you continue to read the booklet, on each page there are several more unphotographed peasants, until the last page where all four of those named are without an image. That deep blankness ends up being the only visual evidence that they ever existed.

These are the true *desaparecidos* of humanity, those who are missing because, in reality, the modern world acts as if, all this while, they had never been there at all, members of orphaned countries that seem to flicker into public consciousness only when they cause trouble, when they upset strategic balances or unhinge the lives of those who watch from the comfort of detached television screens. They were missing before the police came for them. They came late to the distribution of words and techniques and knowledge and, yes, to the saving grace of photography itself, perhaps suspecting that they would merit neither a footnote in the pages of anybody's history book, nor even a few seconds on the nightly news.

I have spent many hours looking at those empty spaces, wondering how those men lived and how they died, who they were, what their eyes might have told me if I had ever met them. The truth is that I know nothing about them. All that I really receive back from that absence is my own reflection.

In the supermarket and superspectacle that our planet is slowly becoming, it is the unknown Salinases and Aninaos of the world who pose the ultimate challenge to globalization. It is one of the great tragedies of our time that we have been unable to organize a world where men like them and their billions of brothers and sisters from all the other continents are included and finally seen, really seen. Everyone on this Earth, I believe, is a member of a vastly interconnected humanity, and the recent terrible events of September 11, 2001, in the United States would seem to confirm that we ignore this fact at our peril.

How to imagine those who live outside the dominant forms of modernity? Is it even possible? Are we too far away to even represent those lost men, those muted women?

Strange as this may sound, I see a dreadful form of hope in the dark blizzard of photos that began to cover the streets of New York precisely after those criminal acts of terror that devastated that city in September 2001. It is an extraordinary recognition of our common humanity that the inhabitants of the most prosperous metropolis in the world, when faced with the infernal dilemma of dealing with the instantaneous and violent disappearance of friends and relatives whose death could be presumed but not ascertained because of the lack of a body, spontaneously recurred to the same methods of memory and defiance that thousands upon thousands of others from the most remote and often impoverished regions of the planet have invented over the last twenty-five years to cope with a similar mental hell.

I am aware, of course, of the distances and differences that separate the missing of New York and their relatives, friends, and community from those who are *desaparecidos* in the rest of the world and am wary of conflating these quite distinct tragedies. It is not their own government that has concealed the bodies incinerated in the Twin Towers or that has mocked those who seek information regarding their whereabouts. And the photos themselves probably originated in a long-standing American tradition that has proliferated images of lost children over the years on milk cartons and on other commercial and postal sites. And yet, the inhabitants of the most modernized society in the world may now be able to connect, in ways that would have been unthinkable before September 11, 2001, to the experience of so many hitherto inaccessible planetary others. How can they not understand, now that they know what it means to have thousands of people suddenly evaporate into nothingness with no body to prove or disprove life or death, how can they not feel closer to an old woman I know in Chile who still awakes after midnight, still awakes, even now, and listens for footsteps that could be her husband's, even though she knows that twenty-seven years have gone by and that it would be better that he not return, who would want him to be tortured for those long years? How can they not empathize more, now that they hold up their photos to search for a sliver of certainty, to find a final witness to their beloved's last moments, those words from some stranger, a message sent to us from the dead? How can their hearts not go out to the grandmothers in Argentina determined to track down the children of their sons and daughters born in captivity and farmed out to sterile military families, those grandmothers who want to see in the eyes of those babies now grown up the ultimate inheritance left behind by their dead offspring? As the operation in the smoldering ruins of the World Trade Center wearily turned from rescue to recovery, as the expectation of one more miracle gave way to the conviction that there can be no more survivors, how can they not have shared the grief of the families of the *desaparecidos* of other lands, when there is no more hope? If New Yorkers are discovering what the women of the missing in Chile and Cyprus and Cambodia and Brazzaville also gradually realized, that their flock of photographs shrouding the entire city are ultimately destined to become a transitory burial ground where the living and the dead can commune, a site of the collective mourning imagination, the only scattered monument immediately possible in the months to come for a city that needs to turn itself into an extended graveyard of its missing dead if it is to go on with life, how can these fundamental, radical experiences of death and vulnerability not open millions of Americans up to the meaning of disappearance in its multiple forms? How can the horror and wonder of breathing an air filled with the oxygen of the absent dead not help them and us to feel linked to the deep suffering and redemption of so many of our faraway kinsmen across the earth?

There is, of course, no guarantee that pain and victimhood lead to empathy, no certainty that this will allow the Salinases of the world to emerge from invisibility. Enormous sorrows can lead to self-absorption and indifference. Horror and pain can lead the powerful to vent upon the innocent in faraway lands their rage and frustration—just look at the campaign against Iraq!

But that is the challenge of the moment: to find ways to make this new global tragedy draw us all closer to each other, not because we can now kill one another more easily and with more devastating effects, but closer because we share the same need to mourn, the same flesh that can be torn, the same impulse toward compassion. And closer also to the day when the most powerful members of humankind can pin to our clothes that blank photo of the disappeared, that image of an emptiness and absence that threatens to devour us all. Yes, perhaps our species is oh so slowly getting ready for the day when enough of us will want to wander the boundaries of this Earth until we have brought the lost souls of modernity, like the other missing of the world, back from death and oblivion.

Love Letter to America

L et me tell you, America, of the hopes I had for you.
     As the smoke was swallowing Manhattan and the build-
ings fell and the terror spread into the farthest recesses of
your land and your hearts, my hopes for you, America.

While around the world many of the past victims of your own
terror, your own attacks, were thinking and often saying, saying
and more often thinking, they deserve it, serves them right, it's
about time they knew what it's like to be on the receiving end. Not
true, I thought, I said. Nobody deserves terror.

Justice. What we deserve, all of us, is some measure of justice.

My hopes for America: not that this was good for you. No, not
that. But I have seen suffering before, I have seen widows wandering remote streets with the photos of their loved ones asking if
anybody knows if they are alive or dead, I have watched men and
women and even countries turn their deepest sorrows into a source
of strength, a form of self-knowledge, a chance to grow.

A chance to grow, America, that was my hope.

Loss turned into maturity.

A chance to understand. Not alone, America, not alone in your
grief. A perpetual valley of terror, that is what most of humanity
is born into day after faraway day. Ignoring if tomorrow we will
once again be assaulted and bombed, humiliated and tormented.
America suddenly living what almost everyone else on this planet
has experienced at some point yesterday or today: the precarious
pit of everyday fear.

My hope for America: empathy, compassion, the capacity to
imagine that you are not unique. Yes, America, if this dreadful
destruction were only to teach you that your citizens and your

The Nation (New York), September 30, 2002.

dead are not the only ones who matter on this planet, if only this experience were to lead you to wage a resolute war on the multiple terrors that haunt our already murderous new century.

An awakening, America.

Not to be. What did not happen.

Your country, hijacked. Your panic, used to take you on a journey of violence from which it is hard to return, the men at the controls not worried about crashing America into the world.

But not just the fault of the men who misgovern you.

They can do only what you have allowed them, responding, those men, to some of your deepest desires.

Above all, this: to be innocent again, to feel good about yourselves, after Vietnam. Vietnam? That country you turned into a mass graveyard?

Innocence, handed back to you, America, on September 11, 2001. A terrible price to pay, but there it is. Those atrocities, that devastation, finally making you all into victims. No ifs, no buts, no listening to the naysayers, no patience for those who suggest you look at your own history, your own interventions across the globe, to understand why so many out there in the crazed world might detest you. No more self-doubt, America.

Beware the plague of victimhood, America.

The finger I point at you, pointed back at my own self. I know that thrill, I have sweetly sucked it in, I have felt the surge of self-righteousness that comes from being unfairly hurt. Anything we do, justified. Any criticism against us, dismissed.

Beware the plague of fear and rage, America.

Nothing more dangerous: a giant who is afraid. Projecting power and terror so the demons within and without will not devour him, so the traumas of the past will not repeat themselves.

Beware the plague of amnesia, America.

Or have you forgotten Chile? Not just a name. Chile? Democratic Chile? Demonized, destabilized by your government in 1973? Chile? That country misruled for seventeen years by a dictator you helped install?

And other countries, other names. Iran, Nicaragua, the Congo, Indonesia, South Africa, Laos, Guatemala. Just names? Just footnotes in history books, your creatures?

But I do not speak to you only from afar.

An insider.

How could I not wish you well? You gave me, an *americano* from the Latino South, this language of love that I return to you. You gave me the hot summer afternoons of my childhood in Queens when my starkest choice was whether to buy a popsicle from the Good Humor Man or from the fat driver of the Bungalow Bar truck. And then back to calculating Jackie Robinson's batting average. How could I not wish you well? You gave me refuge when I was barely a toddler, my family fleeing the fascist thugs in Argentina in the mid-forties. One of you then. Still one of you now. How could I not wish you well? Years later, again it was to America I came with my own family, an exile from the Chile of Pinochet you helped spawn into existence on precisely an 11th of September, another Tuesday of doom. And yet, still wishing you well, America: you offered me the freedom to speak out that I did not have in Santiago, you gave me the opportunity to write and teach, you gave me a *gringa* granddaughter. How could I not love the house she lives in?

Where is that America of mine? Where is that other America? Where is the America of *as I would not be a slave so would I not be a master*, the America of *this land is our land this land was meant for you and me*, the America of all men, and all women, every one of us on this ravaged, glorious Earth of ours, all of us, *created equal*? Created equal: one baby in Afghanistan or Iraq as sacred as one baby in Minneapolis. Where is my America? The America that taught me tolerance of every race and every religion, that filled me with pioneering energy, that is generous to a fault when catastrophes strike?

So was I wrong?

When I hoped you would rise to the challenge as death visited you from the sky? When I believed America the just, the rebellious, the unselfish, was still alive? Not entirely spoiled by excessive wealth? With the courage to conquer its fear?

America learning the lesson of Vietnam.

Vietnam. More, many more than three thousand dead. More, many more than two cities bombed. More, more, more than one day of terror.

And yet, they do not hate you, America.

The enduring lesson of Vietnam. Not next time: obliterate the enemy. Not next time: satanize those who disagree.

What the Vietnamese are whispering to you: they remember and yet they do not hate. Not that easy, America, to forgive the pain. Or can you forget your own September 11 that easily?

Not that easy, America.

To grow.

Or was I wrong? Have I myself become contaminated with your innocence, lived too long among you? Do you need fifty thousand body bags coming home before you start to listen to your own voices of peace and dissent?

Am I wrong to believe that the country that gave the world the blues and Faulkner and Eleanor Roosevelt will be able to look at itself in the cracked mirror of history and join the rest of humanity, not as a city on a separate hill, but as one more city in the shining valleys of sorrow and uncertainty and hope where we all dwell?

Cold Waters

More than thirty years later, what I remember above all is the blond American brat at the pool in Jahuel. He couldn't have been more than three years old, but he was doing all he could to ruin the calm and wonder of our hot, lazy Chilean afternoon. His gringa mother made no attempt to control him. She slept in her bikini, tummy down on a deckchair under a giant eucalyptus, while her son satanically screamed and ran about. My then-girlfriend Angélica (she was not yet my wife, so this must have happened before 1966) kept her eyes tight shut in the hope that, somehow, this would reduce the fanfare. As for me, I tried to concentrate on the sunset as it lit up the slopes of the Andes. Angélica had been brought up a few miles from there, in the small town of Santa María, and I had been looking forward to this visit and to the promise of a quiet time among the rocks and ridges and scrub highlands of the Valle del Aconcagua, which had blessed her childhood and adolescence. I'd just spent half an hour in the pool, which was fed by an icy cold mountain spring and, bizarre as this may sound, I felt that my endurance of this temperature was a sign that I was finally becoming a true Chilean. When I first arrived in Chile from the States in 1954, as a twelve-year-old unable to speak a word of Spanish, whose only desire was to return to the New York from where he had been banished, the fierce chill of the Pacific and southern Chile's equally glacial rivers and lakes struck me as a personal affront. How could I become part of a country that made my body so cold? And yet, gradually, I

First published in *Granta* (London and New York), April 2002. This version, an enlarged and slightly rewritten one prepared for the first anniversary of the criminal events of September 2001, appeared in other papers and journals around the world.

had fallen in love with it: evidence that I belonged here came from my new relish for long, bone-chilling swims.

That may have been the real reason for my annoyance with the kid. If he'd been brown-skinned and yelped in Spanish, I'd probably have forgiven him; who was I to deny him the right to be an exasperating pain-in-the-ass in his own land? Instead, he reminded me of who I had been, of my deep and recently forsaken allegiance to the United States and John Wayne, of my ten joyful years in Manhattan, of the Yankee identity I was trying so hard to repudiate. So I pretended that I didn't understand a word he aimed in my direction and tried to make myself into a monolingual Spanish speaker, a *chileno* whose terrain was being invaded by this foreign spawn. This was the fanatical 1960s and everything was colored by politics, even something as tangential as child misconduct. The odious American boy and his inconsiderate American mother had taken over this serene Chilean pool as if they owned it. Absurd, perhaps, to think this now, but they symbolized to me the many ways in which the United States had dominated Latin America: its ownership of mines and fields and banks and steamers, its proconsuls in Mexico and Buenos Aires and Bogotá, its invasions of Nicaragua and Cuba and Guatemala, its training of torturers, its coups in Brazil and Bolivia and Honduras, its barely concealed idea that that the only thing Latin Americans understood was a kick in the pants. And also, of course, as for all my generation, the horror of Vietnam. But what was most irritating about Americans—to me, who had been one, who had been just as unconscious and insensitive in my own day—was their blind innocence, their inability to grasp how their intrusive bodies and loud mouths and naïve incomprehension grated on the world. Their professed unconcern—"What? Me Worry?"—about what was done in their name in every corner of the planet seemed to me more outrageous than the deeds themselves.

Does this explain what happened next?

A few feet away from me, the boy teetered at the edge of the pool and then fell in.

May God forgive me—or if there is no God, may my two-and-a-half-year-old American-born granddaughter forgive me when she is old enough to read these words—but I hesitated. It isn't easy now to return to that sliver of time to reconstruct what went through my mind, but how I remember it is that for a couple of seconds I let myself lapse into a murderous passivity. The boy didn't flail out; he sank into the blue, icy water, silently. Just his body sinking slowly and my eyes watching just as slowly. What comes back to me is the pang of indifference I felt at the sight—that it was none of my business, that in some perverse sense the kid had it coming to him, as had his mother. It would have been so easy to let those two seconds stretch into three and then four and then more, it would have been so simple for that coolness to devour the world.

I can't be sure that this is what I felt, because I may be associating later events with what happened that day. The CIA had still to engineer a coup against the democratic government of Chile; Washington had still to arm the Contras in Nicaragua and train the death squads in El Salvador. They hadn't bombed a pharmaceutical complex in Sudan or sent missiles to blow up children in Iraq or justified Apartheid in South Africa or . . . Still, my paralysis must have been born of a deep turmoil of grievance and resentment—maybe it was time for them to experience what we experience, maybe they shouldn't presume that when their kids fall in the pool we will rescue them. My anger was on behalf of millions of unfortunate others; it wasn't because my own affluent self had suffered. But that mysteriously made it all the more intense; it was easier to blame the Americans for all the misery that surrounded me than to really do something about it myself.

The two seconds passed.

I plunged in and scooped the boy out and deposited him (sputtering and screaming again) on the rim of the pool. His mother woke up—there must have been some special urgency in his shrieks—and I was so embarrassed by her gratitude that I forgot to pretend that I didn't speak English. She turned out to be a jazz enthusiast. We'd been to the same Louis Armstrong concert in Santiago, which had been sponsored by the then-suspect U.S. Information Service, though that hadn't stopped me bebopping in a most un-Chilean way in the aisles.

That is how effortless it was, and still is, to cross over from Yankee basher to enthralled lover of American culture, a zigzag, back-and-forth path of detestation and adoration that millions of my fellow humans around the world have also been treading for many decades. But more crucially, perhaps, at the poolside in Jahuel I was engaging in an emotional and intellectual exercise that I've been exploring a good part of my life: the attempt to separate the American people from the policies of their government, trying to reconcile, in fact, the two zones of my life and my past.

In the years since, I've come to realize some other truths: how comfortable it is to employ anti-Americanism as a way of avoiding the faults and deficiencies of our own societies, even though such self-criticism should not prevent us from assigning blame to Americans when that blame is due, which it often is. The United States has such incommensurate power to do good or evil, and has set itself high standards of freedom and tolerance by which to be measured.

But what I recall today, precisely when the world tries to measure the consequences we are all suffering because of the terrorist attacks on New York and Washington a year ago, today that violence threatens to contaminate the whole planet, what terrifies me today is how easily we can forget our common humanity, as I did that hot summer afternoon in Chile, how I could automatically forget the humanity we all share as I watched that child descend into the cold quiet maelstrom of those waters.

Pablo Picasso Has Some Words for Colin Powell from the Other Side of Death

Yes, even here, here more than anywhere else,
we know and watch what is going on
what you are doing with the world
we left behind

What else can we do with our time?

Yes, there you were, Mr. Secretary,
I think that is how they call you
there you were
standing in front of my Guernica
a replica it is true
but still my vision of what was done
that day to the men to the women
and to the children to that one child
in Guernica that day in 1937
from the sky

Not really standing in front of it.
It had been covered, our Guernica,
covered so you could speak.
There in the United Nations building.
So you could speak about Iraq.

Undisturbed by Guernica.

First published online on OpenDemocracy.com and TomDispatch.com, February 2003. It first appeared in print in the *San Francisco Chronicle*, March 9, 2003.

Why should it disturb perturb you?
Why did you not ask that the cover
                be removed,
                            the picture
                be revealed?

Why did you not point to the shrieking
the horse dying over and over again
the woman with the child forever dead
the child that I nurse here in this darkness
the child who watches with me
as you speak
                and you speak.
Why did you not say
This is why we must be rid of the dictator.
Why did you not say
This is what Iraq has already done and undone.
Why did you not say
This is what we are trying to save the world from.
Why did you not use
Guernica to make your case?

Were you afraid that the mother
would leap from her image and say
no he is the one
they are the ones who will bomb
                            from afar
they are the ones who will kill
                            the child
no no no
he is the one they them look at them
from the distance the bombs
keeping us always out of sight
inside death and out of sight

Were you afraid that the horse
would show the world the near future
three thousand cruise missiles in the first hour

spinning into Baghdad
ten thousand Guernicas
spinning into Baghdad
                    from the sky

Were you afraid of my art
                    what I am still saying
more than sixty-five years later
the story still being told
the vision still dangerous
the light bulb still hanging
            like an eye from the dead
my eye that looks at you from the dead

beware

beware the eye of the child
in the dark

you will join us
the child and I
the horse and the mother
here on the other side

you will join us soon
you will journey here
            as we all do

            is that why you were
            so afraid of me?

join us
and spend the rest of eternity
watching
watching
watching
        next to us
        next to the remote dead

not only of Iraq
not only of

          is that why you were
          so afraid of that eye?

watching
your own eyes sewn open wide looking
          at the world you left behind

there is nothing else to do
with our time

sentenced to watch
and watch
by our side

          until there will be no Guernicas left
          until the living understand

and then, Mr. Secretary,
and then

          a world with no Guernicas

and then
yes then
          you and I
yes then
          we can rest

you and I and the covered child

Letter to an
Unknown Iraqi Dissident

I do not know your name, and that is already significant. Are you one of the thousands upon thousands who survived Saddam Hussein's chambers of torture, did you see the genitals of one of your sons crushed to punish you, to make you cooperate? Are you a member of a family that has to live with the father who returned, silent and broken, from that inferno, the mother who must remember each morning the daughter taken one night by security forces and who may or may not still be alive? Are you one of the Kurds gassed in the north of Iraq, an Arab from the south displaced from his home, a Shiite clergyman ruthlessly persecuted by the Ba'ath Party, a communist who has been fighting the dictatorship for long decades?

Whoever you are, faceless and suffering, you have been waiting many years for the reign of terror to end. And now, at last, you can see fast approaching the moment you have been praying for, even if you oppose and fear the American invasion that will inevitably kill so many Iraqis and devastate your land, the moment the dictator who has built himself lavish palaces, the man who praises Hitler and Stalin and promises to emulate them, may well be forced out of power.

What right does anyone have to deny you and your fellow Iraqis that liberation from tyranny? What right do we have to oppose the war the United States is about to wage on your country, if it could indeed result in the ouster of Saddam Hussein? Can those countless human-rights activists who, a few years ago, celebrated the trial in London of Chilean General Augusto Pinochet as a victory for all the victims on this Earth, now deny the world the joy of

Washington Post (Washington, D.C.), February 23, 2003, Sunday Outlook section.

seeing the strongman of Iraq indicted and tried for crimes against humanity? It is not fortuitous that I have brought the redoubtable Pinochet into the picture.

As a Chilean who fought against the General's pervasive terror for seventeen years, I can understand the needs, the anguish, the urgency, of those Iraqis inside and outside their homeland who cannot wait, cannot accept any further delay, silently howl for deliverance. I have seen how Chile still suffers, thirteen years after Pinochet left power, from his legacy and can therefore comprehend how every week that passes with the despot in power poisons your collective fate.

Such sympathy for your cause does not exempt me, however, from asking a crucial question: Is that suffering sufficient to justify a war to end it? Because I am unconvinced, along with so many others in the world, that your dictator has sufficient weapons of mass destruction to truly pose a threat to other countries, or ties to criminal groups who could use them for terror, the only possible compelling reason for someone like me to excuse or even support an attack from abroad against Iraq would be the certainty that the people being attacked would ultimately reap the benefits of democracy, freedom, and prosperity.

Despite having spent most of my life as a firm anti-interventionist, protesting American aggression in Latin America and Asia, and Soviet invasions of Eastern Europe and Afghanistan, during the 1990s I gradually came to feel that there might be occasions when incursions by a foreign power could indeed be warranted. I reluctantly agreed with the 1993 American expedition to Haiti to return to power the legally elected president of that republic; I was appalled at the lack of response from the international community to the genocide in Bosnia and Rwanda; I applauded the Australian intervention to stop the massacres in East Timor; and, regarding Kosovo, though I would have preferred that the military action have taken place under the auspices of the United Nations, I eventually came to the agonizing conclusion that ethnic cleansing on such a massive scale could not be tolerated.

I am afraid that none of these cases apply to Iraq.

For starters, there is no guarantee that this military adventure will, in fact, lead to a "regime change," or peace and stability for your region.

Unfortunately, also, the present affliction of your men and women and children must be horribly, perversely, weighed against the impending casualties and enormous losses that the American campaign will surely cause. In the balance are not only the dead and mutilated of Iraq (and who knows how many from the invading force), but the very real possibility that such an act of preemptive, world-destabilizing aggression could spin out of control and lead to other despots preemptively arming themselves with all manner of apocalyptic weapons and, perhaps, to Armaggedon. Not to mention how such an action seems destined to recruit even more fanatics for the terrorist groups who are salivating at the prospect of an American invasion.

I have to say no to war.

It is not easy for me to write these words.

I write, after all, from the comfort and safety of my own life. I write to you in the knowledge that I never did very much for the Iraqi resistance, hardly registered you and your needs, sent a couple of free books to libraries and academics in Baghdad who asked for them, answered one, maybe two, letters from Iraqi women who had been tortured and had found some solace in my plays. I write to you harboring the suspicion that if I had cared more, if we all had, there might not be a tyrant today in Iraq. I write to you knowing that there is no chance that the American government might redirect to a flood of people like you the $200 billion, $300 billion this war would initially cost, that there is no real interest on the part of those who would supposedly liberate you to instead spend that enormous amount of money helping to build a democratic alternative inside your country.

But I also write to you knowing this: If I had been approached, say in the year 1975, when Pinochet was at the height of his murderous spree in Chile, by an emissary of the American government proposing that the United States, the very country that had put our strongman in power, use military force to overthrow the dictatorship, I believe that my answer would have been, I hope it would have been, "No, thank you. We must deal with this monster by ourselves."

I was never given that chance, of course: The Americans would never have wanted to rid themselves, in the midst of the Cold War,

of such an obsequious client. Just as they did not try to eject Saddam Hussein twenty years ago, when he was even more repressive.
Rather, they supported him as a bulwark against militant Iran.

But this exercise in political science fiction (invade Chile to
depose Pinochet?) allows me, at least, to share in the agony created
by my own opposition to this war, forces me to recognize the pain
that is being endured at this very moment in some house in Basra,
some basement in Baghdad, some school in Tarmiyah. Even if I
can do nothing to stop those government thugs in Iraq coming to
arrest you again today, coming for you tomorrow and the next day
and the day after that, knocking once more at your door.

Heaven help me, I am saying that if I had been given a chance
years ago to spare the lives of so many of my dearest friends, given
the chance to end my exile and alleviate the grief of millions of
my fellow citizens, I would have rejected it if the price we would
have had to pay was clusters of bombs killing the innocent, if the
price was years of foreign occupation, if the price was the loss of
control over our own destiny.

Heaven help me, I am saying that I care more about the future
of this sad world than about the future of your unprotected
children.

A Different Drum

A t a time when the world seems to be madly rushing into yet another mad conflagration, I look for signs of peace anywhere I can find them, I look for stories of peace because there is nothing else I can really do to exorcise the demons of destruction.

Why are they so few, these stories about peace, so difficult to find and so difficult to transmit? Is it possible that the peace everybody proclaims as desirable is, in fact, so elusive on our planet precisely because we humans are much better at imagining discord than at imagining harmony? Is it the spectacular and dramatic nature of war that exercises such a fascination on our collective and individual imagination? Is it inevitable that we be seduced and sucked into the whirlwind tales of violence that swamp us everywhere we turn, inevitable that we invariably prefer them to what are all too often pictured as bland stories of monotonous peace? Must that peace always be conjured up as unexciting, the mere yawning absence of hostilities, nothing more than a dull interlude between sensational battles soon to be renewed?

And yet, if we only open our eyes (and perhaps our hearts), we could probably find chronicles of peace, incidents of peace, allegories and yarns and fables of peace everywhere.

Even when we are searching for images of war.

As I was, a bit earlier this year, when I saw a thrilling episode of peace flare up in the town of Iquique in northern Chile, where I had journeyed with my wife in order to write a book for National Geographic. We had timed our visit to that port city to coincide

---

First published in *Le Monde* (Paris), December 23, 2002. The longer version included here first appeared in the *London Guardian Saturday Review* (London), January 11, 2003.

with the May 21 holiday that commemorates the Combate Naval de Iquique, a naval battle in 1879 that gave Chile dominion over the Pacific Ocean and led to victory in my country's war against Peru and Bolivia and the subsequent annexation of a mineral-rich territory previously held by our two neighboring nations. I was curious to see how the May 21 observances of that bloody struggle against fellow Latin Americans would be remembered in the very place where it had occurred—and almost perversely expected that we would be overwhelmed with bellicose images and nationalistic blathering.

After witnessing marches and speeches and patriotic displays all morning, and a flotilla of ships of all sizes strewing flowers on the glorious bay where the naval battle had been fought and won so many years ago, Angélica and I had ended up way past noon in the central plaza of Iquique as part of a boisterous festive crowd bedecked in Chilean flags that was enjoying the performance of two *tamborileros* banging on their drums and dancing in the middle of the street. The word *tamborilero* comes from *tambor* (drum), but to say drummer man or drummer boy does not even approximate what these musicians do. How to describe someone who carries on his back the colossal barrel of a drum that he beats by pumping his leg up and down, accompanying that incessant thud thud thud with all manner of other percussive instruments set into motion by both his arms and his other foot, cymbals and tambourines and chimes? Cousins of every hurdy-gurdy man who ever played his melancholy songs, brothers to the lost organ-grinders of the world, *tamborileros* are in love with rhythm, producing a beat as they whirl and twirl their bodies, merging in their music and their clothes and their cadence the worlds of Andean and Spanish dancing. 'Round and 'round they went that day in Iquique, seemingly lapsing into a trance, oblivious of everything around them, apparently disregardful of the adults celebrating Chile's past military heroics and the children celebrating the ice cream that vendors hawked in loud voices, but particularly heedless, at their peril, of something more ominous. Along Baquedano, the main avenue of Iquique, we could all hear the sound of a naval band that was advancing like an arrow, like a tidal wave, straight from the ceremony that had finished half an hour ago at the monument to the Unknown Sailor by the boardwalk, martially advancing forty or fifty strong toward the square, toward us, toward the *tamborileros* who did not seem to notice, who were not hearing, or pretending not to hear, the trumpets, the kettle drums, the rat-tat-tat of the military parade. A clash appeared inevitable as the band in full array approached, did not slow down, tramping and treading toward the *tamborileros*. I waited, expecting the worse, almost hoping for it, yet another story of conflict and warfare, the confirmation of how these soldiers would, as they had so often before in my life, once again stifle a swirling touch of beauty, smother popular creativity, roll over anything and everything that stood in their way. The fact that these were representatives of the Navy and that they would mow down two men who, with their indigenous features, originated from the mountains and interior of Latin America, projected the upcoming showdown in my mind as one more metaphor, one more small milestone in the conquest of the natives by the technologically more powerful men who had come from the ocean.

Was that going to happen yet one more time? Would the two *tamborileros*, armed with nothing but their music, just keep on playing, invite yet again a confrontation that had played itself out over centuries of Chilean existence, or would those defenseless men withdraw, accepting quietude and meekness and submission as the price to be paid for not being run over? The crowd, sensing a brawl, went suddenly silent, perhaps not exactly lusting for blood but hungry, nevertheless, for a good spectacle, a dramatic denouement, yet one more anecdote of war to add to an endless repertoire.

It was not to be.

When the flag bearer at the head of the naval band was but a few inches from the ragamuffin Andean dervishes, every member of the marine company, as if animated by some secret agreement among themselves or in harmony perhaps with the universe, every one of those men in uniform simultaneously halted their march and their epic music. If there was some sign or hidden order from the officer in charge, I did not catch it. At any rate, I would rather believe that they had all reached, on their own, some inner unanimous accord not to goose-step over those two men.

For a few seconds, and then on and on for another interminable minute, the *tamborileros* stamped and pounded away, under the

very noses of the august band whose progress they were obstruct-
ing, not taunting the naval musicians or provoking them, simply
waiting, the *tamborileros*, just like the soldiers and the spectators,
all of us, tirelessly waiting for the song and cycle to be over. And
then they were done; the gyrations started to wind down, the beat
became less piercing, the dance edged into a shuffle, and the two
men slowly doffed their bedraggled hats and began to weave in and
out of the assemblage to gather a harvest of coins and bills. And
only when they had finally and gently abandoned the street and
the last echo of the last tambourine had been extinguished, did
the naval band strike up its anthem once again and parade off into
the distance, toward the port where they were supposed to greet
the return of the ships from the celebratory waters.

I felt a sense of wonder at this moment of—what could I call
it?—reconciliation, relief, truce? Not just the intimation of some
understanding between the deepest populace of Chile and its soldiers, separated by the many years of the Pinochet dictatorship and
all the massacres that had in the past preceded and in some way
foretold that dictatorship, but of something different, a meeting
of the highlands and the coast, a mutual recognition based on the
sea accepting what the heights would bring, had been bringing for
so many millennia, an inkling of a future where Latin American
antagonists would not inevitably resort to violence as a way of deciding who would rule the air and the avenues. And offering us, also,
a model of conflict resolution: war can be avoided if the weaker
side decides to persist in its dignity and its resistance, conquering
its fear—but only if the other side, the more apparently powerful
one, banishes its automatic presumption of superiority, daring to
allow itself to be challenged.

That peaceful interval was worked out by ordinary human beings
going about their everyday existence. Something similar, I am sure,
must be repeated over and over in thousands of places all around
our murderous globe, even if they are rarely, if ever, reported or
remembered or nourished by those who tell our stories massively.
The deep well of truth of what we all want, each man, each woman,
each child on this earth: that the small space that surrounds our
fragile bodies be respected, that our right to some minimal terri-

toriality or identity or autonomy be afforded recognition by those
who have the power to smash and invade it.

Is it that hard to imagine a world where such respect and such
recognition is the norm and not the exception? Are we so bereft of
stories of peace that none of us could recall even one miraculous
moment in our recent lives when we witnessed humanity demanding
and receiving the right to control its own existence without being
violated? Isn't it time, as war approaches yet again, that each of us
tell those stories of a possible peace over and over again?

Lessons of a Catastrophe

I t can't happen here.
   Thirty years ago that is what we chanted, that is what we sang, on the streets of Santiago de Chile.

It can't happen here. There can never be a dictatorship in this country, we proclaimed to the winds of history that were about to furiously descend on us; our democracy is too solid, our armed forces too committed to popular sovereignty, our people too much in love with freedom.

But it did happen.

On September 11, 1973, the Chilean military overthrew the constitutional government of Salvador Allende, who was trying, for the first time on this planet, to build socialism through peaceful and electoral means. The bombing by the Air Force of the Presidential Palace on that day started a dictatorship that was to last seventeen years and that, today, even after we have recovered democracy, continues to haunt and corrode my country.

The coup, however, left not only pain and loss in its wake but also a legacy of questions that I have been turning over and over in my mind for the past thirty years: How was it possible that a nation with a functioning parliament, a long record of institutional tolerance, a flourishing free press, an independent judiciary, and, most critically, armed forces subjected to civilian rule—how could that country have ended up spawning one of the worst tyrannies of a Latin American continent that is not exactly bereft of infernal regimes? And, more crucially: Why did so many of Chile's men and women, heirs to a vigorous democracy, look the other way while the worst sort of abuses were being perpetrated in their name? Why did they not ask what was being done in the cellars

The Nation (New York), September 30, 2003.

and attics of their howling cities, why did they make believe there
was no torture, no mass executions, no disappearances in the night?
And a final, more dire challenge, one that is not restricted to Chile
and serves as a warning to citizens around our threatened world
today: In the coming years, could something similar befall those
nations with apparently stable democracies? Could the erosion of
freedom that so many in Chile accepted as necessary find a perverse recurrence in the United States or India or Brazil, in France
or Spain or Britain?

I am aware, of course, that it is intellectually dangerous to wildly
project one historical situation onto another thirty years later. The
circumstances that led to the loss of our democracy in Chile were
very specific and do not find an exact replica anywhere in the contemporary world. And yet, even with all the differences and distances, the Chilean tragedy does send us one central message that
needs attention if we are to avoid similar political disasters in the
future: Many otherwise normal, decent human beings in my land
allowed their liberty—and that of their persecuted fellow countrymen—to be stolen in the name of security, in the name of fighting
terror. That was how General Pinochet and his cohorts justified
their military takeover; that is how they built popular support for
their massive violations of human rights. A few days after the coup,
the members of the junta announced that they had "discovered" a
secret Plan Zeta, a bloodbath prepared by Allende and his "hench-
men." The evidence of such a plan was, naturally enough, never
published, nor was even one of the hundreds of thousands of the
former president's followers who were arrested, tortured, and exiled,
not one of the thousands who were executed or "disappeared," put
on trial in a court of law for the conspiracy they were accused of.
But fear, once it begins to eat away at a nation, once it is manipulated by an all-powerful government, is not easily eradicated by
reason. To someone who feels vulnerable, who imagines himself
a perpetual victim, who detects enemies everywhere, no punishment to the potential perpetrators is too excessive and no measure
to insure safety too extreme.

This is the lesson that Chile retains for us thirty years after the
coup that devastated my country, particularly in the aftermath
of that other dreadful September 11, that day in 2001 when death

again fell from the sky and thousands of innocent civilians were again slaughtered. The fact that the terror suffered by the citizens of the United States—which happens to be the most powerful nation on Earth—is not an invention, as our Plan Zeta turned out to be, makes the question of how to deal with fear even more urgent than it was in Chile, a faraway country whose tribulations and mistakes most of humanity could quickly forget.

It is far from encouraging to contemplate what has transpired thus far, in the two years since the disastrous attacks on New York and Washington. In the sacred name of security and as part of an endless and stage-managed war against terrorism, defined in a multitude of ever-shifting and vague forms, a number of civil liberties of American citizens have been perilously curtailed, not to mention the rights of non-Americans inside the borders of the United States. The situation abroad is even worse, as the war against terror is used to excuse an attrition of liberty in democratic and authoritarian societies the world over. Even in Afghanistan and Iraq, the two countries "liberated" by America—and free now of the monstrous autocracies that once misruled them—there are disturbing signs of human rights abuses by the occupiers, old prisons being reopened, civilians being gunned down, men abducted into the night and fog of a bureaucracy that will not answer for them.

I am not suggesting that the United States and its allies are turning themselves into a gigantic police state such as Chile endured for so many years—not yet, at least. But that suffering will have been in vain if we do not today, in other zones of the world, heed the deepest significance of the catastrophe the Chilean people started living thirty years ago.

We also thought, we also shouted, we also assured the planet:

It cannot happen here.

We also thought, on those not-so-remote streets of Santiago, that we could shut our eyes to the terrors that were awaiting us tomorrow.

The Final Temptation of Ivan Karamazov

I s torture ever justified? That is the dirty question left out of the universal protestations of disgust, revulsion, and shame that greeted the recent release of photos showing British soldiers and American military police tormenting helpless prisoners in Iraq.

It is a question that was most unforgettably put forward more than one hundred thirty years ago by Fyodor Dostoevsky in *The Brothers Karamazov*. In that novel, the saintly Alyosha Karamazov is tempted by his brother Ivan, confronted with an unbearable choice. Let us suppose, Ivan says, that in order to bring men eternal happiness, it was essential and inevitable to torture to death one tiny creature, only one small child. Would you consent? Ivan has preceded his question with stories about suffering children—a seven-year-old girl beaten senseless by her parents and then enclosed in a freezing wooden outhouse and made to eat her own excrement; an eight-year-old serf-boy torn to pieces by hounds in front of his mother for the edification of a landowner. True cases plucked from newspapers by Dostoevsky that merely hint at the almost unimaginable cruelty that awaited humanity in the years to come. How would Ivan react to the ways in which the twentieth century ended up refining pain, industrializing pain, producing pain on a massive, rational, technological scale; a century that would produce manuals on pain and how to inflict it, training courses on how to increase it, and catalogues that explained where to acquire the instruments that ensured that pain would be unlimited; a century that handed out medals for those who had written the manuals and commended those who designed the courses and rewarded and enriched those who had produced the instruments in those catalogues of death?

Guardian (London), May 9, 2004, op-ed page.

Ivan Karamazov's question—would you consent?—is just as dreadfully relevant now, in a world where 132 countries routinely practice that sort of humiliation and damage on detainees, because it takes us into the impossible heart of the matter regarding torture, it demands that we confront the real and inexorable dilemma that the existence and persistence of torture poses, particularly after the terrorist attacks of September 11, 2001. Ivan Karamazov's words remind us that torture is justified by those who apply and perform it: This is the price, it is implied, that needs to be paid by the suffering few in order to guarantee happiness for the rest of society, the enormous majority given security and well-being by those horrors inflicted in some dark cellar, some faraway pit, some abominable police station. Make no mistake: every regime that tortures does so in the name of salvation, some superior goal, some promise of paradise. Call it communism, call it the free market, call it the free world, call it the national interest, call it fascism, call it the leader, call it civilization, call it the service of God, call it the need for information, call it what you will, the cost of paradise, the promise of some sort of paradise, Ivan Karamazov continues to whisper to us, will always be hell for at least one person somewhere, sometime.

An uncomfortable truth: the American and British soldiers in Iraq, like torturers everywhere, do not think of themselves as evil, but rather as guardians of the common good, dedicated patriots who get their hands dirty and endure perhaps some sleepless nights in order to deliver the blind ignorant majority from violence and anxiety. Nor are the motives of the demonized enemy significant, that they are naked and under the boot because they dared to resist a foreign power occupying their land. And if it turns out—a statistical certainty—that at least one of the victims is innocent of what he is accused, as blameless as the children mentioned by Ivan Karamazov, that does not matter either. He must suffer the fate of the supposedly guilty. Everything justified in the name of a higher mission, state stability in the time of Saddam, and now, in the post-Saddam era, making the same country and the whole region stable for "democracy." So those who support the present operations in Iraq are no different from citizens in all those other lands where torture is a tedious fact of life, all of them needing to face Ivan's question, whether they would consciously be able to accept that their dreams of heaven depend on an eternal inferno of distress for one innocent human being or whether, like Alyosha, they would softly reply, "No, I do not consent."

What Alyosha is telling Ivan, in the name of humanity, is that he will not accept responsibility for someone else torturing in his name. He is telling us that torture is not a crime committed only against a body, but also a crime committed against the imagination. It presupposes, it requires, it craves the abrogation of our capacity to imagine someone else's suffering, to dehumanize him or her so much that their pain is not our pain. It demands this of the torturer, placing the victim outside and beyond any form of compassion or empathy, but also demands of everyone else the same distancing, the same numbness, those who know and close their eyes, those who do not want to know and close their eyes, those who close their eyes and ears and hearts. Alyosha knows, as we should, that torture does not, therefore, only corrupt those directly involved in the terrible contact between two bodies, one that has all the power and the other that has all the pain, one that can do what it wants and the other that cannot do anything except wait and pray and resist. Torture also corrupts the whole social fabric because it prescribes a silencing of what has been happening between those two bodies; it forces people to make believe that nothing, in fact, has been happening; it necessitates that we lie to ourselves about what is being done not that far, after all, from where we talk, while we munch chocolate, smile at a lover, read a book, listen to a concerto, exercise in the morning. Torture obliges us to be deaf and blind and mute—and that is what Alyosha cannot consent to.

There is, however, a further question, even more troubling, that Ivan does not ask his brother or us: What if the person being endlessly tortured for our well-being is guilty?

What if we could erect a future of love and harmony on the everlasting pain of someone who had himself committed mass murder, who had tortured those children? What if we were invited to enjoy Eden all over again while one despicable human being was incessantly receiving the horrors he imposed upon others? And more urgently: What if the person whose genitals are being crushed and skin is being burnt knows the whereabouts of a bomb that is about to explode and would kill millions?

Would we answer, "Yes, I do consent"? That under certain very limited circumstances, torture is acceptable?

That is the real question to humanity thrown up by the photos of those suffering bodies in the stark rooms of Iraq yesterday, an agony—let us not forget—about to be perpetrated again today and tomorrow in so many prisons everywhere else on our sad, anonymous planet as one man with the power of life and death in his godlike hands approaches another who is totally defenseless.

Are we that scared?

Are we so scared that we are willing to knowingly let others perpetrate, in the dark and in our name, acts of terror which will eternally corrode and corrupt us?

The Last September 11

I have been through this before.

During the last twenty-eight years, Tuesday, September 11, has been a date of mourning, for me and millions of others, ever since that day in 1973 when Chile lost its democracy in a military coup, that day when death irrevocably entered our lives and changed us forever. And now, almost three decades later, the malignant gods of random history have wanted to impose upon another country that dreadful date, again a Tuesday, once again an 11th of September filled with death.

The differences and distances that separate the Chilean date from the American are, one must admit, considerable. The depraved terrorist attack against the most powerful nation on Earth has and will have consequences which affect all humanity. It is possible that it may constitute, as President Bush has stated, the start of World War III, and it is probable that it will be branded in the manuals of the future as the day when the planet's history shifted forever. Whereas very few of the eight billion people alive today remember or would be able to identify what happened in Chile.

And yet, from the moment when, transfigured, I watched on our television screen here in North Carolina that second plane exploding into the World Trade Center's South Tower, I have been haunted by the need to understand and extract the hidden meaning of the juxtaposition and coincidence of these two September 11s, which in my case becomes even more enigmatic and personal because it is a violation that conjoins the two foundational cities of my existence—the New York which gave me refuge and joy during ten years of my infancy and the Santiago which protected my adolescence under its mountains and made me into a man—the two

Los Angeles Times, September 21, 2001, op-ed page.

cities that offered me my two languages, English and Spanish. It has been, therefore, tentatively, breathing slowly to overcome the emotional shock; making every effort not to look again and again at the contaminating photo of the man who falls vertically, so straight, so straight, from the heights of that building; trying to stop thinking about the last seconds of those plane passengers who know that their imminent doom will also kill thousands of their own innocent compatriots; in the midst of frantic phone calls that should tell me if my friends in Manhattan are well and that nobody answers—it is in the middle of all this turmoil that I yield to the gradual realization that there is something horribly familiar, even recognizable, in this experience that North Americans are now passing through.

The resemblance I am evoking goes well beyond a facile and superficial comparison—for instance, that both in Chile in 1973 and in the States today, terror descended from the sky to destroy the symbols of national identity—the Palace of the Presidents in Santiago and the icons of financial and military power in New York and Washington. No, what I recognize is something deeper, a parallel suffering, a similar pain, a commensurate disorientation echoing what we lived through in Chile as of that September 11. Its most extraordinary incarnation—I still cannot believe what I am witnessing—is the hundreds of people wandering the streets of New York, clutching the photos of their sons, fathers, wives, lovers, daughters, begging for information, asking if they are alive or dead, the whole United States forced to look into the abyss of what it means to be *desaparecido*, with no certainty about the fate of those beloved men and women who are missing nor even the possibility of a funeral for them. And I also recognize and repeat that sensation of extreme unreality that invariably accompanies great disasters caused by human iniquity, so much more difficult to cope with than natural catastrophes. Over and over again I hear phrases that remind me of what people like me would mutter to themselves during the 1973 military coup and the days that followed: "This cannot be happening to us. This sort of excessive violence happens to other people and not to us, we have only known this form of destruction through movies and books and remote photographs. If it's a nightmare, why can't we awaken from it?" And words reiterated unceasingly, twenty-eight years ago and now again in 2001: "We have lost our innocence. The world will never be the same."

What has come to an explosive conclusion, of course, is (North) America's famous exceptionalism, the attitude that allowed the citizens of this country to imagine themselves beyond the sorrows and calamities that have plagued less fortunate peoples around the world. None of the great battles of the twentieth century touched the continental United States. Even the Pearl Harbor "Day of Infamy," which is being tiredly extricated from the past as the only possible analogous incident, occurred thousands of miles away. It is that complacent invulnerability which has been fractured forever. Life in these United States will have to share, from now on, the precariousness and uncertainty that is the daily lot of the enormous majority of this planet's other inhabitants.

In spite of the tremendous pain, of the intolerable losses that this apocalyptic crime has visited upon the American public, I wonder if this trial does not constitute one of those opportunities for regeneration and self-knowledge that, from time to time, is given to certain nations. A crisis of this magnitude can lead to renewal or destruction, it can be used for good or for evil, for peace or for war, for aggression or for reconciliation, for vengeance or for justice, for the militarization of a society or its humanization. One of the ways for Americans to overcome their trauma and survive the fear and continue to live and thrive in the midst of the insecurity which has suddenly swallowed them is to admit that their suffering is neither unique nor exclusive, that they are connected, as long as they are willing to look at themselves in the vast mirror of our common humanity, to so many other human beings who, in apparently faraway zones, have suffered similar situations of unanticipated and often protracted injury and fury.

Could this be the hidden and hardly conceivable reason that destiny has decided that the first contemporary attack on the essence and core of the United States would transpire precisely on the very anniversary that commemorates the military takeover in Chile, which a government in Washington nourished and sustained in the name of the American people? Could it be a way to mark the immense challenge that awaits the citizens of this country, particularly its young, now that they know what it really means to be victimized, now that they can grasp the sort of collective hell survivors withstand when their loved ones disappear, leaving them without a body to bury, now that they have been given the chance to draw closer to and to comprehend the multiple variations of the many September 11s that are scattered throughout the globe, the kindred sufferings that so many peoples and countries endure?

The terrorists have wanted to single out and isolate the United States as a satanic state. The rest of the planet, including many nations and men and women who have been the object of American arrogance and intervention, reject—as I categorically do—this demonization. It is enough to see the almost unanimous outpouring of grief of most of the world, the offers of help, the expressions of solidarity, the determination to claim the dead of this mass murder as our dead.

It remains to be seen if this compassion shown to the mightiest power on this planet will be reciprocated, it is still not clear if the United States—a country formed in great measure by those who have themselves escaped vast catastrophes, famines, dictatorships, persecution—will be able to feel that same empathy toward the other outcast members of our species. We will find out in the days and years to come if the new Americans forged in pain and resurrection will be ready and open and willing to participate in the arduous process of repairing our shared, our damaged, humanity. We will find out by creating, all of us together, a world in which we need never again lament one more, not even one more, terrifying September 11.

PART TWO

Yesterday Is Still Here

Hymn for the Unsung

S omewhere in the Saudi Arabian desert, an American corporal is reading *Moby Dick*. He is reading Melville's novel,
a newspaper reports, in order to "understand what drives
people toward destructive obsessions," concentrating above all on
Ahab, "how he kept after the whale," and wondering if "he was
like Saddam Hussein."

How typically American, I thought from my Third World perspective, this need to understand the enemy one is fighting—as
American as his pathetic incapacity to achieve that understanding.
Saddam as Ahab might fit neatly into the current interpretation of
the Iraqi leader as a madman, irrationally pursuing his own downfall in spite of all warnings—but the corporal did not apparently
seem interested in stopping to ask who the whale might be in this
equation or what the whale might have done to Saddam, which
parts of his body and mind had been devoured, to make him act
with such abandon.

Because if Saddam is indeed Ahab, the clues to his present
behavior might fruitfully be searched for in the past, a search that
I doubt the corporal or his fellow Americans are particularly interested in. Instant amnesia seems to have infected the people of the
United States as they devastate a country that a few months ago
hardly any of them could find on a map. It is easier to conceive of
Saddam as Satan—a personification of evil substituting for historical
explanation. No need to ask what has been done to the Arabs—as
to so many other Third World peoples—that makes them feel so
humiliated, enraged, threatened, alienated, that a tyrant such as

First published in the *Los Angeles Times*, February 1, 1991. It also appeared in *The
Gulf War Reader* edited by Micah L. Sifray and Christopher Serf (New York:
New York Times/Random House Books, 1991).

the Iraqi leader can manipulate those feelings to turn himself into their representative. No need to ask why there is a power vacuum in the Middle East which this dictator, like others who will come, thinks he can fill. No need to remember that before this Ahab there was Mossadegh, an elected Iranian leader who nationalized oil and was overthrown with the help of the CIA in 1953. The autocrat who replaced him with a puppet was, of course, the shah. When the shah was in turn swept away by Ayatollah Khomeini's Islamic Revolution, Iraq was encouraged to arm itself to the hilt in order to contain the Iranian menace. Iraq expanded this mandate into a savage war, with America's blessing (and European and Soviet assistance), all human-rights violations and the gassing of Kurds winked at, all condemnations blocked, until some years later when the U.S. ambassador would give Saddam Hussein the go-ahead for the invasion of Kuwait.

But what if Saddam is not Ahab?

How can it be that this young man who faces death so far from his home should be unable to catch even a glimmer of the possibility that Saddam might be the whale and that George Bush might in fact be an Ahab whose search for the monster in the oceans of sand and oil could end up with the ruin, not of the monster, but of those who were bent on its extermination?

Saddam Hussein, of course, is not unique as a monster. He is as monstrous as General Augusto Pinochet, who, having been brought to power by U.S. intervention against an elected democratic government, victimized my own people for seventeen years. And Iraq's aggression against Kuwait is as monstrous as the aggression of the United States against Nicaragua and Panama, against Grenada and Vietnam, as monstrous as the Soviet invasions of Czechoslovakia and Afghanistan. And Saddam Hussein's lobbing of missiles at civilians in Israel is as monstrous as the Israelis' bombing of refugee camps in Lebanon.

For the corporal to understand Saddam Hussein in these terms, as one who has been selectively and conveniently demonized, would necessarily mean condemning his own country's complicity and participation in the pervasive evils of the world today. It would mean seeing the adventure in the Persian Gulf not as a struggle for democracy—which the United States has eroded all over the world by propping up friendly torturers—but as one more sad intervention in the affairs of a region that it knows nothing about, one more step toward the militarization of a world that should be disarming. It would mean denying America's own morality in a conflict that once again finds a superpower technologically assaulting a poor Third World country, no matter how well armed it may be. It would mean that the true connection between Iraq and Vietnam should be made: that the war in the Persian Gulf is being used to refight the war in Indochina with far more lethal weapons—rewriting that American crisis and defeat, proving how it could have been won, having at last the "good war" the Pentagon has been seeking all these years with a single-mindedness that would have astounded even the crew of the *Pequod*.

These connections, alas, are not being made. Pursuing their reflection in the Gulf, Americans are blind to the true meanings of their actions. It is not, however, only their own image that Americans cannot decipher in the nightmare waters of this war.

Not far from the American corporal musing on *Moby Dick* there is an Iraqi corporal.

I know nothing about him, except that he breathes not many miles away and all too soon will be as close as a bayonet thrust, and not even that intimacy of combat will bring closeness or comprehension. It is the very fact that he is nameless, that he has no face, that no newspaper has told us his thoughts, that we have no way of knowing what *Moby Dick*, what Melville of his own culture, he reads in the darkness, what blindness of his own he is submerged in, the fact that his being is a blur that we must imagine; it is the stark fact of his very absence from our awareness that prepares his death. How easy to kill somebody we don't have to mourn because we never dared to imagine him alive.

I want neither Saddam Hussein nor George Bush to win the war in the Gulf. I wish that both of them could be defeated. But I anticipate that these two—Ahab and the whale, the whale and Ahab, George Bush and Saddam Hussein—will emerge unscathed, and that it will be their people who will have to pay for this absurd conflagration. It will be the two corporals who will pay, even if they survive, even if they are not shattered for life, they will be the ones, along with their children, who will pay endlessly for a war that nobody desires and that everybody seems so eager to fight.

Or is the world itself Ahab, suddenly gone mad?

Hammurabi, the Exalted Prince Who Made Great the Name of Babylon, Has Words from the Other Side of Death for Donald Rumsfeld

I bite my tongue and try not to curse you
I bite my tongue and try not to wish upon you
    what you visited on me and mine

my voice that ordered laws
to be engraved for all to see and hear
orphans and widows

        no no do not place that curse upon him they say to me
        they say to Hammurabi the protecting King
        those who accompany me in the green dark of death
        that is not what we do in the green dark of death

my code
even slaves had rights
even women cast out by their husbands
adopted sons prostitutes patients
even the oxen in the fields
builders barbers sailors
they all had rights
even the oxen in the fields

my words that have survived four thousand years
invasions depredations despoilment plunder
Persians Mongols Ottomans Arabs British

First published online on OpenDemocracy.com and TomDispatch.com (both September 5, 2003).

the first written words
                    of history
for all to know and see

Hammurabi shield of the land
that now lies
              broken shattered made dust
the many words of Mesopotamia

You could have stopped this
Rumsfeld Lord of the Looters
Lord of the Black Dawn

the statuettes of birds and goddesses
crushed by hammers sliced by knives
the scrolls painted by these hands
that surround me in the mother dark
gone all gone

only my words written in stone
still with me here on this other side

                not for cursing they say to me
                not what we do here they say

                in the life after the dark of life
                we teach they say to me
                we wait they say to me
                clothed in green gentleness
                the mothering dark

and yet and yet
Rumsfeld Rumsfeld
who did not defend the words and the widow
if I do not curse you, who will?

the tyrant who has fled or is dying dead?
the tyrant who broke my code?
the people of my earth who cannot speak
for fear of the new occupant of the throne?
the far people at your homeland
muzzled by ignorance and dread
who pray to you their protector?

I am Hammurabi
shepherd of the oppressed and the slaves
I am the good shadow spread over the city

Who else is there left to speak?
If any one steal the property of a temple he shall be put to death

If any one steal the minor son of another he shall be put to death

If any one break a hole into a house he shall be put to death

> No no no they say to me
> we do not believe in death
> not an eye for an eye they say

If a fire break out in a house and he who comes to put it out cast
    his
eye upon the property of the owner of the house, he shall be
    thrown
into that self-same fire

He shall be thrown into that self-same fire

> No no no they beg of me
> not a tooth for a tooth they say

He shall read my inscriptions and stand before me

> not a tooth for a tooth they say

may the years of your rule be in groaning
years of scarcity years of famine
darkness without light
the removal of your name and memory from the land

                              not his children they say to me
                              do not say it they say to me

may Nin-tu the sublime mistress of the lands
                the fruitful mother
deny you a son
give you no successor among men
the pouring out of your life
like water into the mouth of the desert

nothing lower than you
day turned into night

If not Hammurabi then who will speak?
Hammurabi the provider of food and drink
Who clothed the gravestones of Malkat with green

If I do not

may the damnation of Shamash overtake you
deprived of water among the living
and spirit below in the earth
day turned into night
thrown into that self-same fire
that fell upon the children and the books

If I do not curse the transgressor

I bite my tongue and try not to say these words
I bite my tongue and try not to say the words
that have lived for four thousand years
and are now smashed in the rubble
of the land that was once Babylon

If I do not curse you

my code and your code broken in the ruins
your glory and my glory gone gone all gone

If I do not curse you, who will dare?

The 19 and the 84

I am about to break one of the resolutions that I made at the beginning of this year.

I had promised myself to go through 1984 without writing about George Orwell, anticipating that his prophetic book set in this year would rapidly be squeezed dry by a deluge of allusions and commentaries that might soon render it meaningless.

I decided to break my resolution this late in the year because, in sifting through the dregs of verbiage on the subject, I have yet to find anyone who has looked at the book—and very few who have looked at the year—from a Third World perspective. That is sad and ironic, since it is the millions of poor in the Third World who are being subjected to the perverse combination of tyranny and deprivation that Orwell implied might someday be the fate of us all.

Those people are absent from the book *1984*. Where their countries do appear they are merely victims, inert slave labor, to be manipulated by the powerful.

But if Orwell left the Third World out of his novel, his publishers did not leave the novel out of the Third World.

I read it in Chile in 1958, ten years after it was written. My English teacher—aware that I was a fervent if adolescent admirer of Salvador Allende, who was then trying to be president of Chile for the first time as a candidate of the left—gave me the book as a way of curing me of what he deemed my socialist delusions.

He did not, of course, give me any of the other books in which Orwell denounces the appalling life of the poor or depicts with sympathy their struggles to be free. "Revolutions," my teacher said, "are failures. They end up creating more misery than they destroy. Read this."

Los Angeles Times, December 31, 1984, op-ed page.

It would be twelve years before Allende finally won the presidency, and when he did, none of Orwell's terrors came true. A multimillion-dollar media campaign, financed from abroad, blared warnings that socialism in Chile would mean the end of human rights and the beginning of an era of extreme hardship and torture. But Allende was scrupulously democratic.

When, three years later and backed by the U.S. government, our enemies came to power and installed a military dictatorship, they did to us what they had accused us of planning to do to them. There was never any proof that we had such plans. There has been, unfortunately, ample proof of their acts. The justification for destabilizing the constitutional government of my country was that people had to be saved from their own irresponsibility, saved in 1973 from the excesses of a hypothetical 1984. So that we could learn the lesson well and never make the same mistake, our whole society was turned into Room 101.

What were we doing to be so maltreated?

We were interpreting those digits—1984—in our own way. In effect, due to one of those delightful coincidences in which history cooperates with literature, 19 happens to be the exact number of countries that make up the First World. Called the Industrial Market Economies by the World Bank, they consume 75 percent of the world's resources, control more than 90 percent of the world's financing and banking, and transmit about 80 percent of the world's information. A curious imbalance appears when those 19 countries are compared with the 84 most deprived countries.

The 19 First World countries seem to have accumulated an amount of wealth and power that would be fair if they were as big and densely populated as the 84 countries of the Third World. And Chile under Allende was quite simply trying to redress the balance and achieve political, economic, and cultural independence.

Eleven years later, of course, the repression has not solved any of the original problems. The same general—Augusto Pinochet—is still in power, and the rebels, the very ones Orwell sided with over and over, can be stopped only by a resurgence of the same old terror he so chillingly depicted.

The cycle begins again. Once again a state of siege has been declared. Moscow and an international conspiracy are repeatedly blamed, and brutal retaliation against dissidents may give the momentary illusion and swift comfort that a solution is being found, but when the guns quiet and the smoke clears, there they are, the same dispossessed or their descendants, protesting the fact that for every one person who eats well there are—to remain within our magical four numbers—1984 who live under subhuman conditions.

Underprivileged people are treated all too often like children. If we are good, we should remain content with our lot and wait until development trickles down from some mythic height—and then we can aspire to an adulthood that has somehow evaded us until now. But if we are bad and disruptive, some corrective violence will be necessary. That brutality can be applied without excessive wear and tear to the conscience, because it is done in the name of anticommunism.

When this sort of terror is exercised against the powerless in a family, it is called child abuse. But when it is not an innocent child who is being beaten but a country such as Chile, too many people tend to shrug their shoulders. To them it must seem inevitable and, in any case, the lesser of two evils. What matters to them is to avoid having the Orwellian terror of 1984 foisted upon them by some foreign conspiracy. Perhaps people do not realize that a big country that cannot live with a disobedient smaller nation nearby—as the United States cannot tolerate an independent Nicaragua, as the Soviets cannot allow the Solidarity movement in Poland—is as insecure and sick as the parents who abuse a recalcitrant child.

Now it will be 1985.

Is there any better year for us to break out of this insane East-West, sick-parent/frightened-child relationship? Is there any better way to start a year than by saying that the 19 and the 84 and the rest of us should share a planet that, it should be remembered, belongs to us all?

The Face, the Voice,
the Eyes of the Enemy

B
ack in 1928, the U.S. Marines were bogged down in Nicaragua, unable to contain the guerrillas led by Augusto Sandino.
Instead, however, of recognizing that Sandino was winning
because he had the support of his people, instead of just packing
up and leaving, the United States initiated the first dive-bombing
missions in aviation history. Not for the first, and unfortunately
not for the last time, the United States was expressing its confidence in victory through technology. But something more disturbing, and equally persistent, was being expressed by those planes.
By deciding to bomb what it could not control, the United States
was setting up a barrier that still stands today. Almost sixty years
later, the United States is still tormenting an adversary, which it
refuses to look in the face, dive-bombing it with more remote, less
visible methods.

Generals and politicians have always known that it is easier to
kill an enemy whom one can portray as a demon. By strange coincidence, the year of the dive-bombing, 1928, happens also to be the
year when Erich Maria Remarque's great antiwar novel, *All Quiet
on the Western Front*, was published. In its culminating scene, the
protagonist, Paul, fatally wounds an enemy soldier and is then
forced to spend a whole day in a trench watching him die. It was
the abstraction of the enemy that Paul stabbed; if he had known
his face, his family, his past, he would have had difficulty killing
him. Half a world away, dive-bombing became one more way in
which the Pauls of this world could be separated from the Diegos
and the Marías they were being asked to massacre.

To fraternize with the enemy is not easy. Even when the will to
do so is present, the practical obstacles may be insuperable. Once

Los Angeles Times Book Review, June 16, 1985.

in a while, however, a book appears that allows us to know the enemy without having to watch him die, a book that reveals to us that the enemy is a human being, a book that, if widely read and profoundly understood, could prevent a war.

Fire from the Mountain by the Nicaraguan Omar Cabezas, is such a book. Though Sandinistas like him have been branded the enemy by the president of the United States, Americans who read his story with an open mind may find it hard to say, after finishing it, "This man is my enemy. This man must be eliminated."

Cabezas is unquestionably a revolutionary. He narrates how he joined the Sandinista movement as a student, was sent into the mountains to train as a guerrilla, survived there, organized the peasants, escaped Somoza's raids. Those Americans who have long forgotten that their country is the product of a revolution tend to find such stories dreary to repellent. But even they, I believe, are in for a surprise.

Even those, in other words, who disagree with the author's politics, will find his story fascinating. It is, after all, the story of how a pitifully small handful of men overthrew a dictator whose family had been in power for forty years. When they began in the 1960s, scarcely anybody could have predicted that the Sandinistas—hounded by the police, surrounded by impoverished people who were too frightened to collaborate—would be able to build up enough support to destroy Somoza's army by 1979. The Sandinistas themselves had difficulty keeping the faith.

In order to explain how this political miracle occurred, Cabezas does not mouth slogans or undertake windy sociological analyses. Instead, he undresses himself in public. He concentrates on his own evolution. War heroes generally shrink from sharing their secrets with us, from letting us into their dreams. But because Cabezas became the man he is by hiding nothing from himself, he hides nothing from the reader. It is all here: the weaknesses, the doubts, the illusions, the mistakes, the machismo, the astonishment. All of it without a shade of narcissism. And because Cabezas has exposed the whole inner landscape of his humanity, the reader believes the author when he gets around to his idealistic commitment to liberation, freedom, and the common good. Nobody who has accompanied Cabezas on this journey into manhood will ever again hear the State Department account of the sinister Sandinistas in quite the same way.

And yet we can find so much more than politics in this book. In Kathleen Weaver's energetically colloquial translation, there is the author's extraordinary sense of humor, the irreverence and earthiness of his language, the sensuality of his imagery. There is his breathtaking, erotic, almost mystical descriptions of nature; his meditations on history and the absurd, on the need for tenderness in the midst of toughness, on the way in which the past traps and forms the present. Such visions seem astounding in a man who does not consider himself a writer at all, until we remember—as Carlos Fuentes does in his striking introduction—that Cabezas comes from the country of Ernesto Cardenal and, above all, of Rubén Darío (1867–1916), the greatest Spanish-language poet of his day. Only Nicaragua, where poetry has survived not in seminars but in the streets, could have produced Cabezas, as only Nicaragua could have produced the eighty-year-old peasant who, when he first saw Cabezas and the guerrillas arrive, said almost nonchalantly that he had been expecting them to pick up the weapons they left the last time. The last time? Sixty years ago. The old man had been waiting sixty years for the sons of Sandino to come again.

To Americans, such a country must seem a mystery. It is a mystery to Cabezas himself, who discovers its secrets slowly, treating it as one would a new lover. Let us hope that rather than destroying Nicaragua from afar or, worse yet, dive-bombing the country a second time, America will start reading Nicaragua's poets—and Omar Cabezas.

Get Rich, Young Man,

or, Uncle Scrooge Through the Looking Glass

When he made his first appearance in a Donald Duck comic back in 1947, he was nothing more than a rich old duck. Carl Barks picked his name out of Dickens's *A Christmas Carol* and added McDuck for good measure. One year later this Scottish surname was put to excellent use when the Duck, a bit wealthier and just as stingy, set out to find a treasure in an ancestor's castle in Scotland, outwitting a crook and some ghosts. This was the first of many criminals he would overcome and one of many treasures he would hunt all over the globe, towing along his reluctant nephew Donald and the three brain-kids Huey, Dewey, and Louie, who always managed to get him out of trouble.

By the time Disney upgraded McDuck to a comic book of his own, in 1952, he was established as not just another opulent barnyard bird, but as the most affluent duck in the world. No, in the universe. He had, after all, accumulated umpteen centrifugilillion dollars or, according to other estimates, one multiplujillion, nine obsquatumatillion, six hundred and twenty-three dollars and sixty-two cents.

But he was so tightfisted that he would never have dished out a dime for his own comic book, as millions of kids did, making it the best-selling children's magazine of the 1950s and 1960s. And, thirty years later, he would certainly not pay $159.95 for a limited edition of twelve of his adventures, now in book form, even if it were a handsome leather-bound publication, recolored in dazzling

---

Review of *Uncle Scrooge McDuck: His Life and Times*, by Carl Barks, and of the United States Post Office twenty-cent stamp of Horatio Alger, in the *Village Voice* (New York), December 28, 1982.

hues by Peter Ledger, with a separate hand-signed lithograph of a painting by Carl Barks.

If McDuck were to read Thorstein Veblen, he'd realize that he was supposed to squander his well-gotten gains on objects of luxury and leisure, thereby distinguishing himself from the needy. But the only thing conceivably larger than Uncle Scrooge's fortune is his avarice. He will not read a paper unless he picks it up in the park; he will not buy the pills the doctor prescribed; he will trek across the Klondike on foot to avoid paying for a plane ticket. It doesn't matter that by refusing to acquire the newspaper he is losing millions in the stock market, nor that those pills will help him make big bucks by keeping his temporary amnesia at bay. It does not even matter that he is the owner of a company that flies all over Alaska. Logic doesn't count.

McDuck's opulence is there to see, to touch, to smell, to taste but never to consume or invest. Though Reagan might cite him as the prototype of the self-made man who will save the country, he is also the nightmare of supply-side prophets. He hoards his gold instead of plowing it back into the economy. If the rest of us were to follow his advice and save our last nickel, the system would flounder for lack of buyers.

Uncle Scrooge, therefore, is a very special sort of capitalist, the kind that strikes it rich by selling more lemonade than the kid next door or by finding a pot of gold at the end of the rainbow. Carl Barks was careful to separate him from those who made their money by exploiting other people: "I purposely tried to make it look as if Uncle Scrooge made most of his money back in the days before the world got so crowded, back in the days when you could go out in the hills and find riches." Scrooge extracts wealth directly from mother nature, without hurting anybody, just by the sweat of his feathers. And each time he increases his fortune he goes about it the same way, rushing off to find a colossal diamond or into space to bring back a twenty-four-carat moon. No one ever possessed or generated this wealth; no human effort ever went into creating it. McDuck's money is as faceless as the inhabitants of the hundreds of valleys from which he has brought back his riches, and as innocent. Just like his namesake, Ebenezer, McDuck has, underneath a flint-skin exterior, a heart of gold truer than what lies in his safe-deposit boxes. Over and over again he will sacrifice his money to save outer-space savages from famine, or an old lady-friend from the poorhouse, or little duckniks in Arabia (the Arabian adventure appears in another Scrooge book published by Abbeyville in 1979).

Even if we were not won over by this sentimentalism, we would still be hard-pressed to see much mischief in his plutocracy. We are told that he owns oil wells, fish shops, peanut stands, shipping companies, and coal mines (in one episode he decides to leave the city because of the smog that his own factories pour forth). But this property of his is never seen in action; we never witness his money "working" for him, as present ads for the savings and loan associations urge. He owns everything, but does not use it. Or rather, he uses it for only one enjoyable purpose, inward and not outward: he likes to dive into his three cubic acres of moolah like a porpoise and scrub his back with tinkling coins and memorize the dates on them. With this sensual, harmless obsession as his only real asset in life, his money, rather than giving him power, renders him vulnerable. He seems more an old grouch than a slave driver, more in need of protection than expropriation. This defenselessness, which makes him endearing, also ignites each adventure.

To save his fortune, fortify it, hide it, compare it, or augment it, Scrooge and company scatter all over the world. A lemming that has run off with a locket containing the secret formula to Scrooge's safe must be pursued to Norway. Earthquakes so worry the old insomniac that he burrows miles into the earth to make sure no cracks are in sight. He sweats out, suffers out, worries out every penny he has earned. And of course, and more important as a trigger for action, he is incessantly set upon by all sorts of cunning operators, from the Beagle Boys to unscrupulously mustachioed pigs, from the witch Magica de Spell, who is out to get the first dime McDuck ever pocketed, to Chisler McSue, who demands that the scurrillionaire deliver a lost crate of horseradish that an ancestor of his should have taken to America three hundred years ago (it lies at the bottom of the sea) or pay for it now with compounded interest.

In this race with crooks of all persuasions and shapes, Scrooge's ample resources do not give him the slightest advantage. He beats his rivals not by overpowering them with his fabulous holdings (as any normal capitalist would); rather, starting from an inferior position, he shows that he *deserves* his wealth, that he is not only the legal but the moral owner of that bonanza. In this sense, he incessantly reconstructs the foundations of his abundance: hard work, frugality, honesty, pluck, and—more than anything else— luck. Again and again, he is returned naked and miserable to beggarhood, then rebuilds his bins of money until every last cent has been recouped. Scrooge embodies one of the most persistent American beliefs: the myth that anyone, with determination and the appropriate ethical standards, can go from rags to riches, the myth that Horatio Alger made famous.

Alger was born 150 years ago, and to commemorate this event, the U.S. Post Office has printed a twenty-cent stamp. It is strange that Alger, whose books are no longer read and have no literary merit, should be given this honor; nineteenth-century writers of the stature of Melville, Hawthorne, and Jack London still have no stamps with their images. And if it is argued that what's being celebrated is the influence of the works and not the skills of the writers, then how about Harriet Beecher Stowe, and Edward Bellamy, and Upton Sinclair, whose works certainly helped change U.S. history? Of course, none of these writers is held up by President Reagan or by corporate America as a model by which the economy can be saved. If everybody acted like a Horatio Alger hero and went out to make himself a fortune and forgot welfare, if everybody had confidence in the wisdom of fate (and the market), like George Gilder preaches to us, if everybody was as generous with his profits as the senior citizens who help Horatio's young heroes when they are down and out, well then the recession would disappear faster than you can say Jack Kemp . . .

The dream that Horatio Alger popularized, the promise this dream holds for everyone, is embedded deep in the American psyche, as these comics of Uncle Scrooge prove. Both Walt Disney and Carl Barks were born in 1901, two years after the death of Horatio Alger. Both of them, like so many others, came from rural communities where adolescents continued to find in Alger's novels a guide to social climbing and success. Disney's life reads like an Alger story, and Alger's stories inspired Bark's most memorable character. And both of them—the entrepreneur and the salaried artist—can be understood only if we see that they spent their life reaching out to what H. L. Mencken called the capitalist that is in every American heart.

This would seem to explain Uncle Scrooge's old-fashioned origins, the fact that—more than his hat, his sideburns, and his spats—it is his mind which is deeply rooted in the nineteenth century. Yet, if ideologically McDuck goes back to Horatio Alger and the mass production of American myths, aesthetically he may be nearer to Charles Dodgson—the real name of the creator of *Alice in Wonderland,* who was, like Alger, born in 1832. I don't think Barks would have had much success with his superbillionaire if he had not developed his art in the tradition opened up by Lewis Carroll. When McDuck and his family go off to search for treasure or to outguess criminals, their ventures begin to feel tiresome. But every so often—and with Barks this is more frequent than with most cartoonists—we come across a delightful exploration of the world of jabberwocky, a feeling that we are on the verge of an insane wild universe more akin to the theater of the absurd than to Mickey Mouse.

Barks pushed back the boundaries of what was called reality and let his imagination go, grow, overflow. His best moments occur when he spawns creatures and situations that not even the most advanced special effects could create. We discover that the causes of earthquakes are not geological: the Fermies, who lift, and the Terries, who roll and push, hold competitions miles underground, to see who can shake the ground the most. They hear about their exploits on the radio, and from it they have learned English . . . in country/western style. How do you distinguish one species from the other? "That's easy! We Terries wear bow-ties. . . . And we Fermies wear four-in-hands!" Similar delights are the Peeweegahs, Indians who speak verse as if they came out of "The Song of Hiawatha"; a giant string-ball contest in the African jungle; and the paradise of Trallalla, destroyed by a six-week rain of bottle caps. In these adventures, as in *Alice in Wonderland* or *Through the Looking Glass,* people can change shape, time can float backward, objects can melt, animals can spout double-talk wisdom, and satire is allowed to grind its axe, which makes Barks much more than just an entertainer.

And yet he had to work within the limits of twentieth-century mass art—a form which Horatio Alger practiced on a vast scale. Alger was among the first to appeal to a mass audience with industrialized fiction, churning out a series of repeated formulas, shallow characters, and quick plots, shutting out all hints of dark doubts and unresolved questions. After the Civil War and until the end of the century, Alger put out three or four novels a year (109 altogether), and from *Ragged Dick* on, they were best sellers. He not only whispered to young men about how to succeed in the evil city without losing their innocence, but he also incarnated in his work the future of the media, the way in which mass entertainment could be produced. *Uncle Tom's Cabin* may have helped precipitate the Civil War, as Abraham Lincoln claimed; Horatio Alger helped stave off another sort of war, between classes, which was brewing in the empire-building decades before World War I. He did it by holding out for millions the goals of success and faith in the system, and by finding the formulas whereby those goals could be marketed and sweetly swallowed. So, ultimately, in the fight for the talent and perhaps the soul of Carl Barks, it is safe to bet that Horatio Alger has beaten Lewis Carroll. After all, nowadays most of the children—and the adults—of the world think that *Alice in Wonderland* is an animated cartoon made by Walt Disney.

Evil Otto and
Other Nuclear Disasters

Millions of people don't need to meditate along with Jonathan Schell to know that the world might end. To them, especially if they are young, the world has ended many times over. Indeed, at this very instant, thousands are at ground zero, watching the world and themselves explode. They press buttons, pull triggers, flick levers, command missiles, look at the bombs raining down, blind the universe. If they stay cool, keep up constant fire, save their ammunition, they can buy two minutes more, another half hour of survival, until finally the enemy has outnumbered them. For a while they are, they were, the target at the center of the laser's eye, the last witness to the storm.

To them, the world is ending, not with a bang or a whimper, but with a zap. They are playing video games.

They put another quarter in another machine, and, once again, they have plugged into the right to fight and keep the world spinning.

Most people, both voyeurs and players, would not agree.

"It's a compelling activity," proclaims a Los Angeles behavioral scientist, "where kids learn to interact with the technology of the future, to solve problems, and experience success. . . . It's a confidence builder." An educational consultant suggests that this is the best road to computer literacy, to growing familiar with machines and trigonometry. It's a game, say others, that helps rid you of aggression. Takes kids off drugs. Lets unathletic youths gain acceptance and status with peers. And, not to be forgotten in these recession times, it's a billion-dollar industry. But in the words of a player, any player:

"Video games? They're just plain fun."

Village Voice (New York), June 15, 1982.

While all of these views, particularly the last one, account for the games' amazing popularity, video games are also, and maybe primarily, a way in which people, most of them teenagers, can press the button which begins a nuclear war. Press the button, and remain alive.

The name of the game is survival. Most of the more addictive ones deal directly with armed conflict. A battle, generally in space, is engaged. When the screen throbs open, deterrence has just failed. Maybe it never existed. Maybe the players always knew, in that deep arcade inside the mind, that it would never work. This is reality: to be thrust, instantaneously, into the abrupt universe where the enemy is about to attack. In spite of flashing lights and pulsating sounds, the inescapable landscape is barren, ecologically on the brink of a void.

There is no history. Communications cannot be opened because the eliminators are absolutely inhuman. The evil they embody lacks a set of values or meaning. Monsters, insectlike skulls, robots, geometric patterns and spikes, subhuman specks out of a Rorschach nightmare, their exclusive function is to destroy. They are *alien*. And armed with nukes, smart-bombs, missiles, laser rays, quarks, and other such friendly weapons. So is the player. But the aliens' power is inexhaustible, forever replenishable, whereas the poor player's resources are limited. It is their vulnerability, the fact that he (90 percent of players are male) is hopelessly outnumbered that makes the primary mission self-preservation. Defense, more than attack, all the video-game books murmur, is the first golden rule; if you're not alive, you can't rack up those points. So anybody who wants to play must expect transformation into a military machine, skilled and instinctual: eyes, fingers, and a nervous system to coordinate them. Sensitivity, emotion, intelligence, culture, we are forewarned, have nothing to do with survival in the face of overkill. This is war, son. But also: this is a war that cannot be won.

It cannot be won.

I can remember no other game where the player knows as a certainty from the start that he will lose, where that irremediable loss is programmed into its very rules.

All the player can do is accumulate time and hysteria, gather bonus ships, stave off extermination, prepare for the next wave of marauders. Each success, each new level gained, makes the enemy and the rhythm faster, more relentless. The expendability of his multiple adversaries and the extinction which awaits him preclude a truce or a breather. Shields, bunkers, nooks where you can hide for a while—all the lulls are transitory, evanescent and may (as in Asteroids when you use hyperspace) mean the risk of death.

Even the best player grows weary and must finally abandon ship.

As of late, it is true, some space-battle games have appeared with a crusading spirit. The hunted apparently become the hunter, off on an offensive mission against a base (Scramble, Super Cobra) or a fortress in the middle of nowhere (Zaxxon, Star Castle). But an attack, a raid, a rescue, no matter how adroit and determined, cannot save you. Just as in Asteroids, Galaxians, Bosconian, and Omega Race, the player finds himself ultimately cornered. The end, when it comes, is always the same; the triangle, the humanoid, the ship is melted, popped, vaporized, shrieked into hell. Just as there was no history that led up to this, there is now no corpse, no fragments, not even dust unto dust.

The war is over, and, as would happen in any nuclear confrontation, we have lost.

ֵ≈

Video games in their present form would be inconceivable if the world did not have the means to blow itself to pieces. Not only because the same computer technology that spawned real missiles with warheads also spawned mock missiles with psychedelic flares on a screen. Nor because the games in the machine imitate the strategy, the targeting, the jargon of the "war games" played in real rooms by real adults in uniform. (*Newsweek* even reported that the Pentagon has been using versions of them as training devices.)

Video games are the product of a society where apocalypse is possible, only a flicker away. Though the scenes supposedly occur under faraway constellations and have indefinable aliens as opponents, I see them in reality as a way of acting out, on another level, the predicament now being called nuclear.

To anybody who has seen the latest catastrophe films or the movies from the 1950s in which monsters from outer space (and nearer-by) arrive in order to ravage "civilization" (usually some small, middle-American town), the proposition that computerized games are a metaphor for social reality or collective consciousness should not come as a shock. Just in case the reader is unconvinced, however, he or she can take a look at the one game, Missile Command, that is overtly, even flagrantly, about nuclear strife. In it the player must defend six American cities, fighting Soviet nukes, sputniks, and ICBMs (in another version, Red Alert, which I have encountered only underneath Penn Station, five foreign cities plus New York are under attack). But what was appropriate in arcades with their floating jetsam of would-be warriors seems to have been deemed uncomfortable for home sweet home. When Atari adapted Missile Command for home video, the attack came from the evil planet Krytol swarming down on the peace-loving and hard-working Zardonians. What Atari did with open atomic conflagration we can do as well, but in reverse. Just baptize the attacking aliens with Russian names, and you'll find out what you've been fighting for all this time. It does not matter what you call the game. Space Invaders is just as much about nuclear warfare as Missile Command.

All these games, in the last analysis, are tools for living through annihilation, of becoming *nihil*, nothing. In Galaxians, a brief dirge accompanies the good-bye bam. Missile Command gives you a mushrooming cloud where a couple of words, THE END, spasmodically flash on before being swallowed. These games of death, then, are a way of dealing with an eventual holocaust, a way of "feeling" and "handling" the unthinkable. They drain nuclear warfare of the remoteness and distance it has assumed, its everyday invisibility, and give the video wizard a function in the end of the world, permitting him some premonition of, and indeed role in, his own extinction. He can visualize in military terms the scene that commences one second after total destruction has been launched. The game lends a framework to a madness that, once unleashed, would break all the rules. The player is afforded, at least, an up-against-the-wall control of the scenario.

But to suppose that these exercises in life and death are only an experience of the unknown, bringing what is vaguely suspected into the apprehensive reach of mind and finger, is to miss half the story. The player is not only a warrior who will die fighting, he is also a witness, who will see, survive, continue breathing. Sports and art seem to combine. The ritual of anticipation shapes the terror, but then dispels it. The ship is extinguished while the real-life body, here in the arcade, remains alert and alive. This immortality is not only physical, but can also be inscribed on the screen. The most adept players of the day, and of the machine, get to carve their initials on the electronic board of fame.

So video games fulfill our fears, but also answer them. The realm of fire is entered, performed, and then postponed. It is the dream we all had as children when we were punished: to die and watch the reactions of those left behind. Many of us still subscribe to these illusions. Video games resurrect them, allowing players to commit collective suicide, while denying and trivializing the ultimate powers of the menace. Computerized games seem to be the safest, most self-gratifying form of facing this predicament.

This possibility of experiencing death safely appears to be a unique case in the history of games. We are a long way from the funfairs, where the passerby could throw eggs or cakes at real people, or bang overstuffed rabbits and cats off their shelf. Then came the shooting galleries, where ducks were massacred against a painted scenery. What was happening was physical, direct violence. The war machines of the 1950s changed that. The enemy you were sniping at from your cabin or the carrier you were blasting from your sub, was a representation of reality. But they never shot back. You were never on the screen, but always in command. Time would run out, and that was it.

Pinball machines came next. There, as in video games, you had to make the experience last. It was up to you to play the ball well and up to your teasing luck as well. (Luck has no place in video games, by the way.) Mastering time wasn't a problem of war, but of sex. Keep the ball from going into the slot, from disappearing. Keep the machine hot and the hand cool, both vibrating. The ball wasn't you, but your appendage. And it was never annihilation that was threatened but—I suspect—jacking off. The craving must have been there all these years. The technology, on the other hand, wasn't.

But it was not inevitable, this sort of evolution. In fact, the first two successful arcade video games, Pong (1972) and Sea Wolf (1976), did not cope with total warfare. Pong was a duel between two paddles and had to be played with a partner. Sea Wolf was an update of the old submarine periscope games of yesteryear. (Battlezone later did the same thing for tanks.) In these first games, you were not destroyed. Indeed, in Shark (1975) the player bites away at four divers, and in Death Race (1976), the merry idea is to run over as many pedestrians as possible. In the beginning, therefore, the player was in the dominant role. Space War, in 1977, made a battle the focus for the first time, but the conclusion was not foreclosed: your money, and not your skill, bought time, and you could finish without losing anything other than your shirt. Only in 1978, when Space Invaders, introduced by Midway from Japan (remember the samurai? remember the name of two cities in Japan in 1946?), hit the United States, did video games become big business. By the way, the end of the world on the screen was the beginning of a new quarter being taken out of the pocket. Commercial interests seem to marry well with ideology, in this case.

But what matters is that the player is turned into a victim, a role he seems to need and enjoy, because all games since then have kept him there. He has also remained a loner. After Pong, home video games, in an attempt to appeal to the family market, have gone back to partnership and have adapted collective sports (baseball and company) for the screen. But in the arcades, only Rip Off, a minor game, needs a team. Two can play other games, but it's not done frequently. Even when they do, they're not playing each other, or with each other. They're both isolated, playing the machine, the aliens. Other humans don't exist, on the screen or as partners. The player is the last man.

The same can be said of nonwar video games, those that are apparently less aggressive. One might almost conjecture that Frogger and Donkey Kong are the civilian side of the space battles raging in the nearby machines, a nonmilitary follow-up of the same dilemma, relying on their quickness and agility to sidestep the menacing, overwhelming world.

A similar picture emerges from the maze games, the most famous of which is Pac-Man. In the labyrinth, the cute mouth of Pac-Man (or Ms. Pac-Man) eats up dots (points), while it is pursued by four devouring ghosts. But Pac-Man is not defenseless. By eating an energizer, he can turn the tables on his adversaries, converting them into momentary victims. During a few seconds, they are chased. But when they die, they are reincarnated—and will come back forever. The player, as usual, does not have infinite lives. So the result can never be a draw or a win. This situation is repeated in other maze games. In Mousetrap, as the player advances, he becomes alternatively mouse, cat, or dog, swallowing inferiors according to his ever-changing identity. The only thing he can never be is the hawk that preys upon all the other animals. In Robotron: 2084 (Orwell, did you hear that?) beware the robots that reprogram humans into "sinister progs."

Indeed, it may well be that those who eat and are eaten in a labyrinth are, in fact, a more complete expression of the contemporary situation of men and women in a nuclear age than those who fire their antiballistic missiles at roving aliens. Under Pac-Man's adorable, smiling guise lurks the reality of total cutthroat competition and the total instability that underlies it. Today you are stronger than your rivals, tomorrow they will hunt you down. The labyrinth is a claustrophobic marketplace. This dance of dominance and subordination, slyness and mobility down long winding corridors gives us an image, not only of the nuclear predicament, but of the paranoid, violent world that gave rise to such a predicament. A world where we do not control the decisions that might lead to our destruction because we do not, to be quite frank, control anything very important in our lives.

Computerized games, therefore, allow the player that which his situation in society has taken from him: some degree of involvement—twisted, vicarious, and tangled as it may be—in the preservation of his own existence. Video games reveal to people, at the fingertips, in a coded, guarded fashion, what they know in their guts: the vulnerability sensed in the dark underbelly of the mind. At the same time, they are getting a handle (or is it a lever?) on life. The game warns them that they are doomed and insecure, and while it tells this tale, it tells them as well that, meanwhile, they must hustle, be suspicious, breed quick reflexes, go it alone. That's the key to stayin' alive, stayin' alive.

Much of the popularity of video games may therefore be due to the way in which they help the young, and their elders, if they are snappy enough, to play out their anxieties and identify them without having to acknowledge the loneliness, the hostility, the grinding terror inside. All mass entertainment, in order to sell and please, must answer not only the hopes, but the fears, of its clients.

Video games are also, however, part of a general process now being called psychic numbing—as if this numbing had not been around much longer than nuclear weapons. It is not a consequence of that sort of armament but its cause. Those who play video games and leave their sensitivity and ethics aside when they deal with fictitious extinction on the blithe screen, when they militarize their free time, do so in the same society that contemplates mass murder as deterrence, corpses as statistics, forty million dead as victory, permanent escalation as peace. Their remoteness from what their fingers are pressing, their failure to seriously imagine what might be happening at the other end, is just a minor product and prolongation of the general remoteness of a system that has lost its capacity for caring about, or even believing in the reality of, other human beings. Video games are anesthetics because we live in a dehumanized society, where suffering has been made invisible by indifference, where the pain of others is simply not real.

When we die on that screen, when we kill on that screen, are we purging that death, are we becoming more sane, more responsible, are we cleansing ourselves of it? Or does the game, instead, wipe out our moral capacity for outrage, bury it even deeper than it is now buried?

Roger Molander was a staff member of the National Security Council for seven years. One day, he asked, he dared to ask, "Where are all the grown-ups?" He had come to the conclusion that those in charge had the adult capacity for destruction, but that they wielded it with the childlike abandon of the very innocent, as if they were not answerable for what they did.

Recently, the film *Atomic Cafe* has awarded us insight into the pressures brought to bear against those who lived through the Cold War. I was surprised to discover that the methods the American government used in the 1950s to create a climate about nuclear war are not that different from those that, twenty years later, General

Pinochet has put into practice against the people of my country, Chile. In both cases, the idea is to terrorize and, at the same time, proclaim normality. The populace must be frightened out of its wits, while suggesting simultaneously that the government and its experts have things under control. The threats from the enemy can be downplayed because the answer to those threats is invariably the same: the accumulation of more power in the hands of the authorities.

The American children who were harrowed by subterranean visions of extermination and superficial reassurances of indifference, the children who heard the siren wailing while they crouched under their desks, the ones who lived through the Cold War, the air raid drills, are the very adults who have invented the buttons on today's video games. Many of the youngsters frantically playing today's video games may be in charge of tomorrow's *real* buttons. People who live life as a video game may, heaven and Pac-Man help us, be in charge of those weapons right now.

Isn't it time we all grew up?

Norteamericanos, *Call Home*

Most people buy a novel based on a movie in order to dupli-
cate an already pleasurable experience. The written word
lets them control the rhythm of the camera and relive
the story in comfort, far from the madding popcorn crowd. My
reasons are different. Knowing that a book cannot manipulate us
as readily as anything audiovisual, search for clues to what really
happened on the screen, almost hoping that the author will have
excluded something vital, that he will have altered enough so I can
discover in retrospect the essential, irreplaceable element that cannot be repeated in another medium. But generally my hopes are
thwarted: we tend to get rehashes performed by hacks.

For once, however, I have been fortunate. William Kotzwinkle's narrative version of *E. T.: The Extra-Terrestrial* has removed
the pulsing, dancing core of the movie. It was not his intention, I
am sure, but he has smuggled us a blueprint with which to interpret the original. By reading his book, we can come to terms with
the real reasons for that film's phenomenal success. Paradoxically,
Kotzwinkle's offshoot is interested in adults. Perhaps there was
no other way a writer as accomplished as the author of *Doctor
Rat* could avoid a dull and parasitic line-by-line repetition of the
screenplay. He had to find a universe of his own to play with, and
the only direction for independent development and depth was
toward the senior characters.

Strange that the producers chose for the novelization of this film,
which is directed to the vast demographic of the "young at heart,"
someone like Kotzwinkle, who does not focus especially on the
children, but is fascinated rather by Mary, the kids' mother, and

Village Voice (New York), August 24, 1982, book review of William Kotzwinkle's
novelization of *E. T., The Extra-Terrestrial*.

by the extraterrestrial himself. The mother is growing old and does not like it. E. T. is ten million years old, "older than Methuselah, as old as old," and loves it. He wants to stay that way. He would also like to return to his interstellar routes before Earth's gravity tears him asunder. Although in the book E. T. has a childlike Wordsworthian worship of living beings, it is pervaded by a "terrible and ancient knowledge," communicating with star-energies and other such elevated and inscrutable beings. Mary is worried about more down-to-earth dilemmas: early menopause, late psychiatry, aching feet at work, pornography, calories and beauty cream, suburbia, and recurring visions of devastating males in bed or at the door. She does not know that Kotzwinkle has injected into the space elf a rather improbable crush on her. While she pines away, a three-footer from the stars debates in her son's closet how best to communicate his feelings. To the story of love between the children and the visitor, which formed the basic plot of the picture, has been added an ironic and sad description of unrequited and impossible love, a reverse fairy tale in which the frog does not gain admittance to the dormitory and never quite becomes the prince.

It is clear that perspectives such as these, from the mature side of life, would have destroyed the film's charm as well as its box-office clout. In the movie, adults are either remote and menacing or close by and ridiculous. They are always useless. They are the real aliens in the camera's laughing lense, not E. T.

So nothing could push the book further from the movie than classifying its extraterrestrial with the adults or trying to give us a notion, as Kotzwinkle does, of how the world might look through the eyes of a more evolved species stranded on our planet. By doing so, Kotzwinkle has acted like someone who, trying to copy Leonardo's *Mona Lisa*, has left out not only the famous smile, but the mouth itself, the framework for the smile. Children are the smile in *E. T.*, the movie. Spielberg's whole strategy has been to strip the universe down to the visions and dimensions of the young. He has also, as is wont to happen in fairy tales, dared the spectators to rejuvenate themselves if they care to enjoy the show. This much has been noted by all—movie critics, spectators, and film executives. Yet what seems to have escaped us and what Kotzwinkle's novelization obliquely reveals by turning E. T. into such a solemn and slow and ponderous old organism, is that the creature from outer space is, in the movie, also a child. His aspect may be ancient and turtlelike, but he is treated like a baby, both by his protectors and his cinematic narrators.

Part of that childishness is, naturally, in the novel as well. It can be attributed to the hostile environment and culture where he has been abandoned. Foreigners invariably have that air of the newborn about them, as they try to adjust to a strange land. But E. T. is purportedly of superior intelligence, agog with magical powers. In theory, he should be able to cope very well. He has all the wisdom of the celestial spheres at his cosmic fingertips and is proficient in telekinesis and telepathy. But what happens to these diverse talents in the movie is significant. They are, in fact, pseudo-powers, bestowed upon him by the script more than by nature so that he may seem mysterious and preeminent, so that he can play with them and with us, give us a thrill or a laugh. Then they are conveniently forgotten for the purposes of the plot. In fact, he is more like a small savage from the Third World or the backlands than a Milky Way wizard. There is no reason why he should be so clumsy, why he should raid the refrigerator and spill everything, why he should get drunk, why he never proceeds beyond a pidgin English ("E. T. phone home") such as Tarzan used in his first film and countless Indians have stuttered in so many others.

Or rather, the reasons have to do with the film's strategy: our boy from out yonder must be vulnerable, an orphan, somebody who provokes our tenderness, with whom we can all identify, full of sitcom gags. The movie does not give us time to ask these questions. We are carried along by the frames, the music, the montage. The book, on the other hand, must try, as literature will, to deliver a certain logical consistency to the character. So Kotzwinkle makes his space runt more wary of his action. The author will not permit him to be dressed up like Miss Piggy. He wants us to feel that we are in the presence of a god from the stars, a nuclear being, and that we should be properly awed. But not even he can explain why E. T. did not simply fly to his spaceship at the beginning instead of letting himself be tripped up by inferior roots and shrubs, turned into a Robinson Crusoe with duck-waddling feet and no Friday to lord it over. Kotzwinkle is trapped, as are we, in the original plot.

The novel has been derived from Melissa Mathison's screenplay, and not from the finished picture. If Kotzwinkle had seen and been enchanted by the creature in all its magic, he might never have been able to transmogrify it into such a consummate adult, and he certainly would not have underlined and exaggerated its deformities: "his hideous shrunken form, his horrible mouth, his long creepy fingers and toes, his grotesque stomach. . . ." This horror is not *our* adorable E. T. It is true that Spielberg has suggested that "only his mother could love him," but he forgot to add that the movie's greatest triumph is turning all of us into mothers. The wondrous mechanical being that Carlo Rambaldi concocted is strange and bizarre, but not at all threatening. It was merely designed to bring out our softest thoughts, to make "everybody love it," as one Hershey executive announced when asked if it was safe to have such a freak promote Reese's Pieces. He could have proved his point with Konrad Lorenz, who noted in *Studies in Animal and Human Behavior* that humans feel affection for animals with juvenile features: enormous eyes, bulging craniums, retreating chins. However much E. T. is beholden to worms, dragons, and insects for his looks, he is above all an overweight fetus, a wise man from outer space in the garb of an infant. This puerile condition is overwhelmingly visual and spectacular, so maybe it was better for Kotzwinkle not to have watched the animated marvel in motion, sucking up our sentiments. The novelist was able to devote himself to more literary whirls of empathy: "His thought patterns were not visible, could not be seen rainbowing above his head in brilliant, subtle waves." In other words, the intellectual glimmerings of a monster are not exactly filmable. But his childishness is.

It is this basic puppy filming, absent from the book, that has made the movie *E. T.* (and, of course, the book as well) such an incredible success. And such a relief. E. T. is so different from all the other fiends, ectoplasms, and psychopaths who have been howling and devouring their way through walls, bodies, and box offices. I have watched with consternation how the mounting curve of American paranoia in international affairs coincides with the mounting hysteria in horror movies. These pictures are laced with dread, insinuating a mental landscape where neither spectators nor characters feel safe. In *Poltergeist*, a typical case, adults try to save the children. *E. T.*, the film, predicates the reverse: it is the children who will save the adults, and they will do it because they comprehend that an alien is not to be inevitably feared, that we do not need to project our terrors upon him. Both the film and the novel refuse to see the stranger as a metaphor for that which must be eliminated, the stranger as an accusation or a blasphemy that can be stilled only through martyrdom or persecution.

This proposition, that we accept creatures unlike us no matter how revolting and ugly, that we stand up against intolerance and extermination, is not new to science-fiction literature. Kotzwinkle's book pursues the idea without adding anything to it. He has written about a Close Encounter of the Fourth Kind. By doing so, he throws into relief, once more, the inventiveness and originality of the Spielberg film. The U.S. audience, starved for affection and openness, is given a tale in which Beauty (the child) kisses the Beast (E. T.) and resurrects him, in which the tired wayfarer of forbidding demeanor but with a bag full of miracles is given hospitality and a hearth. Kotzwinkle, by making his fallen divinity so overwhelmingly superior, leaves us no alternative but to enter into an alliance with him; Spielberg has gone the opposite route, ensuring the monster's acceptance by making him a baby.

And of course the extraterrestrial poses no challenge, in the film and in the book, to the society that harbors him. There is no demand in either of them for a real dialogue with the creature or his civilization. In the book, his world is too mysterious and arcane to be understood, except through impalpable, improbable (and tiresome) waves of light and fingertips of fire, whereas in the film E. T. has no effective civilization, no distinct symbol system. Here is another clue to how an alien can convert the audience to the gospel of love. It is not enough for him to be a child. He must also have about him an air of familiarity, he must possess within himself a desire and capacity for cultural assimilation. In the film, he is not, in fact, alien to Americans at all. This may not seem obvious to people from the States, who tend to view their own habits and images as natural, eternal, and global. But to somebody from the Third World, as I am, to people who are real outsiders and misfits, it is clear that the walking vegetable with the valentine beating openly on his chest as a sign of friendliness, can be accepted as somebody to cuddle and protect, can be sheltered and watched over, because he is easily and comfortably integrated into American mass culture. His very semblance has been prepared by the doll industry, by the Muppets, and by animated cartoons. That is why, when the mother sees him amid a mountain of stuffed toys, he does not stand out.

Spielberg has made sure that all initial contacts between the alien and Elliot are through objects that any kid from the States would recognize, the symbols of the most popular folklife longings of twentieth-century America. The space goblin is enticed out of the foliage by a string of Reese's Pieces, almost as if he were a famished waif in an Asian or African alley. And the first rapport depends on baseball—the boy throws a ball into the toolshed, where the invader is hiding, and the ball bounces back. This may have been too much for Kotzwinkle, who in his quest for universality (a god must be everything to everybody, after all) substitutes an orange for the ball. He also eliminates Buck Rogers as a source of inspiration for phoning home. But Kotzwinkle adds an American trait when he informs us that the spaceship is like a gigantic glowing Christmas tree ornament. Who would guess that intergalactic beings would configure their vessels upon the commercialized American model for the Nativity? Or is this a subtle way of saying that the three kids are the Magi who recognize the Child?

E. T. has been lucky enough to get lost in a rather special, privileged place called California. He never would have made it back home if he had not chosen affluent children who have computer toys, walkie-talkies, record players, and other implements needed for his transmission to the stars. In fact, if E. T. had undergone his unfortunate space wreck among impoverished black girls and boys in Brazil, he never would have made it to the movies or the *New York Times* best-seller list and another sort of stardom.

Kotzwinkle's book allows us to see precisely why the extra-terrestrial in the film is not repulsive to the audience. Not only because of his infantile resonances, but because he has come straight from *Sesame Street*, a second cousin to Yoda. After melting so many nationalities within its borders and exporting its mass culture to so many foreign lands, what is one more space critter to America? The audience can adopt him in the same way that so many small orphans from across the globe, from multiple other very earthly worlds, have been adopted by foster families. An immigrant from another galaxy who does not have to pass through Ellis Island. But I should not complain.

With wars bursting all over the planet like hellfire, with chemicals tormenting our rivers and our vegetation, with whales hunted down to produce tennis racquets, with famine and dictators and a surfeit of rhetorical speeches and reports on how to deal with them, we should be glad that a delight like E. T. is around. Such a mild and lenient message, whether in the film or in the book, is encouraging, especially if the alternative is to watch *Aliens* or *Poltergeist*, or peruse their novelizations. At a time when a lack of trust among nations and human beings is pushing us to disaster, such a message is certainly welcome, and it should not surprise us that people, burdened with responsibilities they cannot handle, are thankful for it and ready to shell out some dollars for the quick comfort they derive. At least a million and a half have been so impressed that they have gone out and bought the book.

Even though Kotzwinkle has not given them the childish fun they expected, they will probably not be disappointed. He tells us again, although without engaging us completely and instantaneously as the film does, that just because somebody is different, it does not give us the right to be indifferent to his sorrows. But surely we do not have to wait for a traveler from outer space to teach us this. Surely there are plenty of people who are different and otherly and much nearer by, waiting under our own sun.

Or does every stranger have to first be infantilized and Americanized in order to gain acceptance?

Down Mexico Way . . . Before the Subcomandante Came Along

The only thing that used to ignite my curiosity about John D. MacDonald was his habit of changing colors for each new title; in the bookstore, out of the corner of my eye, I noticed that here was a writer who seemed to be exhausting the rainbow. Finally, intrigued by Kurt Vonnegut's suggestion that for future archaeologists MacDonald's works "would be a treasure on the order of the tomb of Tutankhamen," I read one of them and, in spite of my absolute devotion to Vonnegut, was not bowled over. Like any enterprising young Latin American writer, I had, back in Chile, devoured the thrillers of Hammett and Chandler. In the rapacious universe of their books, crime was an almost normal activity, for which everyone—victims, killers, and detectives alike—seemed responsible. MacDonald, on the other hand, did not manage to establish a link between evil and the atmosphere in which it takes root. His characters were as adrift in their lives as Travis McGee aboard his houseboat. I had the impression they were joined together like waves: all the same and existing only on the surface.

After that first misadventure, I didn't envisage a second one. But *Cinnamon Skin* seemed enticing because I'd been told that the "Chilean underground" [*sic*] was suspected of blowing up a boat. Having spent the last ten years under the impression that the terrorists in Chile are General Pinochet and his subordinates, I decided to take a look at how my excessively peaceful and patient countrymen were being portrayed. When, a dozen pages into the novel, we Chileans cease to be suspects, I plunged on. The book

---

Review in the *Village Voice*, October 4, 1983, of *The Last Lords of Palenque* by Victor Perera, *Cinnamon Skin* by John D. MacDonald, and *The Sculpture of Palenque*, volume I, by Merle Greene Robertson.

flap promised another sort of Latin American connection—Mexican jungles and pyramids, Mayans and their gods. Unfortunately, McGee doesn't arrive in the Yucatán until the end of the novel. Before that, we trail him and his sidekick, Meyer, across North America's wasteland. Everywhere they go, things fall apart. Though the nexus between MacDonald's troubled homeland and the murderer's lunacy is missing, it is at least clear that MacDonald cares for his country and its ecology.

No such care is lavished on the *Cinnamon* Mayans. There is not a hint that tourism, oil rigs, and acquisitive foreigners are wreaking havoc on their earth and their customs. The characters are clichés: peasants keep a secret network whereby they know everything that happens on their turf; old men worship idols, protected by impenetrable natives; at dawn, a Mayan princess-priestess, heir to the Old Empire, chants the name for the dead from the top of a pyramid. As luck would have it, the Mayan lass was brought up in Canada: McGee can ball her in English, and the other Indians can melt back into the swamps where they belong.

The Mayan hocus-pocus is ritual background: far from the muggy road to Miami Beach, men can "find out" the truth about themselves. This is convenient for Meyer, who is no longer a "one-hundred percent hero" but a real man. Meyer goes from humiliation to release, and his emergence as a whole, even wholesome, person is sure to comfort readers who have no reason to doubt the setting.

For those who do have doubts, who mind the fakery, two recent books movingly depict present-day Mayans and the ruins their ancestors once built. At the moment *Cinnamon Skin* was topping the *New York Times* hardback best-seller list, *The Last Lords of Palenque* by Victor Perera made a rather more modest appearance. And now that the paperback of *Cinnamon Skin* is on the same list, Princeton has brought out the first sumptuous volume of Merle Greene Robertson's *The Sculpture of Palenque*.

Victor Perera's Mayans are the last living descendants of one of the most sophisticated civilizations the world has known; the killer loose in the Mexican jungle is industrial development. After surviving the decline of the Old Mayan Empire, the madness of the Spanish conquest, the intrusion of assorted governments and entrepreneurs, the Lacandons in Nahá are on the brink of depletion. They hold on, tenaciously, tenuously, to their beliefs and their economy. The mahogany trees are being felled; without the rain forest, they lose not only the material base of their lives, but its spiritual foundations as well. They cannot build canoes to cross lakes or ceremonial huts to renew their links with the gods. The animals will disappear along with the trees—first from the diet and then from the cosmology and the dreams. Perera bears witness to the moment when a magnificent and proud culture faces assimilation or death.

For years, tar residues and toxic fumes from oil refineries have been eating away at Palenque, one of the most extraordinary ruins in the world. Hands and feet of tourists climbing the monuments have eroded the surfaces, and now, to this man-made assault volcanic ash has been added. Paint that has remained relatively intact for more than one thousand years is disappearing—not only the sort of color John D. MacDonald alters from book to book, but the mythic meaning behind and inside the colors: "Red seems to have represented the living world. Certain parts of serpents were assigned the color red—scales, teeth, tongue and sometimes beards. This may have been because these were considered the 'humanlike' living parts of serpents that die or are shed, and then are renewed (reborn) by the growing of new parts. Blue was designated the color of things divine, those objects pertaining to worship and the accession of kings. . . . Yellow was reserved for jaguar tails and spots, crosshatched areas, certain plants and portions of serpents. Perhaps they were motifs pertaining to the Underworld."

Archaeologist Merle Greene Robertson has sought to preserve images that no human eye will ever see again. She has worked with the thoroughness and lack of sentimentality of those who salvage ships about to founder. And if the text that accompanies her luxurious photos and precise drawings is dry, if she fails to provide a generous overview of Mayan mythology and society, she does manage to convey the Mayan obsession with resurrection and cycles. This volume, the first of five, deals with the Tomb of the Inscriptions, as important a monument as Tutankhamen's—the burial mound of Pacal, one of the greatest of Mayan statesmen. The sculpture transmits hope: Pacal has died, but a new god is being born. The world may succumb, but it will live again. This culture of rebirth is still alive, but barely, in the last inheritors of the legacy of Palenque. In 1938, when Victor Perera was a child, he saw five Lacandons exhibited like animals at the world's fair in his native Guatemala. He felt instinctively bound to them and later became convinced that his fate—and that of the planet—depended on the survival of these Mayans. In a world where people live in harmony with nature, where the oral tradition keeps the tribe together, where wisdom is not something bookish but a practical means of understanding everyday reality, Perera searched for redemption and guidance. He found them in Chan K'in, the spiritual chieftain of the Nahá community, who is able to interpret the most recent events with the oldest of myths—as if the sculptures in Palenque could explain our predicament.

This is not Castañeda in search of Don Juan. Perera's quest may stem from the same crisis that led Castañeda to invent his sham shaman—it may proceed from a similar desire for nonrational, nonpackaged, anti-industrial explanations of the universe. But though Chan K'in and his people read dreams as we read newspapers and, like Pacal, see animals as their doubles in a shadow world, they are also relentlessly, awkwardly contemporary, caught in the universe of detergents and airstrips, cassette recorders and batteries. The modern world is grinding them down. Perera holds onto his idealization of the Indians, rescues them as examples of dignity in the midst of disintegration, even while he soberly registers the community's decay, the divisions caused by American missionaries, Mexican forestry officials, and consumer goods, the confusion among the sons of Chan K'in about how to resist the alien influence. Chan K'in does not fight that termination. He sees it as part of an inevitable cosmic pattern: the land is weary and must be destroyed before Hachäkyum, the Creator, can revitalize it. But Perera, who knows his ecosystems, makes us sense that we are witnessing more than the end of 250 isolated men, women, and children. He seems to agree with Chan K'in that "when the last Lacandon dies, the world will come to an end."

Victor Perera undergoes rebirth, ventures deeper into the Mayan vision at the moment when the aboriginals who sustain and bequeath it are being suppressed. Though his tone is more poignant than Merle Greene Robertson's, both have an edge of loss, of despair.

They are outsiders testifying about something wonderful which is condemned to dissolution.

As for Travis McGee, needless to say, he doesn't find the real criminal. He doesn't figure out that genocide is going on not far from where he seeks redemption and sex under the Mayan moon. And, like far too many of his readers, he doesn't have a clue about the identity of the real victims.

Finding the Fever

Wallace Shawn's 1985 play, *Aunt Dan and Lemon*, ended with Lemon, the protagonist, defending genocide. She found it refreshing, Lemon told the audience, that Nazis honestly admitted, as she readily did and as everybody alive should, that there was considerable enjoyment to be had in killing other human beings. Besides, there was no other way of protecting one's way of life. And she went on to doubt that such a thing as real compassion could possibly exist. Her ambition was to go around to "loving and sweet" people and ask them: "Could you please describe the particular circumstances in which you felt it and what it actually felt like?"

The disquieting answer to that question can be found in Shawn's first work of fiction, *The Fever*. Compassion has indeed stabbed and entered the heart of the unnamed narrator of this brief, chilling novella—with daunting consequences. Alone in a hotel room in a country "where my language isn't spoken" (though it is implied that we are in a U.S. client state like El Salvador), this person cannot stop imagining the torture, rape, beatings, executions, poverty unfolding just down the street and in the multiple streets and nations beyond the mountains. What sickens the narrator—to the point of shivering and vomiting and hallucinating—is not only the incapacity to turn away from others' suffering, but the fact that those horrors are implacably linked to his or her own lifestyle, are indeed necessary if that comfort is to continue, if the coffee is to percolate in the morning and the garden is to be full of roses and violin sonatas are to be savored.

The mind that Shawn has selected for his voyage is unable, therefore, to carry out that primary exercise in disassociation that allows

Washington Post Book World (Washington, D.C.), April 7, 1991, book review.

people to keep on appreciating life in spite of the sorrows and violence, the strategy that is used by those who bomb civilians from
an airplane and by the torturer who casually presses the button that
will send a new charge of electricity through the sprawled woman
on the cot, all of whom can go home and kiss their children—the
same strategy used to step over the homeless body on the sidewalk
or shrug off the squalor of the inner-city tenement. The narrator
of *The Fever* cannot switch off the world at will as most people do,
nor can he or she, once that world comes howling in, deny complicity in its pain.

Though plotless, the story is compelling, because that voice,
while celebrating life and its wonders, simultaneously hunts down,
ambushes, and strangles every argument that affluent people use
in order to salve their consciences and luxuriate in that life, finally
concluding that

> My life is irredeemably corrupt . . . I keep thinking that
> there's this justification that I've written down some-
> where, on some little piece of paper . . . sitting inside
> the drawer of some desk in some room in some place I
> used to live. But in fact I'll never find that little piece
> of paper, because there isn't one, it doesn't exist.
>
> There's no piece of paper that justifies what the beggar
> has and what I have. Standing naked beside the beggar,
> there's no difference between her and me except a dif-
> ference in luck. I don't actually deserve to have a thou-
> sand times more than the beggar does. I don't deserve
> to have two crusts of bread more.

In an age where morality is so easily on people's lips and so infre-
quently in their acts, where the highest sounding intentions are
invoked to commit the most abominable crimes, at a time when
the Third World is fading from the sight of the comfortable citizens
of humanity except as faraway targets for war, or a nearby target
for commerce, it is encouraging that such an attack on ethical
indifference should not only have been written but that it should,
moreover, have been recently performed as a monologue by Shawn,
himself an accomplished actor.

And, yet, it is disturbing that this solitary voice should be trapped in such an either/or, all-or-nothing mentality, that the only choices are either giving up all one's money or becoming a soul mate of the devil. Coming as I do from a country that has had to suffer seventeen years of savage dictatorship and centuries of the sort of hunger and inequality that nauseates *The Fever*'s protagonist, coming from a land where, in order to survive, one must uneasily coexist with many forms of evil, I feel that putting moral options in this absolute way unavoidably leads to a self-loathing and passivity of little use to the victims for whom one is apparently feeling so much anguish.

This is, I believe, the final tragedy of the voice in *The Fever*. In that country of an unspeakable language, the narrator can see "all those people with the radiant faces . . . dying tonight," but cannot join them and cannot find a way of helping them and cannot hear them telling him, telling her, not to despair, not to let the malignant Lemons of the world have the last say.

Can a Dictator Tell Us
Something About Ourselves?

B ack in 1977, when Miss Margarida, that redoubtable schoolteacher, first strode onto a New York stage, it did not take
the audience long to figure out that they were in the hands
of a rather unusual tyrant.

Two minutes into *Miss Margarida's Way*, the play by the Brazilian writer Roberto Athayde, the protagonist was already getting down to business: abusing the children in her eighth-grade
class—that is, the spectators—idiots, she sneered, who had paid to
enter and now could not leave. Claiming, as all despots do, to be
acting for the good of her defenseless charges, Miss Margarida let
it be known that she would tolerate no disobedience, not a breath
of independent thought.

The self-control she was preaching to her "children," however,
clearly did not apply to her own words or body: two hours of sadis-
tic, hysterical rantings followed, punctuated by profanity, threats
of violence, and, above all, outbursts of suppressed sexuality. Her
lessons were fixated on domination and death: biology ("all of you
are going to die"), mathematics ("to divide means that each one of
you wants to get more than the others"), history ("everyone wants
to be Miss Margarida"), composition (the assignment is "a creative
paper describing your own funeral").

As elsewhere around the world, the New York audience embraced
the play; besides giving affluent theatergoers a chance to safely experience what it means to live under the frenzied eye and mouth of
a schizophrenic autocrat, *Miss Margarida's Way* was darkly, fore-
bodingly hilarious. One month after it opened at the Public Theater, with Estelle Parsons in the title role, it moved to Broadway
for a longer run.

New York Times, February 25, 1990, Sunday Arts and Leisure section.

Thirteen years later, when Big Sister—played by the same acclaimed actress—stomped back into town for a revival, scheduled to be performed at the Helen Hayes Theater at least through today, she faced a dramatically changed world.

ঽ৳

In 1977—a particularly dismal year—the spectators could identify Miss Margarida with a vast variety of favorite dictatorships, starting with Mr. Athayde's Brazil, or the sad neighboring countries of Argentina, Uruguay, Bolivia, Paraguay, or my own Chile. Other United States client dictators abounded: Somoza, the Shah, Duvalier, Marcos, and omnipresent generals in Guatemala and South Korea. In the rival camp, one could cast an eye on a genocidal Pol Pot or the beloved leader Kim Il-Sung or, in Eastern Europe, the gray Brezhnev look-alikes—patriarchal Miss Margaridas, imposing their bureaucratic socialism.

Most of these authoritarian figures have now happily departed from our midst. The most recent and extraordinary changes have, most certainly, been in the Soviet bloc—indeed, Elena Ceausescu's last words at her trial could almost have been lifted verbatim from one of Miss Margarida's monomaniacal monologues. But no less drastic improvements, even if hardly noticed by the media, have been transpiring in Brazil and Chile, where the first free presidential elections in many years were held last December.

The question, of course, given these auspicious global developments toward democracy, is whether the play has not aged irrevocably or, as most of the New York critics seem to feel, is politically irrelevant. Can Miss Margarida's ravings continue to inspire and, yes, "instruct" us?

An easy, preliminary answer is that there are plenty of power-starved oppressors still around—in China, in Haiti, in South Africa, in Albania, just to touch on four parts of the world. And those who have been ousted can't wait to get back into the limelight, determining the limits of possible reform by their mere presence; just look at the Philippines or, again, Chile, where the homicidal General Pinochet, having lost two successive elections, still intends to remain as army commander in chief in a watchdog capacity for the next eight years. So the play could well symbolize the all too numerous candidates ready to reincarnate Miss Margarida's ghost if offered the slightest provocation. And there is bound to be disorder in the coming years if people in such lands seriously believe that their destiny is now really in their own hands.

This first answer, though true, only validates the theatrical experience *Miss Margarida's Way* provides insofar as it may or may not illuminate dictatorships that are comfortably far away. But it ignores what is most important about the play: that it is a subtle allegorical inquiry into the deepest everyday roots of contemporary domination everywhere, what makes people seek power over others and why those others accept and obey.

ᴤ

The metaphorical strength of *Miss Margarida's Way* is paradoxically due to the savage military government that ruled Brazil in 1971, the year the play was written. Barely twenty-one years old at the time, Roberto Athayde was forced to confront a dilemma that so many other playwrights have faced when they try to write under a dictatorship: how to reach the audience with a political message and not be swallowed up by the very violence they are denouncing. On the one hand are the official demands and pressures for silence, complicity, and frivolous entertainment; on the other, the hunger of local audiences to find onstage a hint of the freedom to think and feel that is absent and forbidden in their lives.

Torn between the fear of being repressed and the fear of being irrelevant, many playwrights—such as Mr. Athayde's compatriot Augusto Boal—go into exile. Those who stay can choose between scribbling hidden ferocious words which can be produced, if at all, abroad (the case for the last twenty years of the Czechoslovak Vaclav Havel (that is, before he became the president of his country), or they can adopt Roberto Athayde's solution: investigate life under the ubiquitous boot using the wondrous weapon of allegory, roguishly alluding and eluding, hoping the play is indirect enough to keep the secret police away and transparent enough for the public to recognize the connections.

Roberto Athayde was wrong about the police but right about the public. When his play was finally produced in Rio de Janeiro, in early September 1973, the audience quickly—and nervously—understood that the dictatorship itself was on trial. Unfortunately, so did the dictatorship. A few days after the play opened in a bravura performance by one of Brazil's most famous actresses, Marilia Pera (United States audiences may remember her in *Pixote*, the Hector Babenco film), the authorities in Brasília, acting on complaints from the wives of several generals, banned it. A public scandal ensued, and a week later *Miss Margarida* was back on the boards (and at the blackboard)—though many of the obscenities had been excised along with an unmistakable reference by the crazed schoolteacher to the fact that the students she had sent to the principal's office "never came back," in other words, were tortured and executed.

彩

Not only did Mr. Athayde manage to finally circumvent the censors, but the very censorship that forced him to hide immediate references and invent a surreal, wild representation of mad power was precisely what afforded the work its universal thrust and allowed it to outlive the dictatorial circumstances that had given it birth. Audiences all over the world saw and may continue to see in Miss Margarida an echo of a darkness that lurks inside their own lives and their own societies, no matter how apparently democratic.

The classroom where Miss Margarida, oozing good intentions, cajoles, threatens, browbeats, belittles, seduces is meant to multiply an infinite phalanx of replicant Margaridas, tiny dictators in whom crouch and grow tomorrow's petty smiling ravens of power. Miss Margarida's school is not a peculiarly Brazilian institution but one of many contemporary channels for churning out child and country abusers, robotic accomplices of villainy, the conformists who are the backbone of all antidemocratic movements, scared of being different, scared of bucking the system, scared of their values being called into question by people of other races, other sexual preferences, other political options, other social classes.

彩

Mr. Athayde knows, as do I and so many other writers who have endured the corrosive everyday invasion of a dictatorship, that imperial longings require obedient people to carry out whim and atrocities, and that the terror of our century would not have been possible if children had not been formed—as adults continue to be formed everywhere—by a grinding, almost invisible, chorus of coercion that disguises itself as self-righteous virtue.

And yet, in the play, the power of dictatorship is never seen as total. It foretells the demise and vulnerability of tyrants, large and small, their incapacity to stamp out every external and internal flicker of rebellion. In a way, Roberto Athayde does to Miss Margarida what she most fears—and secretly seems to desire: he leaves her exposed in all her nakedness to the audience. As she covers her victims with abuse, she simultaneously and inadvertently strips for them. To repress others she has had to repress herself, and what shines through her insensate ramblings is an overwhelming need for company and sex and tenderness, the realization that she has lost the magical possibility of using language as a way of freeing people instead of controlling them.

We find ourselves, amazingly, beginning to feel sorry for her. And yet, a word of warning. Before pitying the miserable life she has made for herself, before grieving for someone who can only see her own solitary image reflected back in the mirror of other faces, I would suggest that we first make sure we are well rid of the monstrous Miss Margarida. And rid of the Principal, of course.

Dreams of a Bilingual Nation

Ever since I came to settle in the United States eighteen years ago, I have hoped that this nation might someday become truly multilingual, with everyone here speaking at least two languages.

I am aware, of course, that my dream is not shared by most Americans: if the outcome of California's referendum on bilingual education earlier this month is any indication, the nation will continue to stubbornly prefer to remain monolingual. California voters rejected the bilingual approach—teaching subjects like math and science in the students' native language and gradually introducing English. Instead, they approved what is known as the immersion method, which gives youngsters a year of intensive English, then puts them in regular classrooms.

The referendum was ostensibly about education, but the deeper and perhaps subconscious choice was about the future of America. Will this country speak two languages or merely one?

The bilingual method, in spite of what its detractors claim, does not imprison a child in his or her original language. Rather, it keeps it alive in order to build bridges to English. The immersion method, on the other hand, wants youngsters to cut their ties to the syllables of their past culture.

Both methods can work. I should know. I have endured them both. But my experience was unquestionably better with bilingual education.

I first suffered the immersion method in 1945 when I was two and a half years old. My family had recently moved to New York from my native Argentina, and when I caught pneumonia, I was interned in the isolation ward of a Manhattan hospital. I emerged

New York Times, June 24, 1998, op-ed page.

three weeks later, in shock from having the doctors and nurses speak to me only in English, and didn't utter another word in Spanish for ten years.

That experience turned me into a savagely monolingual child, a xenophobic all-American kid, desperate to differentiate himself from Ricky Ricardo and Chiquita Banana. But when my family moved to Chile in 1954, I could not continue to deny my heritage. I learned Spanish again in a British school in Santiago that used the gradualist method. Thus I became a bilingual adolescent.

Later, during the ideologically charged 1960s, I foolishly willed myself to become monolingual again, branding English the language of an imperial power out to subjugate Latin America. I swore never to speak or write in English again. The 1973 military coup in Chile against the democratically elected government of Salvador Allende Gossens sent me into exile—and back into the arms of English, making me into this hybrid creature who now uses both languages and writes a memoir in English and a play in Spanish as if it were the most ordinary thing to do.

I have developed a linguistic ambidexterity that I will be the first to admit is not at all typical. Even so, it is within reach of others if they start early enough, this thrilling experience of being dual, of taking from one linguistic river and then dipping into the other, until the confluence of the two vocabularies connects distant communities.

This is an experience I wish all Americans could share.

Or maybe I would be satisfied if voters in this country could understand that by introducing children from other lands to the wonders of English while leaving all the variety and marvels of their native languages intact, the American experience and idiom are fertilized and fortified.

If people could realize that immigrant children are better off, and less scarred, by holding on to their first languages as they learn a second one, then perhaps Americans could accept a more drastic change. What if every English-speaking toddler were to start learning a foreign language at an early age, maybe in kindergarten? What if these children were to learn Spanish, for instance, the language already spoken by millions of American citizens, but also by so many neighbors to the South?

Most Americans would respond by asking why it is necessary at all to learn another language, given that the rest of the planet is rapidly turning English into the lingua franca of our time. Isn't it easier, most Americans would say, to have others speak to us in our words and with our grammar? Let them make the mistakes and miss the nuances and subtleties while we occupy the more powerful and secure linguistic ground in any exchange.

But that is a shortsighted strategy. If America doesn't change, it will find itself, say in a few hundred years, to be a monolingual nation in a world that has become gloriously multilingual. It will discover that acquiring a second language not only gives people an economic and political edge, but is also the best way to understand someone else's culture, the most stimulating way to open your life and transform yourself into a more complete member of the species.

No tengan miedo. Don't be afraid.

Your children won't be losing Shakespeare. They'll just be gaining Cervantes.

Questions for Humanity

here were the people of America on February 25, 1969? Where were they on that night long gone when Lieutenant Bob Kerrey and the men in his platoon of Navy SEALs were killing as many as twenty unarmed civilians in the hamlet of Thanh Phong in Vietnam, where was each and every one of the adults of the United States at the moment when women and children halfway across the world were dying?

This is the fundamental question that seems not to have been asked thus far as Americans debate what Bob Kerrey did so many decades ago. It is true that other doubts currently being voiced are just as important: Did Lieutenant Kerrey deliberately order the slaughter of those civilians, or was it just one more accidental atrocity in a war that left over two million Vietnamese dead? And why did Kerrey, who became a U.S. senator from Nebraska, keep quiet all these years about the deaths that he claims have been haunting him since that raid? And what was he doing there anyway, in a country that was not his, under a sky that he did not recognize, closing his ears to the cries of fellow human beings screaming in a language that he could not understand? And how does this fit into a pattern of American intervention in favor of ferocious dictatorships around the world in its fight against communism? And how many more incidents like this one still lurk in the undergrowth of memory, ready to surface and corrode the people of the United States, this war that they lost and that will not go away, coming back to trouble them yet one more time?

This intense focus on Kerrey and what really transpired that night is necessary and unavoidable. As someone who has campaigned for accountability regarding crimes against humanity in my own

Los Angeles Times, May 4, 2001, op-ed page.

native Chile as well as in so many other unfortunate lands, I would be the last to suggest that we dodge the issue of personal responsibility for this kind of outrage. At the moment when the United States is demanding that Slobodan Milosevic be extradited to the Hague to face judgment for his possible participation in brutalities carried out by his troops, it would be the epitome of hypocrisy to overlook or not scrutinize similar offenses committed by the U.S. military. The life of one innocent Vietnamese baby is as valuable as the life of one Bosnian or Kosovar child—or a little girl from Nebraska, for that matter.

And yet to limit our examination of the past only to the officer who gave the order, or to the soldier who wielded the knife, or even to their commanders who did not investigate the incident, is to evade the need to explore the more elusive complicity of the larger collective in whose name those orders were given, those shots were fired, an old man's throat was slit. To truly understand what happened during that moonless night in the Mekong Delta we need to interrogate the responsibility of the nation that sent those young men into war, we need to ask why it took thirty-two years for this story to be told, we need to wonder how many people back then did not want to know of this and other crimes, we need to figure out why, once the war was over, most Americans—even many of those who had, to their honor, magnificently opposed it—could continue to comfortably live without that knowledge, we need to dissect the thousands of days of silence that piled up like dead photographs inside the American people in the years that followed.

Where were they, those faraway bystanders, on February 25, 1969? Where have they been since then, all through the nights that Bob Kerrey was alone with his secret? And now that the knowledge is out in the open, what do they do with it? Not only with the news of the atrocity itself, but with the more terrifying knowledge of their indifference to what was going on—that unbearable indifference which could be considered a greater crime than murder, because those who violate human rights can always argue that there were mitigating circumstances, reasons for losing control. But Bob Kerrey's compatriots cannot claim that they were under extreme duress when so many of them closed their eyes to what was happening. They were not in fear for their lives, they did not stumble with loaded guns and chaotic minds in the panic of darkness, they were not acting under orders when they preferred to remain ignorant of what was being perpetrated on their behalf, nobody forced them to leave Bob Kerrey to face his ghosts all by himself in the heart of his endless nights.

Why did a majority of the American people not care back then? And do they really care now?

These are not questions I should ask only of the people of the United States, and sadly, they cannot refer only to the past.

The century we have just escaped was filled with unspeakable acts of terror and extermination magnified by technology and the power of the State. And all through it, along with the few who protested and refused to collaborate and were courageous or lucky enough to save their dignity and separate themselves from the madness, there were many more, so many countless others, who turned their backs on the remote or nearby devastation that was being visited on their fellows, be it in Stalinist Russia or Nazi-occupied France or the streets of Jakarta under Suharto or the mountains of Anatolia when the Armenians were being annihilated or in a dark cellar in Johannesburg or in Buenos Aires where a man walked toward a woman tied naked to a cot holding an electric prod in his left hand. My own hand trembles to write this, but I am convinced that it was only because of these vast and hushed armies of the silent that such violations of our species could be carried out with impunity, only because of the shrugged shoulders, the averted eyes, the general apathy, that those events of horror could afterward be forgotten and erased. And repeated.

I ask these questions therefore of the damaged brotherhood we call humanity. I ask these questions of myself.

Where was I on May 8, 1994, when I read that two hundred thousand Rwandans had been slaughtered in the last six weeks? Where was I, who call myself a human rights activist, two months later, on July 28, 1994, when the death toll in Rwanda had risen to one million men, women, and children? What did I do to stop that genocide?

Why did I not care?

Bob Kerrey and his men were not alone, after all, in the hut of death that night long ago in Thanh Phong.

Martin Luther King

A Latin American Perspective

Faraway, I was faraway from Washington, D.C., that hot day in August 1963 when Martin Luther King delivered his famous words from the steps of the Lincoln Memorial, I was faraway in Chile. Twenty-one years old at the time and entangled, like so many of my generation, in the struggle to liberate Latin America, the speech by King that was to influence my life so deeply did not even register with me, I cannot even recall having noticed its existence. What I can remember with ferocious precision, however, is the place and the date, and even the hour, when many years later I had occasion to listen for the first time to those "I have a dream" words, to hear that melodious baritone, those incantations, that emotional certainty of victory. I can remember the occasion so clearly because it happened to be the day Martin Luther King was killed, April 4, 1968, and ever since that day, his dream and his death have been grievously linked, conjoined in my mind then as they are now, forty years later, in my memory.

I recall how I was sitting with my wife, Angélica, and our one-year-old child, Rodrigo, in a living room, high up in the hills of Berkeley, the university town in California where we had arrived barely a week before. Our hosts, an American family that had generously offered us temporary lodgings while our apartment was being readied, had switched on the television, and we all solemnly watched the nightly news, probably at seven in the evening, probably Walter Cronkite. And there it was, the murder of Martin Luther King in that Memphis hotel and then came reports of riots all over America and, finally, a long excerpt of his "I have a dream" speech.

Commissioned and transmitted by the BBC; first published in the *Irish Times* (Dublin), August 20, 2003.

It was only then, I think, that I realized, perhaps began to realize, who Martin Luther King had been, what we had lost with
his departure from this world, the legend he was already becoming in front of my very eyes. In the years to come, I would often
return to that speech and would, on each occasion, hew from its
mountain of meanings a different rock upon which to stand and
understand the world.

Beyond my amazement at King's eloquence when I first heard
him back in 1968, my immediate reaction was not so much to be
inspired as to be somber, puzzled, close to despair. After all, the slay-
ing of this man of peace was answered, not by a pledge to persevere
in his legacy, but by furious uprisings in the slums of black America,
the disenfranchised of America avenging their dead leader by burning down the ghettos where they felt imprisoned and impoverished,
using the fire this time to proclaim that the nonviolence King had
advocated was useless, that the only way to end inequity in this
world was through the barrel of a gun, the only way to make the
powerful pay attention was to scare the hell out of them.

King's assassination, therefore, savagely brought up yet one more
time a question that had bedeviled me and so many other activists in the late sixties: what was the best method to achieve radical
change? Could we picture a rebellion in the way that Martin Luther
King had envisioned it, without drinking from the cup of bitter-
ness and hatred, without treating our adversaries as they treated
us? Or does the road into the palace of justice and the bright day
of brotherhood inevitably require violence as its companion, violence as the unavoidable midwife of revolution?

Questions that, back in Chile, I would soon be forced to answer,
not in cloudy theoretical musings, but in the day-to-day reality
of hard history, when Salvador Allende was elected President in
1970, and we became the first country that tried to build socialism
through peaceful means. Allende's vision of social change, elabo-
rated over decades of struggle and thought, was similar to King's,
even though they both came from very different political and cultural origins. Allende, for instance, who was not at all religious,
would not have agreed with Martin Luther King that physical force
must be met with soul force, but rather with the force of social
organizing. At a time when many in Latin America were dazzled

by the armed struggle proposed by Fidel Castro and Che Guevara, it was Allende's singular accomplishment to imagine as inextricably connected the two quests of our era: the quest for more democracy and more civil freedoms, on the one hand, and the parallel quest, on the other, for social justice and economic empowerment of the dispossessed of this earth. And it was to be Allende's fate to echo the fate of Martin Luther King, it was Allende's choice to die three years later. Yes, on September 11, 1973, almost ten years to the day since King's "I have a dream" speech in Washington, Allende chose to die defending his own dream, promising us, in his last speech, that much sooner than later, *más temprano que tarde*, a day would come when the free men and women of Chile would walk through *las amplias alamedas*, the great avenues full of trees, toward a better society.

It was in the immediate aftermath of that terrible defeat, as we watched the powerful of Chile impose upon us the terror that we had not wanted to visit upon them, it was then, as our nonviolence was met with executions and torture and disappearances, it was only then, after the military coup of 1973, that I first began to seriously commune with Martin Luther King, that his speech on the steps of the Lincoln Memorial came back to haunt and to question me. It was as I headed into an exile that would last for many years, that King's voice and message began to filter fully, word by word, into my life.

If ever there was a situation where violence could be justified, after all, it would have been against the junta in Chile. Pinochet and his generals had overthrown a constitutional government and were killing and persecuting citizens whose radical sin had been to imagine a world where you do not need to massacre your opponents in order to allow the waters of justice to flow. And yet, very wisely, almost instinctively, the Chilean resistance embraced a different route: to slowly, resolutely, dangerously, take over the surface of the country, isolate the dictatorship inside and outside our nation, make Chile ungovernable through civil disobedience. Not entirely different from the strategy that the civil rights movement had espoused in the United States. And indeed, I never felt closer to Martin Luther King than during the seventeen years it took us to free Chile of its dictatorship. His words to the militants who thronged to Washington, D.C., in 1963, demanding that they not lose faith, resonated with me, comforted my sad heart. He was speaking prophetically to me, to us, when he said: "I am not unmindful that some of you have come here out of great trials and tribulations. Some of you have come fresh from narrow cells." Speaking to us, Dr. King, speaking to me, when he thundered: "Some of you come from areas where your quest for freedom left you battered by the storms of persecution and staggered by the winds of police brutality. You have been the veterans of creative suffering." He understood that more difficult than going to your first protest was to awaken the next day and go to the next protest and then the next one—the daily grind of small acts that can lead to large and lethal consequences. The dogs and sheriffs of Alabama and Mississippi were alive and well in the streets of Santiago and Valparaiso, and so was the spirit that had encouraged defenseless men and women and children to be mowed down, beaten, bombed, harassed, and yet continue confronting their oppressors with the only weapons available to them: the suffering of their bodies and the conviction that nothing could make them turn back. And just like the blacks in the United States, so in Chile we sang in the streets of the cities that had been stolen from us. Not spirituals, for every land has its own songs. In Chile we sang, over and over, the *Ode to Joy* from Beethoven's Ninth Symphony, with the hope that a day would come when all men would be brothers.

Why were we singing? To give ourselves courage, of course. But not only that, not only that. In Chile, we sang and stood against the hoses and the tear gas and the truncheons because we knew that somebody else was watching. In this, we also followed in the cunning, media-savvy footsteps of Martin Luther King: that mismatched confrontation between the police state and the people was being witnessed, photographed, transmitted to other eyes. In the case of the deep south of the United States, the audience was the majority of the American people, while in that other struggle years later, in the deeper south of Chile, the daily spectacle of peaceful men and women being repressed by the agents of terror targeted the national and international forces whose support Pinochet and his dependent Third World dictatorship needed in order to survive. The tactic worked, of course, because we understood, as Martin

Luther King and Gandhi had before us, that our adversaries could be influenced and shamed by public opinion, could indeed eventually be compelled to relinquish power. That is how segregation was defeated in the south of the United States, that is how the Chilean people beat Pinochet in a plebiscite in 1988 that led to democracy in 1990, that is the story of the downfall of tyrannies in Iran and Poland and the Philippines. Although parallel struggles for liberation—against the apartheid regime in South Africa or the homicidal autocracy in Nicaragua or the murderous Khmer Rouge in Cambodia—also showed how King's premonitory words of nonviolence could not be mechanically applied to every situation.

And what of today? When I return to that speech I first heard thirty-five years ago, the very day King died, is there a message for me, for us, something that we need to hear again, as if we were listening to those words for the first time?

What would Martin Luther King say if he contemplated what his country has become? If he could see how the terror and death brought to bear upon New York and Washington on September 11, 2001, has turned his people into a fearful nation, ready to stop dreaming, ready to abridge its own freedoms in order to be secure? What would he say if he could observe how that fear has been manipulated in order to justify the invasion of a foreign land, the occupation of that land against the will of its own people? What alternative way would he have advised to be rid of a tyrant like Saddam Hussein? And how would he react to the Bush doctrine that states that some people on this planet, Americans to be precise, have more rights than the other citizens of the world? What would he say if he were to see his fellow countrymen proclaiming that because of their pain and their military and economic might they can do as they please, flaunt international law, withdraw from nuclear treaties, deceive and pollute the world? Would he warn them that such arrogance will not go unpunished? Would he tell those who oppose these policies inside the United States to stand up and be counted, to march ahead, to never wallow in the valley of despair?

It is my belief that he would repeat some of the words he delivered on that faraway day in August 1963 in the shadow of the statue of Abraham Lincoln, I believe he would declare again his faith in his country and how deeply his dream is rooted in the American dream, that in spite of the difficulties and frustrations of the moment, his dream is still alive, and that his nation will rise up and live out the true meaning of its creed: "We hold these truths to be self-evident: that all men are created equal."

Let us hope that he is right. Let us hope and pray, for his sake and our sake, that Martin Luther King's faith in his own country was not misplaced and that forty years later his compatriots will once again listen to his fierce and gentle voice calling to them from beyond death and beyond fear, calling on all of us to stand together for freedom and justice in our time.

PART THREE

Troubled Bridges

Who Are the Real Barbarians?

Memory and the Fate of Latin America

When Christopher Columbus, on his first voyage of discovery, sighted a range of hills alive with silver along the coast of what would in the far future be known as the Dominican Republic, he believed—or so the legend goes—that his dreams of unending riches had finally come true. As he was in the habit of baptizing everything he saw, he proceeded, on the eleventh day of January 1493 to give to the largest mount glinting phantasmagorically under the sun the Spanish word for silver—*plata*. Although in fact he continued past those hills without setting foot on them, their present-day inhabitants assure anyone who cares to listen that the admiral did indeed land, and, upon seeing the white shiny leaves of the Ilam-ilam trees turning over with the breeze, winking with sunlight, he morosely understood the illusion under which he had been laboring.

That disappointment of Columbus, as recounted in tales handed down by generation upon generation of Dominicans, may be apocryphal, but the story originates in a core of truths: the truth of the trees that once covered an entire island, the truth of the insatiable Spanish quest for wealth in the lands that were soon to be called New, the truth that things in that World rarely turned out to be what they seemed nor the way they were planned. Because if Columbus were to disembark on that coast today, more than five hundred years later, he would find those hills eroded and treeless, filled with makeshift shacks, open sewers, garbage-littered alleyways. And yet, the name, Puerto Plata, Port of Silver, persists, whispering to its inhabitants, most of them mired in despair and

---

Based on a speech delivered in Sydney in celebration of the Centenary of the Australian Federation, November 2001.

poverty, that perhaps someday things will get better, stubbornly whispering a promise of Paradise.

So the story of Latin America, from the very start, includes both an early utopian longing and its almost immediate frustration. This contradiction has persisted through the ages, coming down to us in two central attitudes between which Latin Americans today wildly swing, summarized in two phrases, *Qué maravilla!* and *Somos un desastre*, that we habitually use to refer to our contemporary condition.

Qué maravilla! could roughly be translated as "How marvelous!" the celebration by Latin Americans of the wonders of their own lands, a fierce attachment to the amazing variety of climates and landscapes, races and languages, cultures and animals and plants that fill and delight our lives. Almost every human ethnic group has found its way to our continent and mingled there—Europeans of every kind, and Africans, of course, and Asians as well, not only the small contingents of Japanese and Chinese and Korean immigrants, but the major waves of wanderers who originally crossed the Bering Straits thousands of years ago and gave birth to the Indians who then proceeded to cover the lands from pole to pole. But more wonderful, perhaps, is another sort of diversity, first spelled out by the Cuban novelist, Alejo Carpentier. In his 1953 novel, *Los Pasos Perdidos*, *The Lost Steps*, a musicologist in search of the origins of humanity takes a trip to the godforsaken interior of Latin America. This odyssey gradually turns into a voyage that, step after step, advances into the successive layers of time past, our continent as the only place on the planet in which all the periods of history still coexist side by side, where all the styles and customs and experiences that the West has developed and exported and imposed upon other lands remain intact and ready to visit as if in a living museum. Carpentier proposes Latin America as a continent where the modern and the prehistoric and everything in between subsist and endure next to each other. *Qué maravilla!* Latin America as a place where anything can happen, everything is possible.

Unfortunately, what did happen was a catastrophe—and we come, therefore, inevitably, as the continent itself did, to that second phrase or attitude or mood—*Somos un desastre*—which can be inadequately translated as "We are a disaster." If the English version sounds strange to our ears, it may be because the Spanish-language formulation is itself rather awkward. Note that we Latin Americans are not demanding to know why we are living a disaster (*¿porqué vivimos un desastre?*), why such a condition has befallen us, but are stating rather that our being is itself a calamity, that we understand existence in the Americas south of the Rio Grande as a permanent ontological cataclysm. Even when we most enjoy life, even when we are at our most sensual and playful and *maravillados*, filled with awe and gratitude and astonishment, it is hard to escape the apprehension that something has gone terribly wrong. We wonder how it can be, now that we approach the bicentenary of our independence, that a continent with such enormous potential wealth and extraordinary human resources has ended up an economic and political—though not a cultural—failure. Oh yes, we have survived up until now, held together under the storm, but what sort of price have we paid for that conjoining, what have we had to do to one another in order to keep from disintegrating? And who is to blame for that inability of Latin America to live up to its originating utopian promise?

The first and most influential answer to these questions was given in 1845 by Domingo Faustino Sarmiento, a young Argentine who had fled the tyranny of Juan Manuel de Rosas, in a book titled *Facundo*, appropriately known as the founding text of Latin American historiography, journalism, and literature, a text indeed so striking and adventurous that it has framed every subsequent debate on the subject, in fact created the paradigm through which our nations have since then conceived and perceived themselves, even for those of us who are critical of Sarmiento's vision.

Sarmiento was thirty-four years old when he created *Facundo* from his Chilean exile, exactly the age, he was quick to point out in later essays, of his country's independence. He therefore found himself in the perfect position to ponder how it was that the rebellion against the Spanish colonial master, that the glorious Enlightenment ideals that had inspired those insurrections all over Latin America, had led to interminable civil wars, economic decline, unyielding backwardness. In order to stem the tide of anarchy and chaos, our republics were increasingly being governed by conservative and dictatorial regimes. How was it that the Latin American revolutions, dedicated to liberty, fraternity and equality, had ended up with the opposite of what they had set out to do? Faced with this enigma, particularly in contrast to the incredible success story of the United States, shining ominously to the North of the same hemisphere, Sarmiento came up with an explanation that was pithily phrased, a dichotomy that served as the subtitle of his book: *Civilización y Barbarie*. We are caught, Sarmiento said, in an epic battle between the forces of Civilization and the forces of Barbarism. The wild natural world of Latin America—specifically the pampas in the case of Argentina—had taken possession of the hearts and minds of far too many inhabitants of the new father-land, and it was this demonic energy that needed to be tamed and domesticated, submitted to white European rationality and indus-try. If we wish to master the disintegrating forces of both the colo-nial past and of savage nature, if we wish to enter, like the United States, the concert of nations, the only way, Sarmiento said, was the disciplined road of progress. In order to catch up with Europe we need to replicate its example and break with the past so that the freedom and spirit of enterprise that have led the established powers of the West to preeminence can be repeated here in a more youthful and creative way.

These were not destined to be merely abstract ideas.

When many years later Sarmiento became president of Argentina (and he served in other administrations as Minister of Education and Minister of Home Affairs), he turned his formula of Civilization or Barbarism into public policy, he tried to exorcise the frightful wildness lurking inside the soul of Latin America, and perhaps his own soul, perhaps subconsciously attempting to separate himself and his Westward-looking Argentina from what he considered the genetically inferior Indian blood which coursed through the veins of so many of his countrymen. Whatever the psychological motives—and there were plenty of economic and political reasons that could also be mentioned—the fact is that Sarmiento helped put into place a series of measures that sought to turn Argentina into one nation and that were vigorously pursued as the century wore on. Primary school instruction was offered to all the children of the republic; technology, capital, and cultural models were imported from abroad; the nomad Indians who roamed the plains were exterminated in *la Campaña del Desierto*; and thousands of European settlers were persuaded to come and colonize those supposedly empty territories. A similar process, of course, was happening not only in the rest of Latin America but all across the globe during the latter half of the nineteenth century, as superior technological military capacity led to the subjugation of indigenous peoples who had held out for centuries against Western incursions. As Sarmiento himself was to write many years later, "If this terrible procedure of civilization is barbaric and cruel to the eyes of justice and reason, it is, like war itself, like conquest, one of the ways Providence has armed diverse human races, and among these the most powerful and advanced, to replace those who, by their organic weakness or backwardness [stand] in civilization's path, [and] cannot achieve the great destinies of man on earth."

Sarmiento recognized that Latin America had arrived late on the world scene and was therefore condemned to be a secondary player on the planetary stage unless its fledgling republics could match the foreign imperial powers, unless its elites could harness the enormous dynamism and resources of these new lands to the freedom and technology necessary for real development. This meant that those impaired inhabitants of the Americas who were holding back the march toward modernization would either have to be eradicated from the Earth or integrated through education into the mainstream, made into citizens, Europeanized.

In the name of the nation, the wandering and dangerous remaining tribes of the Americas were terrorized into submission. They were forced to live thenceforth, in fact, the sedentary experience that most of the other Indians of the continent had suffered through since the Iberian conquest and colonization, since the widespread Aztec, Mayan, and Inca civilizations in Mexico and Central America and the Andean region had been overcome, and its millions upon millions of inhabitants made into a workforce that toiled the mines and the fields and yes, the beds and bedrooms. These enormous masses of indigenous peoples had not been eliminated or assimilated over the centuries. They had continued to breed, to keep (and modify, of course) their languages and cultures, and, from time to time, had burst into major uprisings in Guatemala and Ecuador and Peru and, above all, in Mexico, where they participated in two revolutions that had at their center the need to redistribute land and water. At the end of the nineteenth century and during the first part of the twentieth, the Indian "question" came up again and again. What to do with these people who seemed to live in the past and whose sloth and otherness was blamed for the backwardness of a Latin America lagging ever farther behind the United States and Europe?

This policy differed from the racist and immoral policies set in motion in the United States and other parts of the world, only inasmuch as it *fortunately* did not accomplish what it set out to do. I use that word fortunately because I am part of a countertendency in Latin American intellectual thought that believes that, rather than blaming our rank human diversity for this underdevelopment, responsibility should instead be assigned to the unwillingness of our rulers to include those who are different as real partners in the national consensus and entertain a genuine dialogue with them. And that word, *diversity*, does not, of course, comprise only the so-called Indians, but also the vast throngs of the dispossessed of Latin America: the slaves transported from Africa and their descendants, the workers of whatever color who have fought in the mines and the factories for a decent life for themselves and their children and for national control over the resources owned by foreign companies, the peasants who take over the farmlands from which their ancestors were expelled, the homeless squatters in the cities occupying vacant buildings and empty lots, all these, and also, of course, the many others, the more well-to-do who took up the cause of those excluded millions, students and lawyers and doctors, all those who continue to rebel, generation after pariah generation, incessantly demanding to redefine the nation that has proscribed them. And yet, how not to recognize as well that, in the past, almost every one of the leaders who headed these social movements was killed? They all ended up, my heroes, as martyrs, torn apart, betrayed, invaded, destroyed, overthrown, banished— Tupac Amaru and Zapata and Arbenz and Salvador Allende. It is true that the resisting multitudes have been able to prove by their mere persistence and rejection of the choice between civilization and barbarism, between disappearing and assimilating, that Sarmiento was wrong, showing how fragile and precarious and unstable is the nation, any nation, that would be built without their presence. But it is also incontestable that those legions of the excluded are not the ones who have determined the fundamental direction of Latin America nor have they been able to change the terms that Sarmiento set down so many years ago, nor change, indeed, the very conditions of structural inferiority that shaped Sarmiento's thought and solutions. Even as, decade after decade, an alternative version of Latin America kept on resurfacing, the men in power, the men who decided the rules of the game, the men who kept on dreaming of silver in the trees and of obedient bodies to extract that silver, these men continued to insist, as if they were deaf, that the deep problems of the continent could be solved without taking into account the desires of those bodies and the resistance of those bodies to the plans hatched from above and abroad. The men in power have gone on telling themselves and their nations that at some point those inflexible, recalcitrant populaces needed to be helped into conveniently disappearing.

I got my first taste of this blindness, and perhaps also a hint of its costs, just a few days after I arrived in August 1954 in what was to be my adopted country, Chile.

I was a twelve-year-old lad, born in Argentina and brought up during the last decade in New York, not speaking—by my own volition—even a word of Spanish, not knowing very much about Latin America except that it was a dreaded place to which I would have to resign myself before heading back in a few years' time, or so I thought, to my beloved United States. It was almost as if I had inadvertently been following the secret instructions murmured to me by the dead Sarmiento, that compatriot of mine whose name I did not even know at the time, suggesting that I erase my origins, make myself into a civilized gringo. One of my father's Chilean subordinates at the United Nations' regional offices—an economist who answered to the name of Pepe and whose surname I would rather not reveal—in order to ingratiate himself with the new boss, had taken the family, minus my Dad, on a tour of the city we would henceforth call home. The tour culminated with a climb to the top of a small hill in the center of Santiago, the Cerro Santa Lucía, where the Spanish conquistador Pedro de Valdivia had founded the city in 1540, choosing a place easy to fortify against the encroaching and bellicose Mapuche Indians. They, in return, three years later, ambushed Valdivia and, the legend goes, poured down his dead throat the molten gold that was the primary reason he had journeyed this far South. As we mounted toward the summit, our new friend Pepe offhandedly remarked that, of course, there were no Indians left in Chile today. An opinion, by the way, that I was to hear repeated tirelessly over the years innumerable times by Chilean high society.

I may have known next to nothing back then about that country or any other Latino land, but I did have eyes—and I had seen the dark features of people crowding the streets, I had seen the bronze-skinned workers on the Valparaiso dock where our ship had arrived, my glance had caught the slanted eyes of the slum-dwellers watching our car speed by on the way to Santiago, I had even caught a glimpse of a couple of women in native dress selling herbs and trinkets on a corner. So it was clear to this child who came from what was even then the multicultural city of New York, that Chile was filled to the brim with Indians and their descendants. "Descendants, yes," Pepe answered, when my mother gently voiced out loud the same doubts her son was harboring more quietly, "but no more real Indians, like there were back in the time of the conquistadors. No more pure Indians like this one."

And Pepe stopped in front of a large statue, the replica of a muscular Indian with noble, almost Hollywood features, standing in quiet defiance almost at the summit of the hill that had once, presumably, belonged to him and his people.

"This is Caupolicán," our guide said, "the great Araucanian warrior who resisted the Spanish invasion in the sixteenth century and was martyred by his foes."

"He doesn't look very martyred," I said, pesky kid that I was. "What did they do to him?"

Pepe reddened slightly. His command of English, already clumsy, began to falter even more. "They—they put him on a large wooden stake, you know, from beneath—they—you know, up his—and that made him bleed to death."

"Why didn't the sculptor show the death then?" I persisted, with the typical coarse curiosity of a twelve-year-old. That would have been a sight, I thought to myself: a warrior with a stake up his ass, bleeding into oblivion!

As if he could read my mind, our friend Pepe muttered that it was better to remember heroes in less awkward positions, a matter of public decorum, this effigy was reproduced extensively in school texts and in other public places, etcetera, etcetera. None of which answered another question that had crept into my mind. Why did the statue stir in me a vague reminiscence, as if I had seen it somewhere before—but that was impossible; I knew less about native Chileans than I did about Chile itself, so I held my tongue and did not give the matter a second thought until several decades later when, while doing research for a novel, I discovered the full and perverse story of how the last moments of Caupolicán on this Earth had come to be sanitized in that block of stone.

To begin with, Caupolicán had not been the original name given to the statue by Nicanor Plaza. This Chilean sculptor—born in 1844, a few streets away from where the exiled Sarmiento was writing his *Facundo*—had been commissioned in the late 1860s by some gringos at the U.S. embassy in Santiago to make a likeness of an authentic Araucanian Indian. But Plaza, who then went on to sculpt his work of art shuttered up in a Parisian studio, had no idea what such a primitive specimen might look like, and had probably never even tried to really behold one. So he decided instead to copy an Indian from an engraving he detected in *The Last of the Mohicans*, the novel by the Yankee writer James Fenimore Cooper. This stone likeness, back in Chile, was indignantly rejected by his patrons, who had no desire whatsoever to transport back to the States an American Indian from the North masquerading as an aborigine from the South. And so Nicanor Plaza was left with a slab of useless chiseled stone, useless, that is, unless he . . . Yes, the Cerro Santa Lucía was being remodeled as a distinguished park full of all sorts of imported busts and steps and chapels. And thus, when the new grounds and esplanades were inaugurated in 1873, at the very moment when the Indian warriors were losing the lands they had held on to for centuries and being pushed farther and farther south, away from Santiago, lapsing into a sort of irrelevant stupor of invisibility, Plaza's statue, rebaptized Caupolicán, was exhibited for the edification of visitors, to be thenceforth integrated into the memory of the nation and future schoolchildren.

How was it that the committee that selected monuments for the park could accept that false version of an Araucanian Indian, that copy of what was already a phony North American Indian? At a time when the remote great-grandchildren of Caupolicán were being pushed away from the centers of power and no longer constituted a threat, left to fester in faraway *reducciones indígenas*, what could be more convenient for the elites who wanted to differentiate their recently constituted nations from the former Spanish rulers than to resurrect alternative ancestors under the guise of the noble savage, that Western myth of innocence that had accompanied and complemented the malevolent and satanic versions of the indigenous as the colonial powers expanded across the globe? The committee was able to pay for that statue precisely because it had no connection to any real Indian dreaming under the Chilean moon or resisting under the Chilean sun or working for a Chilean wage, and—more crucially, perhaps—because that statue did not have a large stake jutting into the guts and intestines of its counterfeit Araucanian cacique. I believe it was the absence of torture that gave that statue its real value.

So Caupolicán was killed twice, once by the torments the Spanish visited upon him, and a second time by the forgetting, his trauma masked and disguised and twisted beyond any recognizable form, absorbed into the national mythology so that any adult could casually tell a child of twelve that there were no more Indians, so that every adult could comfortably acknowledge the Indian past without delving into the Indian pain. Forcing us to avoid the question that effectively matters: Where is he? Where is Caupolicán? If there was somebody real, of flesh and blood and bones, who, back in the 1540s, was tortured to death by the marauders who invaded his land, then what is left of him? Where are the other Indians who followed him into death? Where is the Mapuche woman, where is she, the woman who, at the time of the Conquest, not far from where he died, where they died, was thrown down onto the soil of Chile with her legs forced open, where is the woman who was penetrated in a different manner than Caupolicán had been, where is she, how does she fit into the memory of the nation, how does he, how does she, how do they, presently lost in a mirage, claim their share in that nation?

I wish I were only speaking about the long-ago dead, about distant memories, about old battles; I wish I were not speaking about now. But unfortunately I speak of today. What was done to Caupolicán and that unnamed Indian woman and their many brothers and sisters at the dawn of Latin American history has been repeated in many other forms throughout that history. Not only the multiplication of terror, but the incessant forgetting of that terror. Yesterday is today.

Consider what has just happened in Chile, recently emerged a mere twelve years ago from a dictatorship where the sort of suffering inflicted upon Caupolicán was visited upon thousands upon thousands of citizens who had dared in the past to dream of a truly encompassing version of their country. If I have been able to speak about the disappearing of Indians from the consciousness of the powerful of Latin America, it is because the word itself, *desaparecido,* has been forced upon me by history and is now notorious around the globe. It describes what was being perpetrated by the Pinochet regime—not to mention the military regimes in Argentina and Uruguay, Brazil and Guatemala, El Salvador and Honduras—the active disappearance of dissidents, men and women who were arrested and whose whereabouts were denied, whose bodies were not even returned for burial, dumped into the sea or ploughed into the fields, so that there could be no memorial, supposedly no memory, no place to gather and remember and commemorate. What was once done primarily to the Indians, was now imposed upon many others who did not consider themselves indigenous at all, was used against whoever might protest Chile's lack of freedom, Chile's forced modernization, Chile's accelerated integration into the global market.

Shades of Sarmiento, yesterday is today.

When it took over the country in 1990, the newly elected government of Chile was faced with a difficult situation: the victory of the democratic forces had left intact the power of the military and its followers as well as the economic hegemony of a small group of wealthy Chileans who had grown even richer under the dictatorship, leaving the new democratic rulers severely restricted in what they could or could not do. The question of how to hold together a country that was exceptionally divided by decades of civil strife and differing interpretations of the recent past became paramount and closely related to how the new government understood the nation's trauma and how it wanted to present the nation's future, not only to its own people, but to a planet that automatically identified Chile with torture, Chile with arbitrariness, Chile with suffering and insurgency. Not the best sales pitch for a country that beckons enticingly to tourists and investment bankers.

By one of those strange coincidences that history seems to love, particularly in demented Latin America, the first occasion to remake my country's image and export a more positive version of it abroad was the 1992 World's Fair in Sevilla, dedicated to celebrating the five hundred years of the Americas. What the Chilean government bizarrely decided to do, with the assistance of the armed forces and the business community that had enthusiastically gorged itself during the dictatorship, was to choose an iceberg as the representation of the new Chile, proceeding to hack an enormous slab of ice out of the cold mountains of Antarctica and then cart it across the Atlantic to be exhibited in the burning heat of Sevilla. A benevolent observer might construe this snaring of a floating glacier as an extravagant way of reinserting Chile into the magical realist tradition of the rest of Latin America, but in fact, the organizers of the expedition had a symmetrically opposite purpose in mind: to distinguish themselves from the other countries of the continent, lumped together as excessively "tropical" and "violent." The iceberg was a way of shedding the dreadful public image of Chile as a land of tyranny and sorrow, poverty and backwardness, a way of projecting instead the image of a cool country, a country far from even the whiff of a banana republic, a country that was efficient and calculating and rational, a country that you could trust.

Shades of Sarmiento, here we go again, yesterday is tomorrow.

Let me confess that I adored the zaniness of the project, its confidence (not misplaced, by the way) in the capacity of Chileans to autonomously invent the technology that could keep the iceberg from melting in the torrid frying pan of the European summer, let me concede that I adored how unconventional and utopian this adventure was. But even if I found this break with the past and the traps of nostalgia to be refreshing, that does not mean I was unable to simultaneously recognize how the iceberg marketing strategy was also, either overtly or covertly, conceived as a way to avoid any mention of the recent dictatorial past. Wasn't the amnesiac ice of Antarctica attempting to obliterate the pain left over from the Pinochet era, foes and friends of the tyrant supposedly coming together around the desire to sell Chile and Chilean goods abroad? And it was suspicious that the image makers of the new Chile had chosen as their symbol the only piece of the national territory that had never been occupied by previous inhabitants—or by any other living human, for that matter. An iceberg projecting the desire for an immaculate future cheerfully sidestepped the dilemma of how to blend those indigenous troublemakers into the imagined community of the fatherland, erasing not only their presence but the challenge that they predicate. I could see the globalized ghost of Sarmiento silhouetted inside the iceberg, again civilization and technology offering themselves to conquer wild nature, again predicting a Latin America that would work wonderfully well if it were not for those irritating, primitive, antimodern inhabitants and their present-day defenders, so let's simply make believe they are not there, right? And the same questions coming up, yet again, as they have during our almost two hundred years of independence, the need for an answer to those questions even more urgent in an interconnected global marketplace where the poorer lands control their fate even less than they did in the past. The same questions: In order to build a free and prosperous future, did we need, do we need, to make a clean and icy break with the past? In times such as these, what holds a nation together? Can it be the past, if that past has led to so many frustrations and false starts, if it is an incessant source of instability and divisions? Isn't it better to forge the nation's identity by fixing our eyes on where we are going—a shining and radically different future, a future that turns us into a country like—why not?—the United States? Isn't it better to turn the page, forget the laments and the suffering, start all over again, as if we were Columbus himself about to sight the trees full of silver of Puerto Plata, but this time get it right, this time learn from our mistakes? Wouldn't a renascent Sarmiento suggest the same solution all over again, is there any alternative way to catch up, now that it's the internet and the global economy and the cell phone and fiber-optic cable that might allow us to join the virtual concert of nations?

Perhaps I should grant Sarmiento himself a rejoinder to that question. After all, his *Facundo* is not only noteworthy for having so starkly outlined a drastic solution to the mystery of Latin America's economic and political miscarriages. A closer look at the text itself reveals its author's deep ambiguity about his own central thesis. While preaching unity, Northern decorum, and refined harmony, his masterpiece is itself monstrous, a romantic mixture of all possible genres, from history to fiction, from journalism to drama, from diatribes to sociological analysis and biography—a hodgepodge of conflicting narratives that do not conform to any European classification. His book itself is a cracked and fragmented mirror that inadvertently reflects, as it struggles not to fall apart, the very continent that it is, to all appearances, submitting to judicious control. And Sarmiento's best writing subtly celebrates the very barbaric forces he would destroy and subdue. He is fascinated by the excessive marvels—*¡Qué maravilla!*—of the infinite pampas, a majestic lightening storm, the vast and frightful horizons, the tiger that hunts down men and is hunted by them in return, the extraordinary lives of the machos who populate the plains—trackers and scouts and cattle herders and guides and warriors. In short, Sarmiento is in love with the wild—perhaps because he somehow grasps that the backlands are what confer upon him his identity as an American, those distinct characteristics which anchor him as forever divergent and deviant from European normalcy, the peculiar and anguishing crossroads that make him, let us say, marketable in the civilized world he so wishes to join, and yet deeply wedded to that turbulent beauty and tempestuous violence. He may yearn for the salons of Paris and the railroads of England and the textile mills of Massachusetts, but he views his own urgent intellectual task as the joining of the two contradictory halves of his land, the two antagonistic zones of his own being, writing as a heroic way of confederating in a text what reality has irretrievably split asunder, his written words anticipating and pointing the way to a hybrid solution, a mestizo bringing together of disparate elements into something neither entirely

European nor pre-Columbian. So Sarmiento projects Latin America as a space in between.

If history, in the middle of the dangerous disorder of the nineteenth century, did not allow room for that sort of experiment, that quest for a way in which a divided Latin America could meet and mingle and hold together in a novel way, is it possible that now, at this special moment in the history of the planet, when democracy has been given a second breath, is it not conceivable that we might now be ready to build from that reciprocal give and take a new way of engaging the old dilemma of our continent, create Latin America as a beautifully bastardized mixture that would arise out of a dialogue with the submerged zones of our reality?

It is true that one must be cautious, wary of trying to win with highly charged literary words the moral victory that has been denied to us on the battlefields of history. When I look upon the self-delusion of our governments, whose proclamation of their supposedly fresh and original neoliberal ideas is no more than a blind repetition of the formulas of the past, when I see the financial and social debt we have accumulated, when I see the rampant corruption, when I see the United States poised to intervene yet again in the jungles of Colombia, as it has in so many jungles and beaches and deserts of Latin America in the past, when I see how we once again lag behind and once again hear the same voices indicting our culture, our races, our diversity, our chaos, as if we were cursed by our diversity and internal differences instead of blessed by them, let me admit that I find it hard not to despair.

On the other hand, in the last decade, a vast social movement has been shaking Latin America and, at the same time, shaking the very assumptions upon which the national consensus has been built, and this encourages me to be faintly hopeful.

The most well-known of these movements is certainly the uprising in Chiapas, where Subcomandante Marcos and the indigenous people who have accepted him as one of their own have gone beyond the perilous trappings of martyrdom and, I hope, nostalgia as well. But there are many other less publicized groups, just as sophisticated and compelling, that are spreading across the reaches of what was once the Inca Empire, with a particularly potent collective network of indigenous activists in Ecuador and Bolivia. In Brazil,

the MST (the Landless Peasant Movement) has mobilized millions
of landless peasants in a quest for land and also for a different way
of producing food. In my own Chile, nobody today would dare to
articulate the senseless idea that the Mapuches do not exist. During
the last years, the faraway sons and daughters of Caupolicán have
demanded language rights, autonomy, land—demanded memory,
in fact, in ways that would have astounded Nicanor Plaza and the
committee that selected his faux statue to represent the Araucanian
present and past. I could go on about Guatemala and Argentina
and Panamá and Venezuela . . .

What is most interesting about these movements is that they are
attempting to step outside the Sarmiento paradigm, the Sarmiento
debate in which Latin America has become embroiled—in which
my own remarks have been, in fact, entangled all along. These new
movements swell out of a new Indian experience of the world that
no longer projects itself as an impossibly pure and authentic mille-
narian archetype antagonistic to modernity. Rather, these Indians
see themselves as absolutely contemporary, already participating
in the global system but from another set of values and another
source of wisdom, positing an alternative to globalization on its
present scale and model but using all the newest technologies and
instruments available. And this braces them to be the engine of an
array of other movements representing those marginalized by the
ruling classes of Latin America, with needs and interests as vast as
our own flora and fauna and where women are particularly con-
cerned protagonists. Can these movements seriously affect the way
in which Latin America will imagine and recompose its destiny? I
have no crystal ball, but the American CIA, in a report about the
state of the world in the year 2015, warns that the resurgence of
indigenous movements across the Earth—precisely in those areas
where the major sources of the planet's energy are situated—is one
of the most troubling aspects of what the immediate future might
bring. And am I, ever the perennial troublemaker, to doubt the
intelligence experts of the United States?

Or will our future always reflect the past? Does survival inevitably mean, in Latin America and elsewhere, that those who do not
fit in must be sacrificed, must be left to die or die out? Is that the
price every successful nation of our time must pay for its unity, for

its very success, for leaving the past behind? Is that the secret cost of becoming truly modern? Is it hopelessly naïve and idiotically optimistic to suggest that there might be an alternative? Or are we fated to repeat over and over again the same scenarios of self-delusion that have failed in the past? Will we always be as divided as we were when all this started, back in 1492?

For my part, I am hesitant to be excessively prophetic, given that, shadowed, and who knows if mocked, by Sarmiento, I live in the overdeveloped United States, far from the continent I am supposedly representing. But I continue to be thankful that I was given a chance to listen to the drowned voices of history, the dead and repressed and hopeful voices of our history. This aging adult who was once a child of twelve closer to *The Last of the Mohicans* than to the first of the Chileans, who did not even know how to pronounce the name Caupolicán, who was himself blind to his heritage, fell in love with the turbulent variety of Latin America and with the outcasts of its history, and has never felt anything but gratitude and joy at the experience.

I am convinced that the only way that we will escape the curse of our history and go beyond the polarity of civilization and barbarism in which Sarmiento trapped himself, trapping us along with him, is if our variety is celebrated as our ultimate resource, our *maravilla de maravillas*. It is only this celebration of our own people that will allow us to start creating nations of a different sort, nations that are ravishingly beautiful monsters made from all the disparate strands of our being, nations that are finally not afraid to look themselves in the mirror and smile.

Christopher Columbus Has Words from the Other Side of Death for Captain John Whyte, Who Rebaptized Saddam International Airport As His Troops Rolled In

I know something about names, Captain.

Those who conquer must always have a name ready.
Even before the sword, before the gun.

I saw the island and called it San Salvador.
San Salvador because we had been saved.

I did not ask the natives—
they were friendly, they were almost naked, they were brown
    under the
tropical sun—I did not ask them what they called that place
    themselves
I did not ask them what they called their home

And I did not tell them that they would all die
I did not tell them that nobody would ever know
what they spoke
how they spoke

First published online on OpenDemocracy.com and TomDispatch.com (both April 11, 2003).

the words would be swallowed
like boats are swallowed in the tempest
of a sad sea
like bodies are swallowed in a mine

Now they teach me their words and their songs
here in the dark of forever
I study what they called the moon and love and good-bye
I listen to their Carib whispers
and I purse my lips and I whistle and I soften the air
with the language no one has spoken on that island
for over five hundred years

This is my penance

And then Quechua and then Maya and then Tzotzil
and then the thousand and ten tongues that were once alive
in the lands that would not be called my name
that would be called by someone else's name
Amerigo America
and then the learning will go on
Navajo and Guaraní and Nahuatl
and the sounds that once filled the ears
of lovely maidens
to bring forth the crops
and no one today even knows their name
learning learning
until they have taught me to pronounce each last word
how do you say friend
how do you say death
how do you say forever

how do you say penance

they will teach me how they say penance
in their thousand and ten tongues

your penance, Captain?
what awaits you?

You said you came to bring freedom

Freedom. When another can decide for himself.

You said you came to bring democracy.

Democracy. When another can control for herself.

You said you came with liberation.

Liberation. When the people who made the world
name that world and themselves.

Freedom. Democracy. Liberation.
Words.
Your words, the words of your leaders.

And then you called the airport by another name.
It is ours. We took it. We're here.
We killed the men who called it by that other name.
We can call it now what we will.
Under a sky full of bombs another name.
Baghdad now. Not Saddam.

Saddam Airport.
Not a name I like, we like, here on the other side.
a name cursed in the cellars
where the fingers are crushed
where the head is split
where the teeth are pulled

rooted out

the roots of that name Saddam
the striker of the blow
the one who resists
the one who gives grief
the one who prohibits

all all all crying out inside that name

but not for you, Captain,
to change
not for you to decide

your penance?

they wait for you, John Whyte,
here in the glorious dust of words
they once scrolled on paper, parchment, stone
here in the dark light of death

they wait for you
the poets of Iraq

Abu Nuwas and Sa'di
Mutanabbi and Buhturi
waiting like the rugs they used to sit on
waiting like the founts they used to drink from

all the words you did not think to use
Captain John Whyte
all the names you did not know
not even your own
white barakah
barakah related to barak blessing

you will have to learn
pronounce as I have had to pronounce
word for word

the Arabic you did not care to know
like the Nahuatl I never knew
like the Cherokee I never knew

you will have to learn

starting with the hundred words
that pour forth from Allah

Rahman the Compassionate
Rahim the Merciful

Rahman International Airport
Rahim International Airport

can you hear them
even now as you advance towards Baghdad
can you hear their voices

Rahman the Compassionate
Rahim the Merciful

Rahman Rahim
and Salam

Salam
Peace

one of the attributes of God

your penance
John Whyte John Barakah
did you never think

they will treat you with mercy
on the other side

that the people of Iraq
might want to call their land
with the names of Salam
the many names of peace?

your penance
oh white one

it will take you and your leaders
forever
and forever
and forever
it will take you forever

to learn the word for peace

Will the Duendes *Prowl in Santiago?*

Just a few words of warning to the presidents of the Americas as they gather this weekend in my homeland, Chile: Beware of the *duendes*.

Duendes?

Chilean folklore knows them as elflike creatures operating at night, good-natured gremlins who like to play practical jokes on humans and must be appeased from time to time before they do more mischief. Though nobody I've ever met in Chile—or in any other Latin American nation—has ever actually seen one of these elusive imps, their capacity to cause damage in our everyday existence should never be underestimated.

My latest encounter with the *duendes* occurred during a recent visit to Chile, where I no longer live. One Sunday, I noticed that Elba, my mother-in-law, instead of actively perusing the newspaper and muttering imprecations against General Augusto Pinochet, as she is wont to do, was walking around our living room in some agitation. She had lost her reading glasses, it turned out, and soon the whole family—my wife, our two sons, our U.S. daughter-in-law who had come down with us to explore Chile—were all poking around in corners and overturning cushions. Only after half an hour of fruitless probing did Elba tell us to call off the search.

"It's no use," she said. "The *duendes* did it. Last night I didn't leave them their milk. Tonight I'll set out a dish, and tomorrow, you'll see, we'll find the glasses."

My mother-in-law's plan worked. By the next morning, the milk had disappeared—not, I am sure, because of any marauding Chilean cats—and the glasses, of course, were found tucked into the folds of a sofa where I myself had ineffectually looked several times.

Los Angeles Times, April 17, 1998, op-ed page.

It was not the first, and probably will not be the last time that the *duendes* miraculously returned an object they had borrowed, perhaps in order to remind us not to forget their existence.

I fear the presidents may forget them at their gathering in Santiago. They will justifiably celebrate the recent democratization of the continent, they will talk about hemispheric security and free-trade zones, they will proclaim that the frenzied pursuit of profits and the newest technology and the integration of their economies into the global system is the only solution to the recalcitrant ills of Latin America, that the past must be left behind in order to resolutely advance into the consumerist future, and all the while I can imagine the *duendes* nearby, listening and watching these deliberations with dismay and perhaps preparing a mysterious retribution.

The *duendes'* anger at the summit, I expect, does not stem from a stubborn resistance to progress; as their temporary and unelected spokesperson, I am certain they would welcome more hospitals and schools and roads and less hunger and ignorance and violence. What worries the *duendes*—as far as I can tell, that is, and if I am wrong, may they rise from the night and repudiate me—is that the accelerated modernization of Latin America has been done without the real and active participation of the vast population of the hemisphere, without taking into account their beliefs and culture and solidarity and suffering, and by exalting a greed and competitiveness that directly contradicts the value system that *duendes* have been trying to teach humans ever since the dawn of time.

The actions of these demonic and yet ultimately benevolent creatures suggest that we can placate them only if we act gratuitously. Gratuitous, not in the common sense of unnecessary, but in the original meaning of the word: something given for nothing, for which you do not expect a payback, a return, a dividend. The *duendes* hide our belongings and wreak havoc with the harsh order of our daytime routines because we have forgotten to pour some milk into a dish and quench their thirst. They want to remind us of so many others out there in the darkness, so many invisible others we should be feeding and heeding, caring for, embracing into our lives. They are telling us to be wary of a society that does not have space and time for the unpredictable, the compassionate, the magical.

I may believe myself to be the transitory representative on earth of these mischievous underground creatures, but I am not mad enough to suppose that the presidents will set a place for them at the summit banquet table or order their ministers of finance to include the *duendes* as an item in their next budget, under the heading "tenderness" or perhaps "exorcism." The presidents are far too engaged in Important Matters of State.

So how will the *duendes* react to their exclusion?

All I can hope is that on Sunday morning, each and every one of the heads of governments that rule the Americas will be unable to find his reading glasses, will be unable to read the treaties he is about to sign, will desperately send his entire cabinet off on a scrambling, barren search for the missing spectacles, and then, at night, when nobody is looking, when no reporters are around, it is my stubborn hope that the most powerful men in the hemisphere, with simultaneous heartbeats and in all humility, will set out some milk at the foot of the bed and perhaps, who knows, even sleep well for the first time in many years.

Let us hope that the *duendes* have not given up on the presidents of the Americas in their blindness, given up and now won't even deign to play tricks on them, we can only hope they will continue to find a mischievous way to make sure that we listen to their hidden voices in the times of trouble that lie ahead.

The Day I Failed to Be Che Guevara

Once in a while, on a particularly damp day, I am visited by a slight twinge of pain in my shins, the slightest hint of an ache that takes me back to that moment about twenty-nine years ago when somebody in my hometown of Santiago shot me. A man whose name I never knew and whose face I never saw peppered my legs with buckshot and then left me bleeding on a Chilean sidewalk, left me to wander the city looking for a friendly doctor who could extract the small pellets and not report my wounds to the police.

I had anticipated in my imagination the very scene of violence I was later to experience. I was writing a short story at the time—it must have been mid-August of the year 1970—a chapter of a book implausibly called *Ten Variations on the Three Little Pigs*. As a child, growing up in New York in the forties and fifties, I had been raised on Disney fare, and one of my earliest favorites was the cartoon version of how Practical Pig constructed a brick house that could withstand the huffing and puffing of the Big Bad Wolf who was able to blow down the precarious straw and wooden houses of Practical Pig's foolish brothers. As adults are wont to do with their most cherished childhood memories, I ripped into the bland Disney fairy tale with gusto, exploring in my variations the hidden political, sexual, even ecological meanings buried in the original cartoon. In one variation, for instance, I used the succession of the three houses to map out the evolution of humanity from straw to wood to brick and cement, from hunters to farmers to city dwellers, telling the story from the point of view of the building materials themselves as they awaited the buzzsaw of progress, the Big Bad Wolf of modernization that

London Observer, March 28, 1999.

incessantly tears down one house after another in its mad thrust toward the future.

But the story where I predicted my own shooting was the most iconoclastic of them all: I made the wolf one of four brother animals who is a rebel against society, I made him a hero who was on the run and wounded, seeking refuge in one house after another and never finding it. Behind this vision was my infatuation, and that of my generation, with Ernesto Che Guevara, the Argentine-Cuban revolutionary who had been murdered in 1967 while trying to lead a peasant uprising in Bolivia. The villain in my story was Practical Pig who, as far as I can remember, represented some bizarre mix of CIA agent crossed with rampant capitalist, eager to kill the hunted guerrilla wolf.

In my life, as in that of so many writers, fiction has a frightening way of coming true, though often in disguised and twisted ways. As I was putting the finishing touches to that subversive variation on the Three Little Pigs, a news bulletin flashed on the radio. The invented violence of my fiction was interrupted by the deadly violence of the reality of Chile: in the streets of Puente Alto, a small town on the outskirts of Santiago, two high-school students had just been shot to death by the police.

I jumped out of my chair and decided it was no time to adjudicate adjectives and polish my tenses. I was a hot-blooded twenty-eight-year-old and I wasn't going to stand for this sort of murder. Thousands of other Chileans obviously felt the same way, and we poured into the streets to protest the killings. Chile was then a democracy; the word "Pinochet" was not even part of our vocabulary or our nightmares, and the police did no more than hose us down and offer up a dosage of tear gas. As we scrambled away from the police ministrations, I ended up with some other protestors in front of the building that housed the regional headquarters of Jorge Alessandri, the right-wing candidate who, in a month's time, was going to face Salvador Allende in the presidential elections. Allende would go on to win those elections and inspire those of us who were now marching and chanting through the streets to do far more constructive things, but at that instant of exaltation, we did not care about the future. We were full of rage now and had to rid ourselves of that rage quickly and decided that the best way was to insult our enemies where it would hurt them most—at their headquarters—and teach them a lesson or two.

Our enemies were the ones who taught us a lesson. A group of fascist thugs suddenly emerged from the building we had surrounded. They were not armed, as we were, with caustic invective but with shotguns. Instead of running for cover, I had insanely continued to rant at them. I can still see myself, my fist raised in the air as if I were Che Guevara himself. Or maybe, scrolling through my mind back then, I had cast myself as the star of a grotesque revolutionary film. But there was nothing celluloid about the rifle that was fired and the sudden stinging in both my legs or the torn trousers or the blood that started to drip onto the pavement.

It was only birdshot: seven small hard lead pellets that sprinkled my thighs and shins. I didn't even collapse. I just stood there, instantly silent, shocked, in a daze. My high-sounding words had disappeared, swallowed by the bullets.

A friend of mine—his name was Jaime Gómez—pulled me away, limping, to his motorbike. As a poet, Jaime cultivated surreal images and curses à la Baudelaire, but in this case, my friend had his usually feverish head squarely on his shoulders. He knew that I needed medical attention, but that I couldn't check into a hospital or I would immediately be arrested and interrogated. For the next hours, he drove me around Santiago in search of first aid.

As we careened through the city like two bikers from *Easy Rider*, my sense of unreality was heightened by the feeling that I had already lived this situation a few hours earlier in my fiction. Like the Che Guevara wolf of my story, I was on the run. Like him, blood was streaming down my body. Like him, in the first two places we tried, we were turned away.

But this was not Bolivia, and I was not Che Guevara. Santiago was my city, the city I had made mine, with its mountains towering above us and its Mapocho River of an earthy dirty brown, Santiago with its shantytowns where I had worked for so many years as an activist and its cafés where I had debated Sartre and García Márquez, Santiago was the city where I had fallen in love and where my first child had been born, the city that had taught me Spanish and the smell of orange trees in the summer, Santiago was the place on this planet where I wanted to be buried, and Santiago would not let me down, Santiago would find me a doctor as we raced into the wind, Santiago would take care of me.

And Santiago did keep its promise to me: I did not end up like my character. When we finally arrived at the brick house of Dr. Brodsky—was it really brick, or are my memories drunkenly transforming the past to make this story even more singular and amazing?—when we arrived at his house, the doctor, an old friend of the family, came out to greet us and soon, in the safety of his living room, pronounced my wounds minor. I would not die, like Che Guevara, stretched out on a table, captured by a camera that would turn him, for the whole world to gape at, into a Christlike figure. On the contrary, while Dr. Brodsky dressed my wounds, he scolded me in a way that neither Che Guevara nor the wolf would have found tolerable. You really must be more careful, Ariel. "*Tienes que cuidarte más,*" he said.

He wasn't the only one to scold me.

During the next few days, I shuffled my feet conspicuously, more than I needed to. I showed off my seven wounds, I denounced the right-wing ruffians who had done this to poor innocent me, I projected myself as a martyr of the Revolution, but I was also absolutely aware that I was a fool. A point my wife, Angélica, made to me repeatedly. Rather than a red badge of courage, she said, I had decorated myself with seven white bandages of stupidity. I could have lost my eyes, Angélica smoldered as she ministered to my legs several times a day. The pellets could have ricocheted into my lungs or, worse still, into my genitals. All it would have taken for me to limp for life was for one little bullet, just one, to have shattered my kneecap. And for what? What had my fit of infantile indignation accomplished? The two students were dead, and my wounds wouldn't bring them back to life. And the thug who had shot me was free and more than ready to pull the trigger again, as we would find out in the years of dictatorship to come. Nor had my actions influenced anybody's opinion, or drained one ounce of sorrow from the world.

When I was a boy in New York, it had been easy to be a hero. All you needed was two fingers and a mouth: wham, pow, bang, bang. I would run among my friends and rivals killing mercilessly and being just as mercilessly mowed down: gangster, cowboy, warrior,

Indian—it was merely a matter of pointing your finger and spouting onomatopoeia.

Now I had tasted real bullets, had found that they create silence, that violence is not a game.

It was time to grow up.

The years that followed were marked by Salvador Allende's democratic revolution and General Pinochet's military takeover and my wandering the earth for twenty and more years. Those years would teach me much more about violence and survival than I had bargained for, those years would help me figure out when to run and when to stand tall, when solidarity can defeat terror, when bullets cannot impose silence, when bullets need to be answered with words.

I never got to publish my story about the Three Little Pigs and the wolf who was shot, the story in which I had anticipated my own shooting.

But Che Guevara did not leave me alone. The methods he had used in his struggle, his revolutionary zeal, his cult of martyrdom became increasingly out-of-date, unsuccessful, and far from my own options, but the reasons for which he had rebelled and died in the first place had not gone away. The world continued to be a place loaded with injustice, inequality, starving children, massacred Indians, unshackled greed. And so, haunted by Che Guevara, I recently incorporated him into a work of fiction: I invented a character, Gabriel McKenzie, who had been conceived, according to his mother, the very day that Che Guevara was being buried in Bolivia. But I did not make the mistake of having my young character act out my fantasy as a young man of emulating Che. Instead of trying, as I had, to become Che and failing to do so, Gabriel turned out to be cynical and cowardly, desperate to escape Che Guevara's example, totally indifferent to the Revolution. Gabriel's problem is not that the world is full of beggars and inequity and prejudice but that he is, at the age of twenty-three, still a virgin. His energies were not to be spent storming the barricades of heaven, but in desperate and preposterous attempts to find a different sort of heaven and haven—a girl to make love to under the stars. Among other things, I wanted to test the world that had survived Che Guevara and see how much of his rebellion was left in this world where he has become an image on a jug or an icon on a T-shirt. I wondered if the revolutionary guerrilla hero had any message from beyond death for his wayward, neurotic, and virginal godson Gabriel.

So thirty years later, I did finally introduce Che Guevara into my literature. Perhaps he wouldn't mind that he is a character in what is a picaresque comedy, a farce about icebergs and nannies and mistaken identities. Perhaps he is tired of always being portrayed in tragic stories where bullets fly and blood flows. And it is my definite hope that he is glad, wherever he may be, that I did not imitate his life back then in 1970, that I failed to die like he did when somebody whose name I never knew shot me, and I survived to tell this story, this story and so many others.

Rubber Soul

When Fray Juan de Torquemada wrote, in 1615, that Indian tribes in the New World milked trees and then molded the substance they'd extracted into footwear, he could not know that several centuries later human transportation of a more amazing and speedy variety would depend on the process he was describing to Western ears and eyes for the first time.

The vulcanized, pneumatic tires that were set in motion—first in the bicycle craze of the 1890s and, as that fad waned thereafter, wrapped around the churning wheels of the automobile—would have been impossible had there not existed, in the inaccessible Amazon basin, a vast expanse of isolated trees that could be tapped. The result of this insatiable industrial demand was the prodigious rubber boom of the Amazon: from the 1880s to the first decade of the twentieth century, seduced by the promise of extraordinary profits, a fabulous assortment of men, resources, and projects poured into Brazil. The result was bedlam—a region suddenly gone mad with riches and power and illusions. It was symbolized most clamorously by the opera house in Manaus, where the greatest singers of Europe crossed the most dangerous jungle in the world to entertain the rubber barons.

Whose boom would soon turn into a colossal bust.

Those thirty years were so bizarre that an eminent Brazilian intellectual once suggested that a novelist rather than an economic historian was needed to tell the tale. The astounding, apocalyptic story is finally being told, in novel after novel, by one of the most talented writers in Brazil today, Márcio Souza (born in Manaus in 1946).

American readers who were delighted in 1980 by *The Emperor of the Amazon*, his bawdy satire about an adventurer who carves

---

Village Voice (New York), January 14, 1986, book review.

out a short-lived empire in the jungle at the end of the nineteenth century, will welcome *Mad Maria*, superbly translated by Thomas Colchie. Souza's second novel centers on a more somber but equally grotesque event in the annals of the Amazon: the building of the Madeira-Mamoré railroad between 1907 and 1912.

The financers of the railroad promoted it, in its day, as a technical feat to rival the Panama Canal. It would join the landlocked, latex-rich Bolivian region of the Beni with the nearest navigable portion of the Amazon, overcoming almost insurmountable obstacles: 19 foaming cataracts, 227 miles of flooded swamps and gorges, thousands of scorpions and giant trees, millions of malaria-infested mosquitoes. Before it was finished, 3,600 men had died, 30,000 had been hospitalized, and a fortune had been squandered in the oppressive heat of the jungle.

By selecting from the historical records the most macabre and unbelievable episodes of those five years and then concentrating them in a nightmarish three-month span, Souza forces the reader, almost as if he were just one more character tangled up in the undergrowth, to confront that hell:

> The rains would suddenly arrive with a sluttish violence. . . . The whole world was about to dissolve, literally, and nothing provided even the illusion of substance, let alone certainty. Everything grew damp and pulpy, with a pungent smell of aqueous clay exuding the vestiges of life and death. This unmistakable odor would soon penetrate everything and produce in any man a brand of immobility, of glum passivity, as the wetness gradually pervaded his body like a disquietingly sticky, cold sweat.

Souza's refusal to mitigate the horrors by proclaiming some higher meaning to the enterprise closes off what might have been a convenient avenue of escape. He resolutely assaults the myth of the pioneers, romanticized in frontier adventure-fiction, that hardship is the inevitable price for advancing civilization and "vanquishing barbarism." The railroad goes from "no place to no place" and is useless the moment it's inaugurated. The same year,

1912, that a locomotive—the Mad Maria of the title—undertook its triumphant maiden voyage, Southeast Asia became the globe's major rubber exporter, dramatically relegating Brazil to second place and signaling the end of the rubber boom and the decline of the Amazon region.

Because the whole affair is absurd, Souza sees those who try to tame the wild, sensual madhouse of the jungle as fools, at best involuntary suicides, deluding themselves about their motives in order to retain some sanity, unable to perceive what is really happening around them, bamboozled into that green hell by entrepreneur-charlatans. Souza's conviction that they are victims in a con game, played out in faraway Rio de Janeiro by conniving businessmen and politicians, paradoxically saves the narrative from becoming overtruculent and morbid, and gradually tinges it with a farcical, even light, touch.

Just when the reader feels he cannot stand any more of the unrelenting, dismal violence of the jungle scenes, *Mad Maria* switches back, in almost Brechtian style, to the bitter black comedy of the magnates and ministers, all of them historical figures upon whom Souza, on behalf of their forgotten victims, exacts an implacable and posthumous literary revenge. Two of the most powerful men in Brazil at that time, the American millionaire Percival Farquhar and the Minister of Public Works, J. J. Seabra, who have been treated splendidly in official manuals and biographies, are here subjected to ridicule, exposed as hucksters who used the railroad as one more wheel in their multiple deals, savagely fighting each other's public influence while sharing the private delights of the same Brazilian whore. (When the book came out in 1980, this caused quite an uproar in Rio, not least of all because it made public figures fearful that writers would tackle them just as pointedly as soon as military censorship was eased.)

Imperceptibly, advancing as slowly as the railway tracks in the mud, burlesque and satire come to dominate the novel—which, though full of adventure, ends up being essentially plotless. By the time a congressional delegation from the capital chugs up the Amazon for an inspection, we are ready for a hilarious finale. Everybody is enveloped by the absurd. Even the most idealistic characters have been taught by the all-pervading violence that such notions as civilization and progress are of scant help to human beings who are "nothing more than mechanisms of survival."

The closest we come to a protagonist—or, if you will, an axis, in the dizzying movement of the novel—is a young doctor who wants to advance science and cure the sick; he ends up performing autopsies and shooting his would-be patients. A beautiful Bolivian widow, who planned to play Chopin in the backlands as a sign of an illuminated soul, gives her body to any man who promises her relief from that inferno. Even an ingenuous aborigine whose arms have been hacked off by the railway workers, and who might have provided a perspective of innocence or hope, finally ekes out a living playing "Happy Birthday" on the piano with his feet for profit. The last we hear of him he has died of syphilis in a New York circus.

But Souza's diagnosis of the *corps humain* as contaminated does not mean, as one of his characters points out, that we should cease to admire the body itself. Souza may see life as a landscape where yesterday's boom turns into today's inevitable bust, a deception as gigantic as the Amazon itself; he may protest that love is no more than a sexual ensnarement for idiots. Yet there can be no doubt that he is in love with life and in love with the Amazon region as well. This is why *Mad Maria*, despite its cold, relentless vision, is not a bleak book. It is too vital, too sensual, too intense and ribald for that.

Like the Amazon jungle, variously depicted as a bordello, an indifferent mistress, or a colorful crazy womb, its energy and enchantment cannot be denied.

Even as we hear the sobering news day after day that the jungle that inspired this book and gave the world rubber and wheels for so many decades is being despoiled and destroyed, even as we read, the Amazon is in danger of disappearing as we lift our eyes from the insane wanderings of the characters and look out onto the world.

A Hopeful Parable of Doom

I t took Nobel-laureate Gabriel García Márquez thirty years to write his latest novel, *Chronicle of a Death Foretold*. It all started with a murder: early one morning in 1951 one of the Colombian author's best friends, Cayetano Gentile, was hacked to death by two men in front of his house in Sucre, Colombia. They were the brothers of a woman, married the day before, who, having been returned by the bridegroom on their wedding night because she was not a virgin, had falsely named Gentile as her secret lover. And the family's honor had been washed with his blood.

The incident haunted García Márquez ever since. It was one of those crimes that drip from the pages of yellow journals around the world, but behind the superficial sensationalism, García Márquez sensed a deeper drama, where the forces of history and myth were at work. He comes from a country, after all, and a continent where violence has often seemed a fatal god with laws of its own, an almost natural way of settling differences among people, or between people and their rulers.

How could such sudden savagery erupt, almost unpredictably, in the midst of a peaceful celebration? Where had it come from? And how was it possible that the whole town, which knew that the crime was about to occur, had been unable to prevent it?

In a sense, the question he was asking was a wider one: Is Latin America doomed to this sort of everyday civil war on its streets and in its bedrooms?

As if he were one of his own characters, it took García Márquez almost a whole lifetime to answer that question, those questions. Being so near the events and their overwhelming dementia, he could not find the form or the formula, if you will, for transmitting them,

---

Philadelphia Inquirer, March 13, 1983, book review.

which is like saying that he had not yet figured out how a place so familiar could abruptly be transformed into hell.

He also had to discover how to turn the facts into a fiction that would reveal the concealed and more profound structure of truth.

His solution, now that it has come, may not surprise those readers who devoured *One Hundred Years of Solitude*, enthralled by the way excessive, extraordinary, and supposedly exotic situations were made entirely believable and acceptable by a warm and matter-of-fact tone of voice. In *Chronicle of a Death Foretold* they will detect the same style. Using only the most closely observed details of real life, García Márquez manages to construct a landscape with the piercing and visionary quality of dreams, the kind of dreams that remain with us years after we have awakened from them.

But the latest book goes a step further. In his preceding work, García Márquez never let us question the foundations of his world. He acted as a channel for the oral tradition, presenting without any gnawing doubts people who reelaborate their experience, assuming themselves to be the final authority, believing that history and legend are one; memory and fact, inseparable. For the first time, the Colombian author's new novel puts this popular oral tradition to the test.

The narrator himself—a journalist—appears before us, researching the event, attempting its reconstruction from the hundred fragmented and contradictory versions, where time, place, weather, motives shift and lose their anchorage. By blending journalism, so dependent on immediate evidence, with the imaginary, which expands freely according to its own creative laws, that voice will give to the incredible murder a grounding in everyday detail.

These two forms of communication are not incompatible. I remember the almost childlike joy of García Márquez a few years ago—he had just finished the manuscript—when he told me that the coroner's autopsy of the *real* victim's wounds confirmed his imagined version. "The only [wound] he had in the back, at the level of the third lumbar vertebra, had perforated the right kidney," García Márquez said as we sipped our drinks in a resort hotel in Mexico where we were both jurors for a literary prize. Why so jubilant? Because the synthesis of what can be seen and what can be envisioned seemed to be proving his *Chronicle* a prolongation of the original *Crónicas de Indias*, those wild, eyewitness reports with which the first conquistadors recounted the real—and simultaneously fabulous—story of the new world.

García Márquez has invented in this *Death Foretold* a narrator who acts just as a newspaper reporter would, interrogating during twenty-seven years everyone connected with the crime, trying to make sense of the chaos in the witnesses' throats, trying to pinpoint how each person who could have avoided that death ended up contributing to it.

But those witnesses are not allowed to take over the proceedings. Their testimony is rigidly organized within a time frame that lasts exactly one hour and a half. The first sentence tells of the awakening of Santiago Nasar (the name given to Gentile) at 5:30 in the morning of the day he is to die; the book closes, a scant 120 pages later, at 7:00, when he collapses and breathes no more.

Until the very end, the murder could have been avoided. The two killers did everything to force someone to stop them. They bragged of their intentions in the hope that they would be dissuaded or jailed. In fact, they waited for their victim in front of the one door that he was sure not to approach the whole day. But that day Nasar disrupted his habitual itinerary and avoided the door through which he normally entered his house. And his mother, on the other side, was putting up the bar to shut that door against which he would die without being able to enter, believing, that woman, that her son had already arrived home. This confusion is typical of all the events that accumulate like foul, rising water and slowly drown Nasar.

It is as if all the people in the town were doors that might lead to life and instead lead to death. Those who rushed after the victim to warn him were unable to find him. And those who did meet up with him failed, for a variety of reasons, to warn him. We watch the community do the wrong thing, and then we watch the swamp of their justifications, their excuses, their pretexts.

The reader is bedazzled, not only by the chain of coincidences and blunders, not only by the closing of the right doors while the wrong ones are being opened, but by the wizardry with which García Márquez controls his readers and submerges us in the life of a small town and its buzzing, breathless semiconsciousness. Confronted with this double clockwork of life and art, we may succumb to the illusion that what we are witnessing is the working out of a destiny that no man can control.

And yet, this may not be what the *Chronicle* is telling us. In *One Hundred Years of Solitude* and in *The Autumn of the Patriarch* there was no escaping the cyclical wheel of copulation and death. *Chronicle of a Death Foretold* is a political parable that shows the same pressures at work but does not draw the same conclusions.

Gregory Rabassa's translation is as precise and hallucinatory as ever, and yet I beg to disagree with the title. *Foretold* sounds good in English, certainly better than *announced*. But *foretold* has something of the fatal, the Delphic, the solemn, the irrefutable about it. The death was *anunciada*; it was on everybody's mind, near everybody's tongue, but never was uttered to save the victim.

If Santiago Nasar is doomed, it is not because his life is a circle that an oracle has pronounced complete, finished. He will die because of the sum total of rituals, habits, misconceptions, and prejudices that crisscross and corrupt society like shadows. As García Márquez has pointed out in an interview, most people did not intervene because they felt that this was a social rite—the taking back of honor lost, the necessary death of the violator—with which they agreed.

The concatenation of misunderstandings and hesitations that spun Nasar's death are only apparently accidental; they are really an outer expression of a culture that needs, expects, and creates that death, and then stands by passively while it is enacted. The real cause of the murder is the unproclaimed law of war between men, of machismo. Nasar is condemned by his own code. Though he is innocent of having despoiled the bride, he is guilty of sharing the same preconceptions that his murderers will use to justify their act.

It is a network of minds that has set the trap for the victim. The closed blind-alley minds, marooned in their solitude and unable to imagine a different interpretation of what they see and should do, sentence Nasar to his death and themselves to their guilt.

Just one door opening, just one person standing up and shouting what had been announced in murmurs by all would have been enough to turn tragedy into peace. *Chronicle of a Death Foretold* is the story of a collective failure, and it is, at the same time, a challenge to create a collective difference, a story that asks us to open the doors behind which we hide.

If we dare, we may just have the time—and it is García Márquez himself who said so in his Nobel Prize acceptance speech in December 1982—we may just have the time to give the races condemned to one hundred years of solitude a second opportunity on this Earth.

The Clowns Come to the Revolution

WWhen it was originally published in 1965 in Mexico, the late Jorge Ibargüengoitia's *The Lightning of August* caused a considerable literary stir. Until then, the literature dealing with the Mexican Revolution had been somber and solemn—its dominant tone set by the monumental saga of the conflict and the gigantic suffering of the community. History, these works implied, was a serious affair. And then suddenly, for the first time, a novel appeared proclaiming that this shattering, traumatic event was, with all due respect, a laughing matter. It had taken the Mexican Revolution fifty-five years to produce its first satire.

Now, more than twenty years later, American readers can enjoy this funny, bittersweet book in a reasonable translation by Irene del Corral.

The novel is centered on the conspiratorial antics of a group of bumbling generals who, like the Keystone Kops, can do nothing right. But unlike the Keystone Kops, they hold the destiny of a nation in their hands. In their madcap scramble for power, they execute innocent civilians, bombard the wrong towns, and, of course, eventually stab one another in the back—all in the name of the highest ideals.

The man who tells their story is the fictitious Major General Lupe Arroyo, a disarming scoundrel indeed: "Criticism was heaped on me later because I didn't release these hostages although the ransom was paid. I'd like to set the record straight in these pages: The ransom was demanded to keep them from being shot, not to free them."

What differentiates Arroyo from the other generals is that he is brutally open about his motives—and everybody else's as well.

New York Times Book Review, February 23, 1986, book review.

Arroyo knows that in a world of rascals it is not morality that guarantees success, nor integrity that is rewarded: the spoils of the world are distributed by the unpredictable wheel of fortune. He, therefore, has an eye out for the small, unnoticed detail that could trip him up—or save him. No wonder that for him history is a farce in which the goal is not to slip on any of the major banana peels.

But Lupe Arroyo has a talent for slipping. Informed that the watch bequeathed to him by the recently deceased president-elect has been stolen by another general, he punishes the presumed thief at the funeral by pushing him into a muddy open grave—only to discover the next day that the very man he had humiliated has just been elected to the vacant presidency, and that, in fact, the watch in question had never been stolen, but was merely misplaced.

In other words, Arroyo is a born loser hoping for a streak of good luck.

Similar characters can be found in Ibargüengoitia's other novels, two of which are available in English. Although those characters are fighting for more sordid objectives than the generals—a fat share of the family inheritance in *Two Crimes* and keeping a bordello in operation in *The Dead Girls*—they show a similar predisposition to engage lightheartedly in any number of crimes in order to come out on top; and like the generals, they suppose that Lady Luck will bail them out if things go wrong. As in *The Lightning of August*, Ibargüengoitia masterfully situates us inside the skin of his protagonists. It is only after the laughter has subsided that we realize with a chill that the humor has enticed us into accepting on their own terms the characters' cold, almost matter-of-fact violence, the morass of their self-deceptions.

The Lightning of August is much more than a hilarious tour de force. Ibargüengoitia mercilessly forces us to experience his country's corruption and even the language of its corruption. Underneath the smiles, one can feel and share the pain caused by a revolution gone sour.

I wish it were possible to look forward to new works by this subtle, precise novelist. But one day in December 1983 the rotten luck that hounded his characters finally caught up with their author: in Paris he boarded a plane bound for Colombia that several hours later crashed in heavy fog at Madrid Barajas Airport. It is strange and perhaps sadly ironic that in his life, as in that of Lupe Arroyo and so many other characters Ibargüengoitia created, major disasters always originate in human miscalculation.

The fate of Latin America? Where not even the unerring vision of a superb novelist could help him avoid the destiny he had predicted for the creatures of his fantasy?

The Return of Che

By the time Ernesto Guevara, known as Che, was murdered in the jungles of Bolivia in October 1967, he was already a legend to my generation, not only in Latin America, but around the world.

Like so many epics, the story of the obscure Argentine doctor who abandoned his profession and his native land to pursue the emancipation of the poor of the Earth began with a voyage. In 1956, along with Fidel Castro and a handful of others, he had crossed the Caribbean in the rickety yacht *Granma* on the mad mission of invading Cuba and overthrowing the dictator Fulgencio Batista. Landing in a hostile swamp, losing most of their contingent, the survivors fought their way to the Sierra Maestra. A bit over two years later, after a guerrilla campaign in which Guevara displayed such outrageous bravery and skill that he was named comandante, the insurgents entered Havana and launched what was to become the first and only victorious socialist revolution in the Americas. The images were thereafter invariably gigantic. Che the titan standing up to the *Yanquis*, the world's dominant power. Che the moral guru proclaiming that a New Man, no ego and all ferocious love for the other, had to be forcibly created out of the ruins of the Old one, and that it was only a matter of Will Power. Che the romantic mysteriously leaving the revolution to continue, sick though he might be with asthma, the struggle against oppression and tyranny.

His execution in Vallegrande at the age of thirty-nine only enhanced Guevara's mythical stature. That Christlike figure laid out on a bed of death with uncanny eyes almost about to open; those fearless last words ("Shoot, coward, you're only going to kill a

Time magazine (New York), June 14, 1999, special edition, The Hundred Most Famous People of the Twentieth Century.

man") that somebody invented or reported; the anonymous burial and the hacked-off hands, as if his killers feared him more after he was dead than when he had been alive: all of it is scalded into the mind and memory of those defiant times. He would return, young people shouted in the late 1960s; I can remember fervently proclaiming it in the streets of Santiago de Chile while similar vows exploded across Latin America. *No te vamos a olvidar*, we promised. We won't let you be forgotten.

More than thirty years have passed, and the dead hero has indeed persisted in collective memory, but not exactly in the way the majority of us anticipated. Che has become ubiquitous: his figure stares out at us from coffee mugs and posters, jingles at the end of key rings, pops up in rock songs and operas and art shows. The British have even named a beer after him.

The apotheosis of his image has been accompanied by a parallel disappearance of the real man, swallowed by the myth. Most of those who idolize the incendiary guerrilla with the star on his beret were born long after his demise and have only the sketchiest knowledge of his goals or his life. Gone is the generous Che who tended wounded enemy soldiers, gone is the vulnerable warrior who wanted to curtail his love of life lest it make him less effective in combat, and gone is also the darker, more turbulent Che who signed orders to execute prisoners in Cuban jails without a fair trial.

This erasure of complexity is the normal fate of any icon. More paradoxical is that the humanity that worships Che has by and large turned away from just about everything he believed in. The future he predicted has not been kind to his ideals or his ideas. Back in the sixties, we presumed that his self-immolation would be commemorated by social action, the downtrodden rising against the system and creating—to use Che's own words—two, three, many Vietnams. Thousands of luminous young men, particularly in Latin America, followed his example into the hills and were slaughtered there or tortured to death in sad city cellars, never knowing that their dreams of total liberation, like those of Che, would not come true. If Vietnam is being imitated today, it is primarily as a model for how a society forged in insurrection now seeks to be actively integrated into the global market. Nor has Guevara's uncompromising, unrealistic style of struggle, or his ethical absolutism, prevailed. The major revolutions of the last quarter of a century (South Africa, Iran, the Philippines, Nicaragua), not to mention the peaceful transitions to democracy in Latin America, East Asia, and the former communist world, have all entailed negotiations with former adversaries, a give-and-take that could not be further from Che's unyielding demand for confrontation to the death. Even someone like Subcomandante Marcos, the spokesman for the Chiapas Maya revolt, whose charisma and moral stance remind us of Che's, does not espouse his hero's economic or military theories. And Che's beloved Cuba has been kept afloat by agreements made with capitalist Europe.

How to understand, then, Che Guevara's pervasive popularity, especially among the affluent young?

Perhaps in these orphaned times of incessantly shifting identities and allegiances, the fantasy of an adventurer who changed countries and crossed borders and broke down limits without once betraying his basic loyalties provides the restless youth of our era with an optimal combination, grounding them in a fierce center of moral gravity while simultaneously appealing to their contemporary nomadic impulse. (Che is one of our first border-crossers, the first Latin American who became a universal symbol.) To those who will never follow in his footsteps, submerged as they are in a world of cynicism, self-interest, and frantic consumption, nothing could be more vicariously gratifying than Che's disdain for material comfort and everyday desires. One might suggest that it is Che's distance, the apparent impossibility of duplicating his life anymore, that makes him so attractive. And is not Che, with his hippie hair and wispy revolutionary beard, the perfect postmodern conduit to the nonconformist, seditious 1960s, that disruptive past confined to gesture and fashion? Is it conceivable that one of the only two Latin Americans—the other is Pelé—to make it onto *Time*'s list of the one hundred most important figures of the century can be comfortably transmogrified into a symbol of rebellion precisely because he is no longer dangerous?

I wouldn't be too sure. I suspect that the young of the world grasp that the man whose poster beckons to them from their walls cannot be that irrelevant, this secular saint ready to die because he could not tolerate a world where *los pobres de la tierra*, the displaced and dislocated of history, would be eternally relegated to its vast margins.

Even though I have come to mistrust dead heroes. They never grow old, they never had to cut a deal, they never got caught cheating at cards. And they stand in terrible, and perhaps unfair, judgment of those left behind, who are forced to deal with the messy swamp of life. And yet, wary as I am of the overwhelming burden their martyrdom imposes on the living, I will allow myself a prophecy. Or maybe it is a warning. More than three billion human beings on this planet right now live on less than $2.00 a day. And every day that breaks, forty thousand children—more than one every second!—succumb to diseases linked to chronic hunger. They are always there, the terrifying conditions of injustice and inequality that led Che many decades ago to start his journey toward that bullet and that photo awaiting him in Bolivia.

The powerful of the earth should take heed: deep inside that T-shirt where we have tried to trap him, the eyes of Che Guevara are still burning with impatience.

Saying Good-Bye to Pablo

I was there thirty years ago in Santiago de Chile that September 26, 1973, when Pablo Neruda was buried in the Cementerio General, I was there in Santiago, just a few miles away from where his body was being lowered into the earth he had so sensually celebrated. I could have easily walked to that cemetery and joined the men and women chanting next to his coffin, I could have chanted his name with them, I could have said good-bye, but I did not take that walk, I did not join that chant, I did not attend the funeral and final journey of the poet who, more than any author in the world, had taught me to love Chile and the Spanish language.

It is one of the few things in life that I truly regret.

When I had arrived in Chile in 1954 from the United States, a twelve-year-old boy who had been born in Argentina and yet spoke barely a word of Spanish, I had not heard of Neruda and certainly could not have recited one of his verses. During the next decade, however, as I was seduced by Chile and its syllables, Neruda was to slowly seep into my life and then take it by storm.

My first encounter with the great poet, as far as I can recall, was at the age of fourteen. Lovelorn for an impossibly luscious and distant girl a few years my elder, I was counseled by one of my classmates to whisper in her ear—if I could ever get close enough, that is—the words, "*Puedo escribir los versos más tristes esta noche*" (Tonight I can write the saddest lines), and she would, he insisted, fall into my arms and surrender those forbidden lips. I timidly tried, but my delivery and accent must have been as deplorable as my timing because she answered: "Neruda! *Veinte Poemas de Amor*. You're the fifth kid to repeat those same lines to me this month." And she dismissed me with an epitaph for my aspirations:

Washington Post (Washington D.C.), September 26, 2003, Style section.

"Why don't you try 'Una Canción Despesperada,'" referring to "A Desperate Song," a Neruda poem I should have known but did not. Obviously, many other youngsters in Chile were using and abusing the same tactic—and if I wanted to impress the ladies, it seems I would have to dig deeper into Neruda's repertoire. Soon enough I was diligently immersed in the ardent couplets of *Los Versos del Capitan*.

In the years that followed, Neruda was my guide at every step on my faltering road to self-expression and re-invention. Vast and inexhaustible, he was always there, at the tip of my tongue, ready to interpret the hostile, mysterious world, Neruda invariably available for the plucking and the telling, an endless source for every mood and every requirement. *Inagotable*. When I needed to seize the world in all its turmoil, plunge into my own fears of dissolution, my own hopes for a daily resurrection, explore the fluctuating borders between dream and nightmare and the oceanic chaos of every day life, there was *Residencia en la Tierra*. And when it was a matter of naming the América del Sur I had now embraced as my own, there was the *Canto General*, the birds and rivers, the mountains and stones commemorated in all their splendor and complexity—as well as *"sube a nacer conmigo, hermano,"* rise up and be born again with me, my brother, the whole furious history of Latin America retold with outrage for the forgotten and violated lives of the myriad poor and dispossessed, with reverence for their dignity and labors. And when it was a matter of looking at my own feet, of finding words for what it meant to bathe in the icy volcanic sea that Neruda also loved, of discovering the enigmas of the artichoke and the condor and the color blue, it was Neruda in his *Odas Elementales*, always Neruda who opened the exact colloquial window into the exact vocabulary of the heart, like a furtive best friend murmuring to me a world full of wonders, wondering all the while why the world could not be as beautiful for its inhabitants as it was for its poets. Politics, love, fish soup, alleyways, clocks, heroes, brothels, dictators, nuns, breasts, albatrosses, shoes, hands, carpenters—no matter what you wanted to know about life, Neruda had already been there, he had a surfeit and excess of words and most of them (though not all, not every one of them), most of them close to perfection.

And now he was dead and I was not going to his funeral.

He had died of cancer but also of sadness—the sorrow of the coup against democracy on September 11, 1973, the heartbreak of the death of Salvador Allende and of so many other friends and compatriots being rounded up, tortured, executed, all of it too much for Neruda who had spent most of his life fighting, as a communist, for the social justice and economic sovereignty that were being crushed by the military. A climate of fear—of the suffocating sort Neruda himself had so often described in his poems, the blood he had denounced in Republican Spain in 1936 and invited the whole world to come and see flowing in the streets—had now descended over his own peaceful Chile, invading and silencing every inhabitant. It was that fear that kept me from Neruda's last rites. I had gone into hiding after the coup and was looking for a way to leave the country alive—and the most foolish thing I could have done, I muttered to myself, was to make an appearance at a funeral sure to be crawling with soldiers and government spies.

Thousands of other Chileans, perhaps more desperate than I was, certainly more imprudent, definitely more valiant, decided to defy the authorities and conquer their own dread. From all over Santiago, they converged upon the Cementerio General that day thirty years ago. Friends of mine later told me that it was at first a mute and desolate multitude—and then a voice had emerged from the depths of the crowd and called out, *Compañero Pablo Neruda,* and hundreds of voices had thundered back, *Presente!*—and the nearby troops had not known what to do, how to react to this homage to Chile's greatest poet, Latin America's most popular writer, one of the most extraordinary voices of the twentieth century or any other century; and then the same baritone had blared out, *Compañero Salvador Allende,* demanding the presence and recognition of the dead president who had been buried anonymously two weeks before, and again *Presente*! came the cry of those who had been unable to mourn publicly their dead dreams and would have far too much to mourn in the next seventeen years of the Pinochet dictatorship.

Neruda must have smiled from the other side of death. He believed, above all, in the body—its juices, its bones, its genitalia, its hairs and nostrils and skin—and it must have been a vindication of his vision to realize that his supposedly dead body had become the spark and starting point for the Chilean resistance, that this funeral gathering turned out to be the first attempt by the people Neruda had devoted his life to singing about to take back the public spaces forbidden to them. And symbolic, too, that this inaugural challenge to the forces of darkness and doom and authority from on high would surge from the farewell ceremony to a wordsmith who had himself always proclaimed that poets were not gods but more like bakers of bread or builders of houses, entangled in the everyday underlife of the ordinary men and women with whom they shared their fate.

Yes, it was fitting that it should be those men and those women, who had, like me, been nurtured and nourished all through their existence by the verses of Pablo Neruda, it was somehow right that they should be the first ones to tell the world that their bard had not really left them, swear that they would keep him alive merely by remembering the hot shadow of his words when they made love and they drank red wine and breathed in the dazzling light of the sea, recall him when they were saddened at twilight and exalted at dawn, I believe Neruda would have wanted his last act on this earth to have been a prelude or maybe an intimation of something better, of that remote day when the planet would be worthy of the poems he offered us so generously and that still resonate and endure beyond his death and ours and, who knows, maybe even beyond the death of the tumultuous universe itself.

Neruda and the Terror in Madrid

Madrid is no stranger to bombs.

Almost seventy years ago, as the Civil War was beginning, Spain's capital suffered devastating attacks from the air. With the support of Hitler and Mussolini, the insurgent forces commanded by Francisco Franco targeted the civilian population of Madrid in the hope that the democratically elected government of Spain would capitulate.

Living in that city at the time was the great Chilean poet Pablo Neruda, and he left behind a series of memorable poems denouncing those assaults and commemorating the resistance of ordinary people.

By a strange coincidence—not the first time history and literature, tragedy and words, collude in my life—one of those poems was on my desk at the very moment I heard about the terrorist attacks on Madrid on March 11 that left more than two hundred dead and so many more wounded. I had been reading that poem, "Explico algunas cosas" ("I *explain a few* things"), over and over again, in preparation for a homage to Neruda to be held at the Kennedy Center on March 15 in celebration of the centenary of his birth.

I had originally chosen to recite that specific poem because I felt it was a way of allowing Neruda to condemn the invasion and occupation of Iraq, the bombs falling upon the innocent, the blood of children that runs, today as yesterday, *simply like blood of children*. And I also wanted Neruda's verses to howl against the destruction of so many other cities and lives. *Look at my dead house, look at broken Spain* could just as well refer to Santiago de Chile, which Neruda inhabited for so many years, which I had fallen in love with when I arrived there as an adolescent, the city I

Op-ed, *Los Angeles Times*, March 21, 2004.

saw bombed on September 11, 1973, while Neruda was dying not far away, dying of cancer and sorrow at his seaside house in Isla Negra. And also New York on fire, on that other September 11, the New York Neruda treasured, the New York that fascinated his friend, Federico García Lorca, the Spanish poet killed by the fascists in 1936, the New York that had also been visited by smoke and pain and widows. It is always one small group, *jackals that a jackal would despise,* that sows death and always others, the many others, overflowing with light, who die, simply die.

I wanted Neruda to speak to us from beyond his own death, to be our contemporary.

The poem ended up being more relevant than I had planned. When I finally read it at the Kennedy Center on March 15, I understood, as did the audience, those five hundred Americans there in the U.S. capital, that Neruda had decided to capture my mouth, steal my throat, in order to whisper something far more urgent. The recent bombings in Madrid transformed his words into a requiem for the recent dead: it was Madrid that was once again aflame, again the Madrileños were being attacked by *vipers that vipers would abominate*, again the innocent were paying for a war they had not desired or deserved. It was my own beloved Madrid, that city so open to wanderers, the city of Velazquez and Goya and Lope de Vega, where *one morning everything was burning / and one morning bonfires / came out of the earth / devouring humans /,* it was Madrid, *and from then on fire, / gunpowder from then on, / and from then on blood.*

Oh yes, the audience at the Kennedy Center understood the message. In every conversation after the homage, once and again, spectators came up to me to give me thanks (why me, if it had been Neruda who had written those words, if it was Neruda who had chosen me from beyond death to repeat his defiant verses?), to thank us and the gods of poetry for expressing how these victims of terror replicate and multiply with their deaths so many earlier deaths, so much terror that goes on and on, Madrid today and yesterday, Santiago yesterday and Baghdad today, New York and Srebenica and Rwanda and Cambodia.

But that was not all Neruda was telling us. There are American commentators—as well as in Spain—who have declared that the Spanish people, by punishing the Aznar government and electing a leader opposed to war, have offered up a victory to terrorism, that from now on fanatics will be able to use their lethal weapons to intimidate the free citizens of the world and blackmail the electorate. Such a claim is not only an insult to the maturity and courage of the Spanish people but also an insult to the intelligence of the world itself. They dare to say that of a citizenry that has confronted and isolated the criminal ETA organization. They dare to sustain such nonsense about the men and women whose parents and grandparents resisted for three years the fascist forces, Mussolini's troops and Hitler's air force, while the world watched with distance and indifference?

Those who believe the Spaniards are afraid would do well to listen to Neruda.

In his poem, he makes the following prophecy: the blood of Spain will rise to drown its murderers *in one single wave / of pride and knives*, he promises us that *from each dead house burning metal will come.*

We should not be confused. Just because a sovereign nation decides to reject and oppose an unnecessary, unjust, and deceitful war, does not mean that the people of that nation are not willing to defend themselves, more than ready to fight to return Madrid to that moment before the bombs exploded and that Neruda also remembered:

I lived in a barrio
of Madrid, with bells
with clocks, with trees.

My house was called
the house of flowers.
Raúl, do you remember?
Do you remember, Rafael?
Federico, do you remember,
dead under the ground,
do you remember my house with balconies
where the June light drowned the flowers in your mouth?
Brother, brother!

Yes. Brother, brother! Said to the murdered García Lorca and now, so many years later, to those who have again died, said to all those senselessly slaughtered all over the world and who are remembered ceaselessly by a poet who was born a hundred years ago and lives now only in the legacy of his words, tendering us consolation and rage and hope once more in these times of tragedy and terror.

The Latin American Aesthetics of Hope

One morning in early August of 1987, I descended into the bowels of the Buenos Aires subway system not, as might be imagined, to seek a means of transportation, but to mail a letter. I vaguely remembered from a previous trip to Argentina that this particular station had a small post office.

The office, unfortunately, was closed. On its shuttered windows, competing for attention with political and sexual graffiti, was a crudely handwritten sign: CERRADO DESDE OCTUBRE 1986, SHUT SINCE OCTOBER 1986."

I could not guess at the moment who had scrawled that message, whether a thwarted client or a weary employee. My first reaction was puzzlement: the sign hardly served any immediately discernible practical objective. If you wanted to post something, it was informing you not when service would be available, but only how long you had been forced to endure its absence. For endless streams of commuters fruitlessly carrying unmailable letters during ten or eleven months, the words seemed to be above all mocking them, a reminder of what they had been forced to confirm, and indeed suffer through, day by day.

Because they are produced in the Buenos Aires that gave us both the tango and Borges, it is tempting to interpret those words as an attempt, albeit a modest one, in the anonymous exercise of a nostalgia that has been, for many years, one of the salient characteristics of a city that loves to look backward.

And yet, the real underlying thrust of those words may refer, once we meditate on them, not to the past, but to the future. The sign may have been put up in, say, September 1986, warning pro-

---

First published in Spanish under the title "Entre el Subte y la Esperanza" in *Página Treinta* (Buenos Aires), February 1991.

spective clients what was going to happen: the DESDE meaning "AS OF OCTOBER" and not "SINCE OCTOBER." If so, it has long lost that pragmatic meaning—the fact that no one has taken it down, that no one has come to explain when service will be renewed, inevitably drives you to read the message as useless. Those words now announce that it is impossible to fix a date—tomorrow, the day after, one month from now—when letters will again be mailed from that location. Because October 1986, in that context, has ceased to be a real date and is more like a never-never land, a yesteryear of almost mythical proportions, a once-upon-a-time moment: October 1986 is infinitely far away. The author of the sign has ended up suggesting, no matter what his original intentions were, that this insignificant office has been closed down for so long, almost a year, that one should abandon all hope of ever seeing it open again, that one should cease to inquire about its fate. If the words, therefore, now speak of the past, they do so in order to postulate that past as weighing down so strongly on the future that days to come cannot discover any possible alteration. Nothing will be born tomorrow that can be significantly different from what we have already encountered in the past.

I am aware, of course, that I could be accused of exaggerating the meaning of those four brief words, *Cerrado Desde Octubre 1986*. But make no mistake: that unknown scribbler of hopelessness and stasis is responding to an experience embedded deep in the Latin American psyche. One of the prevalent visions in our lands is that of a continent where the past devours the future and forces eternal repetition. A continent where, appearances and calendars to the contrary, it is always October 1986, or October 1886, or October 1816—any October except October 1492 when it seemed that everything would be born all over again. A continent where the prophecy of a different future comes back later to haunt us with its cyclical sameness. A continent that, like Macondo, or like the post office, or like Rulfo's Comala in *Pedro Páramo*, or like Onetti's Santa Maria, closes in on itself, biting its own tail. Or is it its own tale, its own story-tale?

How to convince the writer of those words, and the thousands of readers of those words, of an opposite version of reality that stipulates a radically diverse future where not only postoffices announce their opening—opening that would, astonishment of astonishments, take place according to schedule—but where one could normally expect other things to open, such as schools and mouths and hospitals and books and whole societies. Or to put it in other terms: how to convince the author of that minimalist miraculous opus of linguistic expression, CERRADO DESDE OCTUBRE 1986, that there is such a thing as hope—when everything hammers into him that hope is an illusion and that all efforts to change the way things run is not only condemned to failure but probably will only make things worse?

The question is one with vast literary implications, because I belong to a generation that subscribed, some of whom indeed still subscribe, to a basically divergent proposition: that we can, in spite of the chains of our legacy, modify reality and create a different tomorrow. This utopian strain in contemporary art and literature (not to mention theology, sociology, and many other *ologies* that swarm around) is, of course, not something exclusive to this generation. Its roots go back to the beginnings of Latin American history, before we called ourselves in this way, when the very word *new*, as in New World, promised birth and renovation. That subsequent waves of newborn children inherited, instead, an inferno (or, at best, a purgatorio), only made all the more urgent, when they grew up, the challenge of imagining a different future.

If there was a difference with my generation, it was that in the wake of the Cuban Revolution and of the vast awakening of Latin American consciousness which came after it, we thought that the revolution was not only just around the corner, but that it was already here. Twenty, twenty-five, thirty years ago, if I had come across them, I would have considered those words, CERRADO DESDE OCTUBRE 1986, aberrant, outdated, and outside of history, on the verge of being proven wrong. Many of us, in particular in the Southern Cone and Brazil, quite consciously set out to explore the possibility of joyful renovation—in life and love, in society and streets, in language and fictional procedures, and, above all, in our work. At the time, I wrote, for instance, that we were going to *"abrirle el marruecos a la literatura"* (unzipper the pants of literature). Let it all hang out, I would have said, during my days in Berkeley in the late sixties. Insolent, buoyant, and enthusiastic, we were preparing what I would tentatively call an *estética de la esperanza*—an aesthetic based on hope, based on the proposition that the dead do not choose for us, but that we choose for them, that we change the past as we forge into the future. Of course, we promised ourselves as well that we would break out of the small circles where literature had hitherto, in general, been confined, not only because of how we wrote but because the radical social earthquake that we anticipated would at the same time liberate millions of potential *testimonio* voices and also—why not?—readers. What loomed on the horizon was a vast exercise in democratic participation, including, quite naturally, all forms of artistic expression.

I thought we would dance forever in the streets of Santiago.

Things did not turn out quite that way. The dictatorships that ravaged our lands in the last decades did not fulfill our prophecies. Or to put it in the words of a character in one of my novels, somebody was persistently (*minuciosamente*) breaking every bone in the body that had been told it would dance forever.

Repression, terror, exile, and particularly the overriding presence of evil were going to put us and put our hope to the test. This is not the place to enter into a detailed examination of how my generation confronted this new situation, but in a nutshell, some of the literature of the so-called *novisimos* in the last fifteen to twenty years has been a descent into skepticism and ambiguity while others have continued a search for the foundations of that hope, for what Humberto Constantini, a member of an older age-group, calls "*la parte más hermosa y más perdurable*" (the most beautiful and most enduring part) of every human being subjected to dehumanization. How do you keep that hope alive, how do you continue to renew your faith when everything seems to be saying CERRADO DESDE SIEMPRE Y PARA SIEMPRE, all the post offices and forms of communication CERRADOS forever and since ever? How do you convince the person who wrote those words that there continues to be a chance for change and openness?

But this last question hides false presuppositions, because before you can convince anybody, you must be able to reach that person—and it turns out that the distances between the public and the writer have grown instead of diminished. To the old forms of isolation of the artist in Latin America—structural illiteracy, differences in education, the widespread poverty of the potential readers, a reduced industrial publishing network—have been added the new forms of authoritarian control of public space, the *mordazas* and censors, not to speak of the fact that many of us have been physically removed from our hypothetical *dialogantes* by banishment.

Perhaps, however, the greatest problem is that the people who, according to our grandiose plans and dreams past, should now be reading us are, in fact, not reading at all or, if they are, find themselves reading *subliteratura*. The colossal audience that we had foretasted with such relish is, in fact, absorbing its fictions from the mass media, the *novela rosa*, the television series, the far west *folletines*, the cheap thrillers, the *fotonovelas*, the *historietas*, the movies, the *radioteatros*. This situation is not, as might be thought, merely a dilemma of how to communicate with that blocked-off public. Because those mass creations that are so popular also happen to have a particularly hopeful structure, if not an *estética de la esperanza*, then at least an *estética del* happy ending.

I can imagine that very person who wrote those anonymous words, CERRADO DESDE OCTUBRE 1986, settling down to a reverie of better times, a world where the smiling Technicolor finale is guaranteed, where it is never OCTUBRE 1986 and everything has been worked out, where the good are rewarded and the evil are punished. He may be immersed in the certainty of collective hopelessness and probably would doubt the efficacy of any participation in history or social action to change the world, but I have no doubt that at this very moment he, or millions like him, are vicariously living an individualistic answer to their communal frustration, living the happy ending in some fictitious version of what is the undeniable, unhappy repetition of post offices and communications closed over and over again, continuously. What a comfort for them to be able to sing, as Annie does, "Tomorrow, tomorrow, tomorrow—it's only a day away," while their real days disappear into the dismal stagnation of today.

If all this sounds rather pessimistic, let's not forget that my generation has one major advantage in that quest for the despairing reader who dreams of sugary salvations and saviors, fictional heavens and havens: we have been brought up on the media just as our audience has, we share the myths, the characters, the slang, the techniques, the perceptions, the whole subculture. Indeed, one of the most significant characteristics of my generation (MY GENERA-TION, AS THE "WHO" WOULD PUT IT) is the constant use of the media—as a framework, as a challenge, as a source of inspiration, as a purveyor of characters, as a dilemma. That these uses have often been ironic does not mean that we do not feel comfortable in the proximity of those popular genres. We hold in common a series of cultural experiences with our potential readers, from the bolero to Woody Woodpecker, from Batman to Cantinflas and, of course, to Manuel Puig's Spiderwoman. I believe that even those authors who have withdrawn into their own pure cocoons of art, rejecting contamination by the media monsters, are unavoidably shaped by the overwhelming existence of those messages.

Our relationship with the media, however, is inevitably ambivalent. Because it exists as a major molder of public consciousness, it leads to a major temptation: in order to reach those people, we are tempted to oversimplify our literature, to subscribe to a falsification of the future, to reduce all ambiguities, to punish in our fiction what we cannot set right in our reality, the sort of temptation, by the way, that structures socialist realism. (That is why I have proposed, sometimes as a joke, sometimes as a deeper direction, the idea of socialist irrealism, *el irrealismo socialista*.)

Needless to say, the *estética de la esperanza* rarely, if ever, has a happy ending. On the contrary, if the future exists and informs the present, it takes on the painful form of a struggle to imagine something different and demands the courage that such a struggle entails—even if it means death, defeat, and disaster now. If there is hope, it is the hope that others will come and hear the message and transmit it, that in times such as these what matters is to rescue one flicker of dignity in the midst of the tempest to keep alive one adjective "as clear as a ray of light," to "ask for the verse our lovers will still need/if we are ever again to bathe/in the same river."

Because the *estética de la esperanza* bases its ultimate existence on the experience of other people, those who, with their back against the wall, use that wall to find identity and another hand, because the *estética de la esperanza* must be renewed in social movements to really exist beyond the hollow of rhetoric and paeans to faith and almost mystical beliefs in "el pueblo"; because the *estética de la esperanza* seeks the utopia in each human being and believes it to be an irreducible part of humanity—because of all of this it remains to be seen how long it can survive without being accompanied by a breakthrough into history by the outcast and marginalized millions. It remains to be seen if the millions of people who, in spite of reading CERRADO into each corner of their lives, in spite of reading ABIERTO into an individual future that will statistically only be visited upon a tiny portion of them, it remains to be seen if our readers will turn the *espera* into *esperanza*.

PART FOUR

Imagining a Way Out

The Wandering Bigamists
of Language

It may have been García Márquez who once told me the story of entire Colombian villages that had migrated as if they were birds. Fleeing from catastrophes or perhaps plagues or recurrent floods or merely the desolation of never-ending civil wars, these villages had seemingly decided, at some point in history, to uproot themselves. And as they packed every transportable belonging and moved to a remote location in search of peace, these future fugitives did not forget what was, to them, the most crucial of all things: their dead. In effect, according to García Márquez, these villagers on the verge of becoming nomads dug up the bones in the cemetery and carried their ancestors on that journey into the unknown, probably animated by the need to defy the fluctuations of time and geography with the illusion that something from the past endures and abides and permeates the present, seeking to keep at least one hard physical link to memory at a time of devastating change.

Not all migrants can push to such extremes, of course, their desire to stay connected to the men and women who generated them, who coupled distant descendants into life. Most migrants are barely able to bring along a photo, a clipping, the keys to a house that is no longer theirs and that may, in time, be demolished, its address lost. But every last one of the migrants will inevitably take on his travels, her travels, another sort of possession, one that invisibly preserves those faraway dead and their past and their receding land better than any bones can. All migrants through history have

First published under the title "The Nomads of Language" in the *American Scholar* (Washington, D.C.), January 2002. This version, which has been slightly rewritten, appeared in the anthology *Lives in Translation: Bilingual Writers on Identity and Creativity* edited by Isabelle de Courtivron (New York: Palgrave Macmillan, 2003).

invariably transferred with them the syllables and significances enclosed in the language they learned as they grew, the language which gave them a slow second birth as surely as their mother gave them a relatively rapid first one. That language, which contains the seeds of their most intimate identity, will be put to the test once the voyage is over, especially if those displaced happen to be unfortunate enough to move to a foreign land. Because waiting for them at the new location are multiple others with their own dead, their own ceremonies and cemeteries and, of course, their own tongue. If it were to be the same language—let's say, for instance, an Uruguayan who migrates to Spain or to the Dominican Republic, or a French-speaking woman from Côte d'Ivoire who comes to Lyons—there will still be a valley of distances and misunderstandings between she who arrives and he who greets her, he who arrives and she who sells him bread, but it is more frequent in our globalizing world that those who arrive on a hostile shore are faced with an alien tongue.

And will therefore be condemned to live a bilingual fate.

They will not be able to avoid the need to live for many years in two languages, torn between the public dominant language, on the one hand, in which the police interrogate, the school principal complains about a child's conduct, bank accounts are opened and all too often closed, groceries are bought, jobs are proffered, signs and advertisements are written, and, on the other hand, the private subjective set of words that keep the newcomers in touch with the old home and homeland and with the persons they once used to be, the persons they believe they still might once again become.

How to deal with this incessant and often perverse doubleness, how to protect the fragile shell of the self bombarded by two needs and two communities that read opposite meanings into every mouthful at every meal? From the beginning of history, migrants have wavered between extremes that promise to resolve and even abolish this fragmented, anguished condition. These possibilities are not always available to everyone, but they do tend to be phantasmagorically there, temptations that call to us, suggesting wholeness, a delusion of completeness.

One strategy, of course, is assimilation: the wayfarer seeks to become an integral part of the new society, tries to forget or hide the mother tongue, wants to blur the accent, fantasizes that all bonds to the past can be cut, makes believe the dead are really, entirely dead. And if the originating migrant cannot always do this—because languages cannot be cast off like old socks—there is always the reverie that this full status in the new society will materialize with the children or, eventually, the grandchildren, conjecturing that some acquiescent offspring will overcome the curse of a bilingual, duplicated existence. The opposite of this solution is what could be called the rejectionist model: I have seen Chilean compatriots of mine who, twenty-five years after they were first banished from their land, continue to stubbornly refuse learning more than a few words of their host country's language, their faces and their hearts nostalgically fixed on their remote country, their tongues repeating colloquialisms that, in fact, have fallen out of use back home. It is not necessarily a tactic doomed to failure. They plan to return to Chile someday, to make the trip back, and indulge, therefore, like so many Kurdish and Moroccan, Indonesian and Korean, Nigerian and Mexican émigrés in a similar situation, in a tactic of cultural survival that holds on to the native language as a pure and intact entity, a bridge, a down payment on that ticket home.

These two strategies, assimilation or rejection, represent the two extremes with which monolingualism and its temptation of immaculateness tugs at the heart and mind of every potential migrant, attempting to avoid the Janus-like existence that haunts most wanderers. Of the two, it is assimilation that is the more pow-erful. Influential and effective institutions align themselves behind this monolingual alternative, first and foremost the nation-state with all its history and resources brought to bear on creating and enforcing borders and boundaries, imposing them on geography and bodies, on flags and hymns, as well as on syllables and relative clauses and interjections, identifying the nation with a language as a bulwark against foreign contamination, always alert to the need to control and homogenize its population in the name of security and internal order. And that national language also thrives by its alliance with those structures in which it is embedded—religion, literature, family rituals, newspapers, schools—all of them allow-ing citizens to imagine themselves as members of a vast community. As if this were not enough, there is another inner confederate: the ingrained psychological need of each and every human to belong and blend in and succeed, the enticement to erase that pain in the past that reminds us of failure.

I happen to disagree with the monolingual option, both for countries and for human beings. But I also happen to understand the wellsprings from which flow the desire to be whole and indivisible in one language. I have myself been a fundamentalist of language, someone who, for decades, tried to escape the bifurcation of tongue and vocabulary, a back-and-forth that was determined by exile and repression and geography. Born in Argentina to a Spanish-speaking mother and father and forced into my first migration—to New York—at the age of two, I all too soon used a childhood sickness and trauma to jettison my native tongue for the English that was, in those post–World War II years, beginning its triumphant domination of worldwide business and popular culture that would make it the global lingua franca of the planetary elites. But when, at the age of twelve, I had to follow my father into yet another exile, this time to a Chile that I did not want to live in and whose language I could not speak or write, I found myself at the mercy of Spanish—and it treated me, not like a spurned mistress, but rather as a lover who had been patiently awaiting my torrid return. I was—in a word—*seducido*, seduced. *Totalmente, enloquecidamente*, seduced, and it was not long before I decided to refuse to speak any English whatsoever, a political choice that was meant to cement and proclaim my identity as a *Latinoamericano* opposed in any way he could to the encroachments of the Yankee I had once been on the land I had now come to call my own, including encroachments on the intricate inner domains of language. Like so many converts, I made a point of burning my bridges, even if I called them *puentes*—maybe so my snubbed Anglo language would not understand what I was doing and retaliate against me in a fit of jealousy. Though English also knew how to wait for the wayward husband to come home, patiently let history ambush me. I wonder at times if it could read the future, my English, if it anticipated that once Chile fell to a dictatorship and I was sent into exile, I would need its refuge, its skills, the very words with which I am writing this essay, perhaps these words in English were inside me, predicting the moment when they would be allowed to materialize. Though what I finally arrived at was not the victory of one tongue over the other, but rather a cohabitation, my two languages reaching a truce in order to help the body they were lodged in survive.

This is where I write from now, embracing the need to live in two dimensions, pledging loyalty to two cultures, using one language to speak to the mailman and the other to read the mail from home that he brings to our door. It is as a resident of this dual existence, married to two tongues, inhabited by both English and Spanish in equal measures, in love with them both now that they have called off the war for my throat, it is as an adulterer of language that I presently trust that the distress of being double and somewhat homeless is overshadowed by the glory of being hybrid and open. It is as a fluid bigamist of language—indeed, as someone who has to write everything first in one and then in the other tongue, who corrects the Spanish text sent to *El País* in Madrid with its English transliteration and re-creation that will appear in the *Los Angeles Times*, who has to explain to himself and others why the novel *Terapia* is called *Blake's Therapy* in its rival incarnation—it is as a confessed grammatical philanderer that I now encourage migrants and the states in which they dwell to embark fully and without fear upon the adventure of being bilingual and ask them to celebrate as well, as so many of the young do, the many intermediate, wonderful, full-fledged patois that prosper in the spaces in between established linguistic systems, the myriad Creole zones of confluence and mixture where languages can mingle and experiment and express the fluctuating frontiers of a hybrid humanity.

This call of mine is not merely, I believe, the fruit of my own personal seesaw romance with two languages. Just as there are institutions that compel us toward the defense and adoption of only one language for our identities under siege, there are also equally strong forces in the world today that are pushing us toward multilingualism as a real alternative.

The primary factor, I would wager, is the sheer mass of migration, all those bodies and minds inside those bodies smuggling foreign syntax across the borders under the noses of immigration officers and customs officials, penetrating the stockades of the nation-state, invading the fields and the kitchens and the elementary schools. In the case of the country where I now live, the United States, the

Latino influx is so enormous and unstoppable that within a century I anticipate that exploding demographics will force bilingualism to be the norm rather than the exception—as it is in some of the major cities in America today.

A second major condition favoring bilingualism is the compression of the immense distances that used to separate migrants from their native lands. The feasibility of ever more frequent circular journeys back and forth to Ithacas from which we no longer need to be absent for twenty years is undeniable, not to mention the manner in which technology invites us to connect to the simultaneous words being spoken back in the motherland, as well as to ever wider international networks of linguistic partners across the globe, inciting communities to organize in diasporic webs that could not have been even imagined thirty years ago. Which leads us to a third factor: the world itself, because of this incessant movement of bodies and goods and capital, is producing speakers who are increasingly plurilingual. It is true that a great deal of this linguistic traffic is transpiring in English. I greet this circumstance warily, even if this predominance of one of my languages allows me personally to break down travel and intellectual barriers (and make a better living). Any excessive hegemony has always filled me with suspicion: English's ascendancy, like so many phenomena associated with globalization, leaves too many invisible losers, too many people silenced. Regarding languages and migration, I never forget the questions that are so often neglected when progress is abstractly celebrated, the questions that the real suffering human subjects face, one by one by one. Do you come from a place that is poor, that is not fully incorporated into modernity, that does not control a language that commands respect, do you inhabit a language that does not have armies behind it and bombs and modems and technology, do you reside in a language that will one day be extinct or whose existence does not have value in the marketplace and can get you a good job and help you in the everyday struggle to survive? Do you dwell in a language that is wonderful only for making love or teaching your children the difference between right and wrong or serves to pray to God? Is your language perfumed with unpronounceable words by poets with unpronounceable names describing their unpronounceable forests and guttural maidens? How does such a language defend itself in our globalizing world?

I hold no effortless answers to this quandary of globalization, but regarding the empire of language, I can at least console myself with the reminder that English, or whatever other international language will be used by many men and women from many nations, will itself undergo—is, indeed, undergoing at this very moment—the slings and joys of outrageous appropriation, the mongrelization that inevitably comes when transnational clans breed bodies and breed syllables. But perhaps more crucial: the new global disorder enacts a world where more and more people, submitted to the obligation of dividing their brain between two (or more) linguistic systems, end up de-territorializing language, unlinking it from the power of the nation and the coercion of the state, allowing other tormented bilinguals to feel less alone in their own quests for the sort of multiple pluralistic beings that I hope will constitute a model for tomorrow's new humanity.

If I am (tragically) optimistic about the prospect of bilingualism, it is because I believe that languages—in spite of an innate and inevitable conservative tendency which answers a hunger in us for stability and continuity—have themselves also always been maddeningly migrant, borrowing from here and there and everywhere, plundering and bringing home the most beautiful, the strangest, the most exciting objects, learning, learning, taking words out on loan and returning them in a different wonderfully twisted and often funny guise, pawning those words, punning them, stealing them, renting them out, eating them, making love to them, and spawning splendidly unrecognizable children.

Indeed, the first bilingual experiences at the origin of our species must have flourished in the intersections between groups that had already evolved divergent and mutually incomprehensible linguistic systems. The intersection of trade, certainly, the bartering of goods that had to be accompanied, at some point, by the bartering of words and the dawning discovery that anyone who knew both tongues would be able to sell and buy, swap and acquire on much better terms, trading stories first and then desires and finally goods. And that other intersection, the dire intersection and crossroads of battle, when captives were taken as booty and warriors were spared

and enslaved and women were brought back for breeding and plea-
sure. I think of those captives as the first nonvoluntary bilinguals
of history and prehistory, though they may also have been the
first to educate their captors in the delights of another language
and another viewpoint, Scheherazades of the forked tongue. And
then, the ultimate intersection, the intersection of languages due
to the sweeter intersection of love and reproduction, the biologi-
cal and cultural and personal and epic need for exogamy, the need
for the other, the age-old impulse toward mixture and miscegena-
tion, cells that want to fertilize by expanding, the need to leave
the suffocating inner circle of what is familiar and plant yourself
in the wider world. And languages were there, had to be there, in
those love affairs at the beginning of time, one language for the
man, another language for the woman, coupling the bodies and
coupling the minds and coupling the tribes.

Languages, two of them, both of them, there, at the very start
of the first journey out of Eden—an immediate, almost automatic,
way of challenging death, telling us still today that we need not
excavate the cemetery as those mythical villagers in Colombia did,
we need not carry the physical bones with us into the future, to
stay in touch with our origins and dispute death's rule over us. If
this vision of the bilingual origins of our humanity is correct, then
the chances of our living simultaneously in multiple linguistic systems may not only be daringly contemporary but could presumably
have its roots in our most ancient mirrors. If language is, finally,
in its deepest essence and meaning, our first and last attempt to
defy and defeat death, then perhaps a bilingual humanity is the
best way of fooling death when it comes for us, fooling it not once,
but twice and perhaps even three times and more. Perhaps before
we disappear from this earth we can at least force death itself to
speak all our tongues.

Moving Away from the Known

For exiles, memory brings the first consolation. During the years of banishment, distance needs to be defeated by an incessant act of remembering, keeping alive inside what is being despoiled by the dictator in the faraway forbidden land. That this process of recollection can also be a trap only becomes apparent when the exiles return and the past they patiently built in the ideal home of their minds ends up not corresponding to what they find entangled in faces and trees and houses that should be familiar and yet are unrecognizable. For many refugees, therefore, the voyage back to the native land is often transformed into an attempt at restitution, a constant questioning of the foundations of the past hidden under the flicker of the present.

It is this search for stable ground upon which to walk and perhaps someday be buried in, that animates and drives *Dog Heart*, a recounting by the great expatriate Afrikaner poet Breyten Breytenbach of a prolonged visit from abroad to the South African valley that saw his birth sixty years ago.

The author's quest for permanence and meaning will not be made any easier by his disappointment with the post-Apartheid era. In his indictment of a society plagued by confusion and violence, mutilation and sloganeering, crime and uncertainty, we detect none of the subtlety and ambiguity that laces such works as Antjie Krog's superb *Country of My Skull* or André Brink's fervent *Reinventing a Continent*, both authors fellow Afrikaners writing in English about South Africa's transition to democracy. Breytenbach's sardonic tone is that of a man who once believed enough in liberation to risk his life for it, suffering seven years of incarceration as a political prisoner, and who is now a bitter outsider who does not like the future he

New York Times Book Review, November 28, 1999.

struggled for. It is this hunt by someone who has been away too long and who needs to get under the skin of the country, which informs the compelling core of this dreamlike memoir.

It is an emotional journey. Breytenbach circles his immediate and remote origins like a dog who has survived an earthquake and sniffs for bones in the rubble, ready to chew up anything that can keep him going. The poet zigzags between personal memories and tribal chronicles, sifts through photos and clippings, queries portraits on walls and medicine bags in museums, listens to tales of ghosts and suicides and family migrations, slowly delineating a stark and mysterious silhouette of South African history. And all around him, while he interrogates his many beginnings, people are dying—old friends, mentors, painters, relatives, an unending succession of fading apparitions who carry away with them another possible mirror for the author's life.

This fragmented pursuit of identity can be disorienting at first, but ultimately mesmerizes and rewards us because it enacts for the reader the very wandering which neither the author nor the memories that devour him can escape, forces us to experience the dizzy "moving away from the known" (175) that created the mixed bastardized language that is Afrikaans and turns out to be the only final "community of understanding" to which Breytenbach pledges allegiance. The fluctuating narrative is also anchored by the recurring presence of the author's great-grandmother, Rachel Susanna Keet, to whom the book is dedicated, a woman who tended the sick with cheerfulness and acted as midwife to hundreds of women of all races. It is her symbolic burial among the unclaimed anonymous graves of a cemetery at the end of *Dog Heart* that helps Breytenbach reach some sort of transitory reconciliation with his troubled lineage: "We'll take this one, the one lying in the open with a view all around on the immensity of mountains. . . . I'm planting a beacon in Africa. A landmark. Am I not allowed to mark out my history? May one not adopt a dead person?" (196).

In his expedition to the past, Breytenbach adopts a host of those long gone, including his own self, the dead child he might have been or the dead cousin whose name he bears. Or his grandfather who, as an old man, climbed a tree and decided to stay there, fearful of a snake that might come for him as it did for his first wife.

Or an old beggar, "a sad nomad with filthy rags twisted around his head" (103). Or a legendary native shaman who dies and is reborn incessantly in a different form and who reminds the author of what his task should be: "It brings good luck to the traveler to pass by a grave, and add a pebble to the pile of stones there, or leave a branch, some clothing, maybe a skin of his own" (143).

It is this tenderness which finally pervades the bleak, breath-taking landscape of Breytenbach's South Africa, the hope that it is possible to rescue the distant dead who "left only the flutter of a shadow behind, a whisper in the leaves on branches" (103). By not abandoning them to dust, the exile—Breytenbach as well as so many of the expatriates of history—has perhaps managed to finally come home.

Final and First Words on
Death and the Maiden

Eight or nine years ago, when General Augusto Pinochet was still the dictator of Chile and I was still in exile, I began tentatively exploring in my mind a dramatic situation that was someday to become the core of *Death and the Maiden*. A man whose car breaks down on the highway is given a lift home by a friendly stranger. The man's wife, believing she recognizes in the stranger the voice of the torturer who raped her some years before, kidnaps him and decides to put him on trial. On several occasions I sat down to scribble what I then imagined would be a novel. A few hours and a couple of unsatisfactory pages later, I would give up in frustration. Something essential was missing. I could not figure out, for instance, who the woman's husband was, how he would react to her violence, if he would believe her. Nor were the historical circumstances under which the story developed clear to me, the symbolic and secret connections to the larger life of the country itself, the world beyond the narrow, claustrophobic boundaries of that woman's home. The use of a forceps may be necessary to ensure the birth of a child that needs help out of the womb, but I had by then blessedly learned that when characters do not want to be born, forceps may scar them and twist their lives irreparably. My trio would, unfortunately, have to wait.

They were forced to wait a long time. It was not until Chile returned to democracy in 1990 and I myself therefore returned to resettle there with my family after seventeen years of exile, that I finally understood how the story had to be told.

My country was at the time (and still is now as I write this) living an uneasy transition to democracy, with Pinochet no longer

---

Afterword to my play *Death and the Maiden* (London: Nick Hern Books, 1991, and New York: Penguin, 1992).

the president but still in command of the armed forces, still able
to threaten another coup if people became unruly or, more specifically, if attempts were made to punish the human rights violations
of the outgoing regime. And in order to avoid chaos and constant
confrontation, the new government had to find a way of not alien-
ating Pinochet supporters who continued occupying significant
areas of power in the judiciary, the senate, the town councils—
and particularly in the economy. In the area of human rights, our
democratically elected president, Patricio Aylwin, responded to this
quandary by naming a commission—called the Rettig Commission, after the eighty-year-old lawyer who headed it—that would
investigate the crimes of the dictatorship that had ended in death
or its presumption, but which would neither name the perpetrators nor judge them. This was an important step toward healing
a sick country: the truth of the terror unleashed upon us, which
we had always known in a private and fragmented fashion, would
finally receive public recognition, established forever as official history, re-creating a community fractured by divisions and hatred
that we wished to leave behind. On the other hand, justice would
not be done, and the traumatic experience of hundreds of thousands of other victims, those who had survived, would not even
be addressed. Aylwin was steering a prudent but valiant course
between those who wanted past terror totally buried and those
who wanted it totally revealed.

As I watched with fascination how the commission carried out
its difficult task, it slowly dawned on me that here might be the key
to the unresolved story that had been buzzing inside my head for
so many years: that fictitious kidnapping and trial should occur,
not in a nation under the boot of a dictator, but in one that was in
transition to democracy, where many of its citizens were grappling
with the hidden traumas of what had been done to them while others wondered if their crimes would now be revealed. It also became
clear that the way to make the husband of the tortured woman
have a tremendous stake in the outcome of that kidnapping was to
make him a member of a commission similar to the one headed by
Rettig. And it did not take me long to conclude that, rather than
a novel, what needed to be written was a play.

It was a risky idea. I knew from experience that distance is often the best ally of an author and that when we deal with events that are being enacted and multiplied in immediate history, the danger always exists of succumbing to a "documentary" or overly realistic approach, losing universality and creative freedom, trying to adjust the characters to the events unfolding around us rather than letting them emerge on their own, letting them surprise and disturb us. I also knew that I would be savagely criticized by some in my own country for "rocking the boat" by reminding everyone about the long-term effects of terror and violence on people precisely at a time when we were being asked to be notably cautious.

I felt, however, that if as a citizen I had to be responsible and reasonable, as an artist I had to answer the wild mating call of my characters and break the silence that was weighing upon so many of my self-censored compatriots, fearful of creating "trouble" for the new democracy. It was then and is now more than ever my belief that a fragile democracy is strengthened by expressing for all to see the deep dramas and sorrows and hopes that underlie its existence and that it is not by hiding the damage we have inflicted on ourselves that we will avoid its repetition.

As I began to write I found the characters trying to figure out the sort of questions that so many Chileans were asking themselves privately, but that hardly anyone seemed interested in posing in public: How can those who tortured and those who were tortured co-exist in the same land? How to heal a country that has been traumatized by repression if the fear to speak out is still omnipresent everywhere? And how do you reach the truth if lying has become a habit? How do we keep the past alive without becoming its prisoner? How do we forget it without risking its repetition in the future? Is it legitimate to sacrifice the truth to ensure peace? And what are the consequences of suppressing that past and the truth it is whispering or howling to us? Are people free to search for justice and equality if the threat of a military intervention haunts them? And given these circumstances, can violence be avoided? And how guilty are we all of what happened to those who suffered most? And perhaps the most urgent dilemma of them all: how to confront these issues without destroying the national consensus which creates democratic stability?

Three feverish weeks later, *Death and the Maiden* was ready.

If the play revealed many of the hidden conflicts that were just under the surface of the nation and therefore posed a clear threat to people's psychological security, it could also be an instrument through which we explored our identity and the contradictory options available to us in the years to come.

A multitude of messages from the contemporary imagination, specifically those that are channeled through the mass entertainment media, assure us, over and over, that there is an easy, even facile, comforting, answer to most of our problems. Such an aesthetic strategy seems to me not only to falsify and disdain human experience but, in the case of Chile or of any country that is coming out of a period of enormous conflict and pain, it turns out to be counterproductive for the community, freezing its maturity and growth. I felt that *Death and the Maiden* touched upon tragedy in an almost Aristotelian sense, a work of art that might help a collective to purge itself, through pity and terror, in other words, to force the spectators to confront those predicaments that, if not brought into the light of day, could lead to their ruin.

Which is a way of stating that this piece of fiction, like so much of what I had written previously in my novels, stories, poems, and other plays, was not merely Chilean in scope but addressed problems that could be found all over the world, all over the twentieth century, all over the face of humanity through the ages. It was not only about a country that is afraid and simultaneously needful of understanding its fear and its scars, not only about the long-term effects of torture and violence on human beings and the beautiful body of their land, but also about other themes that have always obsessed me: What happens when women take power? How can you tell the truth if the mask you have adopted ends up being identical to your face? How does memory beguile and save and guide us? How can we keep our innocence once we have tasted evil? How to forgive those who have hurt us irreparably? How do we find a language that is political but not pamphletary? How to tell stories that are both popular and ambiguous, stories that can be understood by large audiences and yet contain stylistic experimentation, that are mythical and also about immediate human beings?

Death and the Maiden appears in English at a moment when
humanity is undergoing extraordinary changes, when there is great
hope for the future and great confusion about what that future
may bring. In the current debate, little is being heard from that
submerged zone of our species who live far from the centers of
power but are often near the quick center of suffering where ethical choices determine the immediate shape of things to come and
things to be postponed. In times such as these, when the more
miserable and distant lands seem to disappear from the horizon,
it may help us a bit, perhaps a teensy-weensy bit, I would hope, to
think of the Paulinas, the Gerardos, the Robertos, of the world—to
figure out for ourselves which of these three we most resemble, how
much of our secluded lives are expressed in each of these characters and in all of them. Until finally, I would also hope, we would
realize that what we feel when we watch and whisper and ache
with these faraway people from faraway Chile could well be that
strange trembling state of humanity we call recognition, a bridge
across our divided globe.

A Message from a King of Troy

A few days ago, I was drawn, for a reason I did not immediately understand, to read Homer's *Iliad* again. As I reached the ending, where Achilles, having heaped abuse on the body of his fallen enemy, Hector, slowly finds the humanity in himself to give the corpse back to Priam, Hector's grieving father, I was deeply moved. Those words written thousands of years ago brought to life that warrior who was able to repress his rage and acknowledge the pain of others, those parents finally able to touch the white bones of their child and honor his existence and his passing away.

My emotion may have been deepened by the fact that I hold in my memory, as many Chileans do, a number of friends who were presumably killed years ago during the military dictatorship that plagued my country from 1973 to 1990. I say presumably because the bodies of my friends, like those of thousands of other Chileans who disappeared without a trace, have never been returned to their families. Mothers and fathers, brothers and friends still wait for something—a bone, some hair, anything—to be restored to them by the military who took their loved ones away. Like Priam or his wife, Hecuba, we cannot rest until our missing, our *desaparecidos*, are themselves set to rest. Unlike Priam, we do not have an Achilles to turn to.

And yet, there is one man who could remedy their circumstance, the one man in the world who, like Achilles, could render the dead to the living. That man bizarrely came into my thoughts as I reached the final strophes of Homer's epic, and I dismissed him, dismissed the possibility that he would want to do anything, drove him from my thoughts just as Priam had driven his foremost enemy Achilles from his mind when the gods had first suggested the idea.

Guardian (London), September 17, 1997.

That man is General Augusto Pinochet. Twenty-four years ago, on September 11, 1973, he launched a bloody coup and was for the following seventeen years the ferocious dictator of Chile until he reluctantly relinquished the presidency. He, and he alone, as the present commander in chief of that country's army, has the power to order his subordinates to investigate their own misdeeds, search their records, reveal where the bodies of the disappeared lie, what happened to them, who killed them. He is the only man alive who could force the Chilean army, an institution that fervently believes in hierarchy and obedience, to discover the truth. He is also, unfortunately, the man least likely on this Earth to imitate the nobility and compassion of Achilles. Rather than using his leadership to bring reconciliation to Chile, Pinochet has mocked the dead—and their relatives.

A few years ago, for instance, when a hundred or so mutilated bodies were located in a cemetery, packed two to a coffin, he quipped that those who had buried those victims should be congratulated for having spared the state the expense of an extra coffin and extra nails.

Even so, as I closed the *Iliad*, I wondered if that general, whom I detest above all people on this Earth, was totally beyond the reach of Homer's words. I wondered if this is not the time, the only time, when somebody must ask Pinochet to meditate upon Achilles and Priam, if now is not the precise moment when the Chilean general may be open to the message from the plains of Troy. Because it turns out that Pinochet is about to lose power. Six months from now, on March 11, 1998, he will retire from the army and will no longer exercise the authority that would enable him to right, however slightly, the wrongs he has done and begin to repair the consequences of his reign.

Quite frankly, I do not expect him to heed these words. He has shown himself to be a man outside the common bonds of humanity. And yet I have forced myself to swallow my pride and write them, many miles from home and thousands of years after Hector was buried outside the walls of Troy.

General Pinochet: you have reiterated over and over that you executed the 1973 coup in order to save Chile for Western civilization. Here is the first epic, the warrior epic of the Western world you say you are defending. In it, the man who has insulted and shamed the corpse of his enemy ends up restoring it to the bereaved family. General Pinochet: if you have not listened to the thousands of relatives of the missing all these years, perhaps you will attend to the call of King Priam of Troy, who reminded Achilles that there are laws that oblige us all, merely because we belong to the same species.

General Pinochet: before you leave power, read the *Iliad* and think about tomorrow.

. . . And They Lived Heartlessly Ever After

T his stark, disquieting first novel opens with a scene that was common enough in Europe during World War II: a mother deposits her twin sons at their grandmother's house in the country as a way of saving them from starvation and bombs in the city. But from here on, *The Notebook* by Agota Kristof, a Hungarian who immigrated to Switzerland in 1956, is anything but common; the young twins who are its narrators are far from ordinary children.

Abandoned like Hansel and Gretel to an avaricious, tyrannical old woman the local people call the Witch (because, it is rumored, she poisoned her husband many years earlier) and orphaned like so many fairy-tale heroes in a cruel and vindictive world, they will draw the sort of implacable conclusion we do not normally expect to find in such stories: that the only way to survive is to become completely unfeeling and merciless, that unless they are free from hunger, pain, and emotion they will be unable to endure what is in store for them.

With horrifying logic, the twins set about programming—indeed, strengthening—their capacity to suffer. They systematically submit their bodies and minds to a calculated series of exercises. They beat and scald and tear at each other: "After a while, we really don't feel anything anymore. It's someone else who gets hurt, someone else who gets burned, who gets cut, who feels pain." They fast for several days in order to habituate themselves to hunger. They insult each other to get used to offensive words. They go out begging, not to obtain food but to test and observe the hypocrisy of adults when confronted with destitution.

This behavior is understandable. It emerges from a basic impulse of human beings under siege: at the very moment when incompre-

New York Times Book Review, January 15, 1989.

hensible forces savage our lives, it is essential to have some muffled say over our own fate, to keep some semblance of control and dignity. But the twins do not seem to realize—and it only gradually dawns on the distressed reader—that the training they are undergoing is simultaneously cutting them off from humanity, a development that is perhaps best symbolized by a game they play in which one of them pretends he is blind and the other pretends he is deaf. Later on, they note that people are being killed all around them, so they decide they must learn how to kill without flinching and proceed to torture chickens and rabbits and string up their pet cat. Since they don't want to feel sorrow, they eliminate the word *love* from their vocabulary. It "is not a reliable word," they explain. "It lacks precision and objectivity."

As the two boys drain meaning from all words that do not have an immediate and visible equivalent in the world, they also withdraw from morality. And this is no abstract withdrawal; they will end up blackmailing, stealing, defiling the dead, murdering—acts they have learned from their "betters," acts without which they would be dead themselves. Watching these youngsters grow, we are reminded of what the great Italian chronicler of Auschwitz, Primo Levi, wrote shortly before he committed suicide: that those who were delivered from the concentration camps "were not the best, those predestined to do good, the bearers of a message." Instead, "the worst survived, the selfish, the violent, the insensitive, the collaborators . . . the spies."

What makes this anti–fairy tale of twins lost in our contemporary forest so alarming—and believable—is that the voice with which they childishly bear witness to their transformation into monsters has itself been contaminated by the cold, relentless distance that has possessed their lives. As if they were voyeurs of their own bodies, they describe, for instance, several scenes in which they are sexually abused by adults, and they do so in the same remote, dispassionate tone they use elsewhere to report digging for potatoes or buying paper and pencils so they can continue their studies.

It is this taut, unsparing vision, eloquently rendered from the French by Alan Sheridan, that gives an almost lyrical intensity to those brief flickers in the text when the humanity of the twins is able to faintly express itself. They befriend a harelipped, hounded girl and her derelict mother. They offer a deserter food so he may continue his trek homeward. When she is sick, they even save their ruthless, illiterate grandmother, who has sold off their clothes and burned their mother's letters. However, as if they are afraid of recognizing in themselves a reserve of pity or solidarity toward others that would weaken their resolve and leave them open to manipulation, the two boys justify their kindnesses for one reason alone: these people "absolutely need" help and must therefore be assisted.

In a faint echo from a faraway life, the twins themselves are touched once in a while—a long while—by some transitory gentleness, some caring gesture: an unknown woman stroking their hair, a cobbler (who is about to be deported) giving them boots for the winter. But because these signs of benevolence are arbitrary and unpredictable, the exception rather than the rule, they ultimately prove of no use to these children of war. By the wrenching end of the novel, the twins have become as devoid of loyalty and trust as the adults who surround them, as ready to decide, godlike, who should live and who should die.

There is something deeply disturbing about this dark parable, but not because of the catastrophes it deals with. War, famine, extermination camps, endless waves of refugees, liberating armies that turn into oppressors—all of these afflict the people in so many books written in our troubled century. However, we have managed to comfort ourselves with the belief that the human spirit has not been destroyed by the madness it has seen and suffered, and we point, often convincingly, at the survivors themselves as proof that there is still hope, that there will always be some fierce zone, some frontier in us, that resists evil. In the very act of writing about such horrors, it has been said over and over again, there is a faint intimation of victory, a stubborn refusal to let those who oppressed others have the last word. The children, we say, will be different.

In the bleak landscape of Agota Kristof, even that pale consolation has been taken from us. She pries open the innocent eyes of the very young only to reveal a sick world where the sole redemption, if it may be called so, is the courage to look the inferno in the face and not blink.

Surviving the Century

Filming with Roman Polanski

Something is wrong with the lamp. Roman examines it carefully. We are only a few days away from principal photography, but Roman Polanski acts as if he had all the time in the world. It is an ordinary kerosene lamp, the swinging sort you take on camping trips or you carry around the house when there's a blackout, the sort you would never give a second glance to. But Roman is giving it more than a second glance. He is spending long silent valuable minutes, observing it as if it were about to come alive and pounce on him.

We are on the set of *Death and the Maiden* in the studios of Boulogne, just outside Paris. The legendary art director Pierre Guffroy (a regular on many Polanski films, including *Tess*, for which Guffroy received an Academy Award) has painstakingly recreated a Latin American beach house down to the last detail. It is what Roman loves in Guffroy's work, enhanced and fine-tuned during a career at the service of Cocteau, Buñuel, and Bresson: the set is a character that whispers, shifts, lies in ambush, assists the protagonists, betrays them, comments on their blindness and hopes. And every object in that house—all the props that Roman is now inspecting with an unrelenting gaze—must blend into that atmosphere, must be consistent. Polanski puts the lamp down, then picks it up again, touches it, turns it around. It is almost as if he suspects the lamp of trickery, as if it were about to pull a fast one on him, like a fraudulent second-rate actor trying out for a starring role when he

Commissioned by Susan Gray for her book *Writers on Directors* (New York: Watson-Guptill Publications, 1999), for which each director chose the writer he or she wanted to profile their work. Prepublication in *Tin House* (Portland, Oreg.), vol. 1, no. 1, spring 1999.

doesn't even deserve to be an extra. Roman looks up at the four or five people who surround him, who have been watching him watch the elusive lamp. He does not want help. He intends to figure this one out by himself. Briefly, his eyes fall on me. But they do not ask anything, do not confirm or interrogate. Has he guessed that I happen to know what's wrong with the lamp? Not because I am especially good at visuals. In fact, overly devoted as I am to words and literature, I tend to be extremely, almost stubbornly, inept at images. If I understand how this particular lamp should look, it is only because, as a Chilean, I have seen countless replicas of it in my own country. In every beach house like this one, far away on that savage Pacific coast, lamps like this one await the night—except they display an added nuance of gray, are more banged up, more tired looking. The lamp that Roman is scrutinizing is a shade too bright, untinged, perhaps clean-cut to a fault.

"The silver tint needs to be darkened," Roman declares finally. "It shouldn't shine like this."

He's right, of course. But how can he know? How can he possibly perceive something that subtle?

Polanski has never been to Chile, never stepped into the beach houses where I have spent months, never seen a photo of the sort of sad and tarnished lamp that occupies my mind. It is not research that gives him the right clues. He can, quite simply, grasp how the lamp should look, because for the last few months—and indeed for several years now—he has been imagining, object by object, board by board, the haunted and yet strangely ordinary place where Paulina will encounter and put on trial the man she thinks raped and tortured her fifteen years before. Now that the film is nearing the end of preproduction, he is taking his obsession with making everything coherent, inhabited, perfect to unlikely extremes. Just to give one crazy example: Paulina's simulacrum of a kitchen is lined with closed cupboards. In them, filled to the brim, are mountains of authentic Chilean food staples in Chilean bags and tins imported specially from Santiago, halfway across the world. There is not one shot that calls for one of these cupboards to ever be opened, for the contents to be even remotely glimpsed through the shadows. But Roman needs them to be there, filling the corners of the unseen, lurking beyond the mere surface of perception, beyond what the

camera captures, making the house breathe, secretly telling the
characters where they are and who they have been and what they
have eaten. It is this mania of Polanski's, the extended construc-
tion of a reliable imaginary, that warns him that the lamp with its
healthy look would stand out, given all these other details—these
billowing curtains, this light brown loaf of bread, these threatening
knives, this sort of old-fashioned telephone, this Neruda woodcut,
this stained table. He sees that the lamp would call excessive attention to itself, would divert attention from what really matters: the
madness and dissonances and troubles that are just underneath the
surface of the world and that are about to explode. What really
matters: human beings are trapped in that house with that lamp
and with everything else in their lives, and we are going to watch
them during the next few hours trying to escape from the tyranny
of that reality, we are going to watch them try to bend that world
to their desires, we are going to watch them succeed, and we are
going to watch them fail.

This is what Polanski does, has done, in film after stunning
film: *Knife in the Water, Cul-de-Sac, Repulsion, Rosemary's Baby,
Chinatown, Macbeth, Tess, The Tenant, Frantic, Bitter Moon.* Put us
inside, deep inside the world he has created, on the frontier where
illusion and pain meet, at times separate, and at time merge. And
this is the paradox: Roman builds each space, each universe, to be
absolutely, incontrovertibly recognizable, unflinchingly familiar,
horribly believable, so as to explore what is hidden, what is bizarre,
what is absurd, so that the grid of reality can be tested against the
inner demons of his characters, so that we can experience the liq-
uid terror of being that person in that room, in that story, so that
we can accompany that protagonist as he, as she, tries to change a
destiny that has been imposed from somewhere else. Roman has
spent his life mastering and using the techniques of realism in the
service of the unspeakable.

So the lamp is there to help us understand what the lamp does
not know, what cannot be seen immediately through its glow: the
almost inaccessible world of the mind and the heart, desperate for
love, unable finally to touch others deeply enough to break out of
solitude or delusion. And Polanski, once he has launched us on
this voyage, will not relieve us with conclusive answers: his endings

are almost invariably ambiguous, his heroes and heroines (if they may even be called that) haunted by the bite of uncertainty even as they dash their heads against the mirror of life. At times, as in *Repulsion* or *The Tenant*, they end up lost in insanity. But most of the time, as in *Knife in the Water* or *Tess* or *Death and the Maiden*, they end up lost in the bitter opposite of insanity: they end up lost in awareness, learning how vulnerable they are (they always were), how difficult it is to be moral, to be loved, in a world controlled by more powerful others. Donald Pleasance on his lonely rock in *Cul-de-Sac* or Mia Farrow alone with her devil's child in *Rosemary's Baby* or Jack Nicholson finally understanding who owns Los Angeles in *Chinatown*—all of them face-to-face with who they are, what the world is. The ferocious pull of Polanski's best films comes from his ability to implacably place us inside the impossible fantasies of his feverish protagonists and simultaneously force us to acknowledge them coldly, from afar, from the outside, from the history they cannot change. It is a vision Polanski rehearsed in his first short, *Two Men and a Wardrobe*, where the two Beckett-like fools emerge from the sea with their enormous wardrobe, are rejected by everyone as they wander the cruel city, and, unable to fit their oversized burden of the imagination anywhere, return to the waters and are swallowed by them.

Except that Roman was not swallowed. The waters did not close over him. In his art, he found the one option not open to his characters: a way of turning his vision away from the abyss of hallucination or the blind alley of frustration and into the shared and joyful realm of communal experience. This he has done at great personal expense, paying for the consequences of his independence, aggressively and often rambunctiously rejecting all compromises, refusing to apologize for the mystery of what he was seeing or the tangle of what he was communicating or the transgressions he lived, treading the dangerous line between the commercial and the artistic in a century that has not been kind to visionaries.

That is why Roman Polanski is the ultimate survivor: he has earned the right to inflict this vision on his spectators because he has always been willing to inflict it on himself.

Now, here, on the set of *Death and the Maiden*, he hands the lamp that is too pleasant and cheery to the prop master so that it can be darkened, so that it can help entice millions of eyes into his dreams, so that he can then close the door and not let those eyes out until they have caught a terrifying glimpse of what Roman's mind and life contain. He picks up some ropes. He looks at them for a while. He handles them. He ties them into a knot. He unties them. He makes a different knot. In a few more weeks, Sigourney Weaver will be using them to tie Ben Kingsley's hands. Are the ropes the right color? Are they too long? Are the edges too frayed? Would they be the sort a woman would have in her kitchen drawer at a beach house? He looks around at us. His eyes squint at me, at all of us. He is looking at me, but also through me, past me, some-where else. He turns back to the ropes.

"There's something wrong," Roman says. "But you know, I can't figure out yet what it is, what's not right."

He will. He will.

Conjuros

The Bull in the Labyrinth of Spain and Chile

Yes, Velázquez was there in all his glorious depth, his *Meninas* and also that forest of opposing lances at the Breda battlefield and, of course, the gaunt mystical figures of El Greco twisting toward a sky about to crack open, but what I most remember of my inaugural 1951 visit to the Prado Museum in Madrid were the infernal landscapes of Hieronymus Bosch and, above all, the turbulent nightmares of the black Goya paintings transposed from the Quinta del Sordo, the House of the Deaf Man. I was only nine years old at the time and intended, at that point in my life, to be a painter rather than a writer and may have hoped that growing familiar with those vivid scenes of torment would exorcize them from my life. Attracted and repelled by these visions from the past that corresponded so disturbingly to my fears for the future or perhaps for what I dreaded might be lurking that very night under my bed or behind the nearest walls of my mind ready to emerge from my sleep, I convinced my mother to take me back to the museum two, maybe three times that week.

Not knowing, of course, that many years later (it must have been the seventies) the eyes of a young Spanish painter and draughtsman born in Madrid and called Pedro Sánchez would insistently repeat that same itinerary, be lured by those same paintings in the Prado, grant Goya and Bosch each a corresponding grasp on his sanity. His path eventually intersected with mine in 1988 when Pedro Sánchez, weary of the drab and predictable post-Franco realm his nation had become, traveled to my country, Chile, as part of a human-

First published in the brochure accompanying an exhibition of works by Pedro Sánchez, curated by the author, at the Duke University Museum of Art, Durham, North Carolina (April 4–June 2, 2002).

rights team that monitored the plebiscite that General Augusto
Pinochet held as a way of consolidating his rule. But the General's
plans went awry: the people of Chile rejected him at the ballot box,
opening the road for a return to democracy. One of the unintended
consequences of that exceptional event—history seldom offers us
the spectacle of a tyrant routed in an election when he controls all
the levers of power!—was that Pedro Sánchez stayed on in Chile,
finding there the solidarity and excitement missing from his native
land. Just as crucial may have been the discovery that here was a
country where art was being challenged to respond on a daily basis
to life-and-death issues, a country where the consequences of making art truly seemed to matter beyond small elite circles. Though
many of the Sánchez etchings and paintings during those first
years in his adopted country were, naturally enough, explorations
of social themes, a search for the images that could accompany a
vast community fiercely determined not to forget past sufferings
as it sought a way out of decades of repression—other representa-
tions delved into a series of less immediately relevant themes, such
as an effulgent series of jazz paintings where Sánchez re-created
from extant photographs several smoke-filled jam sessions that
mimicked and echoed in an extemporizing splash of vivid colors
the beat and improvisation of the original music.

It is not strange that most of Sánchez's energy, throughout those
initial years of settling in a foreign land, went into workshops and
lectures and national tours that he himself organized for a collective of Chilean artists who had raucously welcomed him as a new
member of their *Taller*. Indeed, he got to know the country better than most of his Chilean contemporary artists. Like so many
expatriates—in fact, in ways that recall how I was myself seduced
by Chile when at the age of twelve I moved there from the States
in 1954, coincidentally the very year of Pedro's birth—he ardently
embraced his newfound home and tried to turn his back on what
had constituted up until then his previous life and inspiration. And
yet—also typical of exiles—from time to time, reminiscences of
Pedro Sánchez's apparently receding Spanish past would crop up:
a 1991 Goya-like circle of fiery figures celebrating an initiation rite
(*Ritual de Fuego*) and in subsequent years some preliminary sketches
and lithographs of bulls.

The turning point came in 1995, when a touring collection of Goya's prints were exhibited in Santiago and Sánchez participated in a workshop at the Catholic University, demonstrating to high-school teachers and students the varied techniques that Goya employed to produce his graphic works. In retrospect, it seems that this experience—being transformed into a bridge which joined that favorite artist from his own land with the eyes and hands of Chileans whose fate and everyday existence he now shared—stimulated Pedro Sánchez (or liberated him?) to start on a journey of rediscovery of his roots, creating the collection we are now privileged to display at Duke Museum.

Disparatado Capricho, from 1996, opens an extended series of homages to Goya. The title couples Goya's Disparates (Absurdities) with his Caprichos (Follies/Stubborn Fancies), while the composition itself alludes back to a third group of etchings by him, the Tauromaquia. Sánchez not only makes every effort to pursue with painstaking skill Goya's own methods and procedures for manufacturing prints, but places the great Spanish artist himself in the precarious center of the pictorial arrangement. Goya vaults above a crowd of his own grotesque creatures and characters, not sure—nor are we—whether he will be able to avoid crashing into them, whether he is on his way up or down. And the heavens he is reaching for are themselves full of danger, those earthiest of animals threatening to descend upon him from what would appear at first glance to be a circus tent propped up by trifling dark figures and that, as we look further, seems more and more like the disquieting underbelly of a thrusting bull. Vaulting into darkness, our Goya finds himself, like our Sánchez so many centuries later, jabbed into the caverns of an upside-down world where the artist, any artist, is at the mercy of his own dreams and mad inventions. Vaulting into the underground, because in the universe that Pedro Sánchez is about to unfold for himself and for us, there is barely any sky—only an arena, increasingly closed off, where, if we are lucky, we get to perform and where, if we happen to be very lucky, really lucky, we might conceivably be allowed to extract some sense from the visions that besiege us.

That same year, 1996, Sánchez portrays yet another man suspended in midair in *El Pelele*. This flayed carcass of a barely human

DISPARATADO CAPRICHO

body—which recalls, rather than the dandyishly dressed Goya of *Disparatado Capricho*, the spasmodic movements of one of the flapping bulls—is being mocked below by three demons who have thrown him upward, and above by three angel-winged devils who, instead of catching our hapless protagonist, are offering him through an open manhole a variety of objects in the process of being peeled: a clump of hair, an orange, a chicken. Without trying to reduce an inevitably enigmatic scene to its immediate social context, it is worth pointing out that in Chile, *pelar*—to peel—also describes the act whereby transgressors to the status quo are submitted to the merciless attention (and malignant gossip) of the rest of society. So we are witnessing someone—the artist? a prisoner? a representative of the people?—being punished for having dared to . . . dared to what? Fly? Escape? Dream? Dissent?

Taken together, these two 1996 etchings of anguish and deracination may help us to peer, albeit sideways, into the sort of crisis that was corroding Sánchez in the mid-nineties, an increasing disaffection—personal and political—with the Latin American country he had decided to make his own. This period of distress derives from an estrangement from some of his colleagues in the *Taller* where he had been laboring so selflessly, but also, more crucially, from the sinking realization that the Chilean transition to democracy was losing much of the flair and enthusiasm and collective spark that had distinguished it during the first post-Pinochet years, the perception that a deep and unacknowledged damage had been done to the psyche of the country's citizens during the dictatorship, leaving them fearful and at the mercy of the market economy and the malls that were sprouting up everywhere, equating life with consuming and destiny with shopping, almost like a twisted underdeveloped parody of the contemporary Spain that Sánchez had fled from and that he now had to face all over again—this time far from his old network of family and friends.

My interpretation of this crisis may be colored by the fact that it runs parallel to my own disappointment during those years with the grayness and compromises of the Chilean transition (and also coincides with my deepening friendship with Pedro Sánchez), but I cannot help suggesting that it is this gradual slipping away of the surface of certainty, this admission that Chile is not the paradise or refuge he had supposed fuels our artist's need over the course of the next five years to recover a heritage of Hispanic themes, images, and portents from his past that can accompany his quest for understanding what is happening both to him and to the world around him.

Central to this quest, an anchor in an otherwise confusing universe, is the iconic figure of the bull. Goya and his *Tauromaquia* (a title Sánchez changes in one of his prints, not exhibited, to *Tauro-*

magia, the magic of bulls) is just as important as an artistic source from the past as for its association with a childhood memory. As a boy, Sánchez and his brother would go to the *corridas* with their uncle; the two boys would run ahead of the bulls in the street and then later participate as spectators in the sacrificial rite enacted in the ring. Referring to this ritual, García Lorca has written that Spain is the only country in the world where death is the national spectacle, and Hemingway added, some years later, that bullfighting is the only art where the artist is himself in danger of being killed. There can be no drama, therefore, unless those who watch identify with the bull as well as the torero, with the animal as well as the human—and it is this ambivalence that Pedro Sánchez impels us to confront. By placing us behind the animal as it rushes toward a fate that it cannot foretell (see, for example, *Encuentro, Buscando la Salida, Urotauro*), we are included in its passion and vitality, its desire to endure, its mythic incarnation of the same lifeforce that pulses inside each and every one of us—and inside, of course, the matador who awaits the bull on the other side of the blinding light, at the final stop in the one-way tunnel of existence. For an instant, we are transported to the origins of our species, that moment when we had to thwart what was primitive around and in us, and control it and slay it in order to survive as a species, when we then had to recapture it through memory and art, if we were to survive with any sanity. Pedro Sánchez does not merely refer to that moment and its ritual reiteration, but attempts in *Altamira* to re-create that origin with a technique, communing with the aboriginal hunters who, in those caves in Spain, fathomed the magical power that art confers in the struggle to snare the wild bull (in fact, a bison). Using granulated paper that simulates the irregular walls of rock upon which those first paintings were executed, he applied a blood-colored ink that imitates the red earthiness of the primeval caves, probing and fixing it into the image with his fingers and a cork. Perhaps trying to touch that which we have lost in our mad race towards progress, art understood as a form of reaching for the place where the sacred and the profane, the beast and man used to meet and still might meet again if we only allowed time enough and space.

It is an encounter and fusion we are still able to imagine in all our loneliness (*Minotauro en el Laberinto*), even as we are forced to

MINOTAURO EN EL LABERINTO

realize, as that other Spanish artists, Picasso, also did, that these
two zones of our reality and our desires have been tragically and
repeatedly separated from each other and now face *la hora de la
verdad*, the hour of truth, the hour when truth will come out, when
the matador and the *toro* look across the divide with murderous
intentions, each a serene shadow and projection of the other, each
trying to kill the other as a way of becoming whole, integral, complete. In this masterful print we now see the bull from the front,
and it is the man who turns his back to us and raises his arm in an
apparent attempt to greet and placate . . . who? Who is up there?

Who are those three figures, as well as those other three, and that one solitary man; who are these people who watch this drama unfold from above?

At the same time that Sánchez re-creates the mythical and mythological possibilities of this encounter with the past and with our own deepest psychic needs, he is also aware that today this rite persists more as parody (*Ensayo General, Ensayo en el Laberinto*) than as reality, indeed as a spectacle that has been degraded and is gradually being stripped of its meaning. A spectacle because up there, in the gallery, we can catch a glimpse of those who gaze with mocking eyes and mouths upon the savage confrontation of man and the animal territory of his being, those who are only there to be entertained. That is why, I believe, Sánchez's next step is to present us (and himself) with two close-ups—like a camera that does not want to witness what it has captured, like a camera coming into focus in spite of its own wishes—of the audience. Again, harkening back to *El Pelele*, we have two disquieting groups of three. In *Circunloquio I* and *Circunloquio II* we gaze up into the unholy faces of masked men who press down upon us, press down upon both the bull and the torero, perhaps down upon the unseen Minotaur, letting us know that they hold the key, they have the power, they persist, yes, but at the price of having become a caricature; and they can see, yes, and not be identified, yes, but one among them is also horribly blind, all of them—reminding us of Goya's blind beggars—expose their white empty orbits shining in the dark, all of them threaten some manner of unspeakable retribution. The subtitles say it all: "El Burladero"—the place where people mock those down below—and "El Respetable," an ironical reference to the Public as Respetable, the Public as composed of those who must be pleased, appeased, propitiated. Though these figures bear a resemblance to the figures spilling out from the Goyaesque Spanish past, they also seem to refer—or at least that is how they resonate with me—to their contemporary Chilean counterparts, the shadowy torsos and facades of the men who decide, from some supposedly higher and inaccessible region, who lives and who dies.

These mysterious, even ghoulish, bystanders provide a chilling context to what are arguably the two most original and compelling pictures of the exhibition: *Círculo Iniciático* and *Tientos y Diferencias*.

Here, as in a series of other works that have not been included in the presentation at Duke (*Punto de Encuentro*, *El Rito y la Máscara*, *Puntos de Fuga* among them), Sánchez lets his imagination run riot. The flayed figure that we first met in *El Pelele*—all naked and red and exposed flesh is still surrounded by strange men and omens, and still marooned in midair—still looking for a way out of his predicament. But now stilts or a high chair furnish a tenuous connection to the earth. In *Círculo Iniciático*, the protagonist, in the midst of an initiation rite that has no clear outcome or outlet, must content himself with conjuring up the conflicting traditions that call to his body from the wells of yesterday: the mythical Minotaur of the deep Mediterranean, the screaming cardinal of the repressive Spanish theological past, while the apparently interchangeable angel and devil dancing above with hands interlocked provide no real protection or guidance.

A similar uncertainty pervades the even more enigmatic *Tientos y Diferencias*. Where are they headed, those two figures on the move, the man on stilts and the mutilated upper body of that other man on wheels, perverse complements of each other, how do they expect to escape? Why is each of them being watched—though even this is not clear—by those other two iconic representatives of old Spain: the sad trapped man who wears the conical hat of Inquisitorial times and the gigantic *Cabezón*, another masked form that comes straight out of the childhood street memories of Pedro Sánchez? Beyond that strange room, what city of cupola and tower calls to them?

In search of a response, my eyes go back again and again to the man on stilts, perhaps because he seems the most hopeful of the four as he tentatively crawls through the air on some sort of quest, but also because in him I see a Chilean incarnation of a Spanish tradition. Sánchez himself has informed me of how, at his first enormous public gathering in Santiago (to cheer the victory of the people against the dictatorship in the 1988 plebiscite) and also at subsequent massive meetings, he had been thrilled at the sight of participants who were celebrating on stilts, walking along above the multitudes with their baby steps and their desire to be birds and their need to reach for the sky. His Spanish past persisting playfully into his Chilean present—a past also echoed, although more ominously, in the deformed half-man wheeling his corroded

TIENTOS Y DIFERENCIAS

body exactly underneath the stilts, a reminder of all the beggars and rabble that populate the streets of contemporary Santiago as they did in the yesteryear of Madrid, ironically undercutting all these Attempts (*Tientos*), this temporary groping toward something better. Is that why Sánchez added *Diferencias* (Differences) to the title? Because something was telling him that he was exploring the ambiguous intersection of Spain and Chile, two countries that have been through parallel forms of misery and excoriation in this century, countries that still have so much to communicate to each other?

A quandary which brings us full circle—or is it a semicircle, so loved by Sánchez, that we are executing here?—back to Goya and the question of what he still has to offer us, what he continues to whisper to his faraway disciple in a foreign land two centuries later. Though the answer is scattered throughout this rich and varied exhibition, it may be encapsulated or at least summarized in the ambitious pencil-ink-etching *Entuertos (Homenaje a Goya)*.

To translate the word *entuertos* as wrongs does not do justice to the way in which the Spanish resounds with damages and injuries (*tuerto* is he who has lost an eye). At the top of his etching, Sánchez has reproduced three figures from Goya's *Caprichos*—and "reproduced" here should be taken quite literally, as Sánchez uses the same reddish brown watercolors with which Goya himself prepared his drawings before turning them into prints. The three penitents that Sánchez has plucked from the vast repertory of suffering men and women Goya immortalized are significant: one of them is being punished because he has no legs (like the flesh-eaten man on wheels of *Tientos y Diferencias*); another because, like Sánchez himself, he was born somewhere else; and finally, the third one, stretched out on the torture rack, because he dared to dream. All three of them as alive and relevant and chastised in today's Chile—and today's many other sorry lands—as they were in Goya's time; and all of them deserving of the artist's eyes and heart and skill and rage. The portrait of Goya that Sánchez has chosen to place at the very center of his homage is one that appeared as the frontispiece of the 1799 *Caprichos*, where the great Spanish master has been careful to offset his so-coveted bourgeois respectability with that slitted, sideways glance of vigilance, irony, maybe even admonition, wary of being caught by the Inquisition and who knows what other more secular powers. But defiant, yes, definitely defiant and sure of what he has seen and has yet to see. Asking us if we are willing to see it all over again.

The way in which Sánchez emphasizes how much more difficult it is today to be a witness to that suffering and to be true to the subterranean inner visions that accompany it from another dimension, is by taking one of Goya's most famous paintings from the House of the Deaf Man, *El Aquelarre*, in which a group of witches sit around a great he-goat, and turning it into a commentary on

globalization and the role of the mass media. The 1823 original is
a scene of collective madness under the moon. But Sánchez has
replaced the devil seducing the frenzied swirl of gaping women with
a television screen, the goat's horns with an antennae stand, and the
monk's cloak with a black table; light no longer filters down from
the lunar powers above but emanates from the cold cathode rays of
technology. There is a final humorous touch: the most monstrous
of all the demonic helpers, a dwarfish figure shrouded in white,
now has earphones affixed to her head. The dreams of Reason do
indeed create monsters!

Having traveled halfway across the planet to escape the effects
of post-Franco Spain, Pedro Sánchez finds himself facing, in his
adopted Chile, the same forces of cultural and economic homog-
enization, the same stupefying disregard for those who are left
behind and left outside, the same inability to face the pain of
the past and the challenges of the future. Instead of reacting to
this crisis by physically returning to Spain, he decides to recover,
through his art, those elements in his remote and recent origins that
illuminate his current predicament—the predicament of most of
humanity today as it confronts forms of accelerated modernization
cutting us off from the rituals and wisdom of the past. By doing
this in stunning colors and incantatory visions, Sánchez offers us
an extraordinary synthesis of the sacred and the profane, of light
and shadows, and perhaps, who knows, may Goya bless us, a way
out of the maze. Because it is already a start to be told in such a
warm multitude of ways that we humans, all of us, are still in a
labyrinth where we must figure out our deepest identity, yes, we
must figure out when and where we lost our way or die the slow
death of the truly blind.

Confessions from
Another South, Other Wars

I n the late 1960s, Antonio Lobo Antunes was sent to Angola
to serve as a medic in the war that Portugal was fighting in a
useless attempt to retain its African colonies. Out of that experience came an extraordinary fictionalized memoir published in
1979 that was translated into English four years later as *South of
Nowhere*. Through a hallucinatory monologue set in a Lisbon bar,
its protagonist managed not only to explore the degrading consequences of that specific war, but also the bitter homecoming of
so many soldiers of other countries and other times, searching for
their lost innocence in the refracted mirrors of multiple Penelopes
and Circes.

The same obsessive scrutiny of the nightmare world of the colonial war veteran, the same brutal lyrical language, the same maelstrom of erotic violence and guilt can be found in *Fado Alexandrino*,
Antunes's second novel published in English. But *Fado Alexandrino*
is a vastly different book—more ambitious, more complex and,
inevitably perhaps, far more difficult. The one lonely narrator of
South of Nowhere has been fractured here into four failed combat-
ants who, as they expose their own crisscrossed lives during one
tumultuous night, also recount the sprawling epic of their country
in the ten years after its troops came home from Africa.

Although of different rank and social class, all four men share
a common destiny of frustration that seems emblematic of their
national history. Somewhat in the same way that, even after they
have crumbled, the country's four-hundred-year-old Empire and its
recently deposed dictatorship of forty years continue to influence the
present, so the past mistakes of these men drown and haunt them,
contaminating not only their efforts to alter their society and start

New York Times Book Review, July 29, 1990.

anew, but also the many bodies of love they compulsively grope for as anchors in the midst of decay. The bedchambers of Portugal end up being as much a battle zone as the jungles of Mozambique.

Antunes has chosen to transmit his characters' stories through a dense web of confessions spilled into the ears of a silent and enigmatic captain—an army investigator, a psychoanalyst, maybe the author himself?—who accompanies them on a long orgiastic night out on the town with five prostitutes. Though this technique, which juxtaposes Africa and Lisbon, a rape and a funeral, yesterday and today and anticipations of a possible tomorrow, can be confusing and even tiresome at times, it is crucial to the author's intention of revealing the hidden mingled layers of his nation's subconscious, how far it has traveled from the legendary Vasco da Gama who many centuries ago set sail to claim the world for Portugal and inspired Camões's great epic, *The Lusiads* (1572). Now all that is left of that archetypal unity are the splintered masks and voices of these bankrupt Portuguese males, and the only exploratory journey a descent into a series of shattered private hells.

Before the night is over, Antunes will have revealed how they are secretly connected to the same women, how they have been making love to each other's wives and mistresses and fiancées. And one of them, because of that connection, will be murdered, "the body lying face down on the sidewalk . . . amid the indifference or the fright or the hunger of the birds, among the chimneys, the trees, the garrets, and roof after roof after roof that hid the river" (419).

Will it be the lieutenant colonel who has spent his years in the army serving whichever faction happens to be in power, drifting like jetsam from bed to bed in an attempt to exorcise a wife who died of cancer the day before he returned from the war? Or will it be the second lieutenant who, divorced by his high-society lesbian wife, returns to his country from Brazil to marry a deformed and jealous dwarf? Or will it be a noncom who was tortured and imprisoned for belonging to a Maoist sect, but has since lost all belief in the revolution and is left with nothing but his sexual urge to stop feeling like "dinner leftovers" (290)? Or the soldier, selling his body to strangers in order to have enough money to impress the young woman he loved and who dumped him anyway, almost as soon as they finally married? Ultimately, it does not really matter:

the turmoil of their society will, like the primeval sex they fear so much, end up swallowing them all.

What is miraculous in *Fado Alexandrino*, which often reads like a mad amalgam of Dos Passos and Céline, is that its readers are not themselves devoured by the chaos. The author, with the very energy and vision that he denies his blindly cynical characters, narrates their lives with a remarkable savage swirl of imagery that controls and sustains the wandering threads of their jumbled fates, allowing us to look deep into the predatory origins of their incessant violence—a revelation made possible, in English, by Gregory Rabassa's splendid translation.

South of Nowhere was a masterpiece which, unfortunately, did not catch on in America, not even making it into a paperback edition. The more arduous and disturbing *Fado Alexandrino* gives readers in the United States a second chance to plunge into the strange and yet oddly familiar world created by one of Portugal's preeminent writers as a way of demanding that his country and his compatriots finally come to terms with the many wars they have lost.

Writing Voices from Beyond the Dark

W hy is there so much needless suffering in the world today? Why do so many remain silent? How is it that a few men and women break that silence, find themselves struggling against exile and prison and censorship? Where do they find the courage to speak out, to continue speaking out even after they have been repressed and threatened by the authorities of their lands? And what is it that those defenders of the rights of all humanity most fear—fear more than death—in the secret shadows of their heart?

These are not easy questions to answer and not even easy to ask.

Though I had been pondering similar issues for most of my adult life, both as an artist and as an activist myself, let me confess that when the opportunity arose fifteen months ago to write a play about the men and women who interrogate and address those problems, I almost decided to reject that opportunity. It was offered to me by the prominent American human-rights lawyer Kerry Kennedy-Cuomo, who had written a book of interviews with more than fifty human-rights defenders from around the world and wanted to know if I would be interested in assembling some sort of stage adaptation of her conversations. She envisaged major presentations by distinguished actors in many countries, starting with the United States, with the exciting possibility of eventually placing the play in thousands of schools where youngsters would be able to interpret and discuss those topics. This also meant that the work had to be relatively brief—one hour or so—because too much terror and too much saintly opposition to it could end up boring audiences that, after all, are not overly enthusiastic to approach these questions to begin with.

Guardian (London), June 2, 2001.

Which was precisely why such a play was urgently required. It was enough to look out upon the desolate landscape of our recent history—the wars and brutality, the child labor and female bondage, the unrelenting poverty, the excess of pollution and greed and tyranny and lies—to feel that I had to say yes, of course, I would do anything I could to bring to the world's attention the voices of those who refused to be stilled and cowed by that overwhelming violence and by fear, its malignant twin. Who had heard of Kailash Satyarthi, that quiet man who over persistent decades has liberated forty thousand children in India from child labor, who has tried to make faraway consumers aware of the tiny wasted hands that interlace and braid the rugs that adorn well-to-do living rooms? Who knows how Van Jones heals and protects the victims of police brutality in the United States, who has even heard his name? Who has heard, for that matter, of Rana Husseini, a Jordanian journalist who has denounced the "honor" killings of pregnant women by close relatives, who is aware that these women, if they survive, may languish for years in protective custody? Who has listened to the story of Digna Ochoa, a nun who became a lawyer in Mexico in order to confront the disappearance of trade-union militants and was herself tortured? Or Harry Wu, determined to make the planet understand how many of the innocent toys we cheerfully give to our progeny have been created by prison labor in China's humiliating and devastating Laogai? Or Ka Hsaw Wa, who spent years in the jungles of Burma, merely collecting the sad stories of peasants nobody cared to listen to? Or Koigi wa Wamwere and Freedom Neruda and Wangari Maathai and Juliana Dogbadzi and Abucar Sultan, who will not let Africa turn into a continent of despair, who have rescued child soldiers and planted trees and insisted on freedom of the press and . . . Need I go on?

Yes, I did need to go on. I needed to help those voices and so many more extend and stretch so they could influence the world. And yet, I hesitated—and the reasons for this hesitation were above all aesthetic reasons. I have always been wary of art that tries to prove a point and convince or harangue an audience, I tend to be suspicious of theater and indeed other forms of intervention in the public sphere that reduce complex issues to simple and heroic answers. I prefer to obliquely disturb spectators and leave them

unsettled and uncertain, mired—as I am—in the moral flaws of
my protagonists who do not themselves have good answers to their
dilemmas, perhaps because history has not yet provided them, perhaps because at times I wonder if there are any permanent answers.
Could I find a dramatic form that remained true to the valor, the
purity, the righteousness of these champions of human values, while
at the same time taking into account the frailty and darkness of
our contemporary condition? Can the hope and inspiration necessary, indeed essential, for social activism be married to the mistrust
and transgression, the linguistic experimentation and playfulness,
the blurring of the lines between good and evil that nurtures the
most significant literature of our times? What, if anything, do the
Dalai Lama and Samuel Beckett have in common?

If I finally decided to write the play, it was because the voices
themselves, their boundless variety of causes and continents, ide-
ologies and adversaries, gave me guidance, slowly whispered to me
ways in which the stories could be staged. It was the very fact that
only a handful of the defenders interviewed by Kerry were well
known globally (Elie Wiesel and Rigoberta Menchú, Vaclav Havel
and Desmond Tutu), the acknowledgment that the vast majority
of those who risk their lives for freedom struggle in the darkness,
almost anonymously, far from the spotlight of celebrity, undiscov-
ered by the media, their voices barely heard, hardly discerned, it
was their very absence, the very shame of their distance from those
of us who watched (or failed to do so) from the safety of our seats,
the difficulty of bringing them into the light, it was that unrelenting quest for voicehood denied that would carve the language that
would give them a theatrical home. The play, to be called *Speak
Truth to Power: Voices from Beyond the Dark*, would be modeled on
a cantata form, with clusters of narrators reciting their tribulations
and commitment at some length, telling each other how they had
come to consciousness, one story after another interspersed with
short lyrical interludes by other defenders, a collage of verses and
phrases and incantations garnered from their own words, weaving
a tapestry of utterances, commenting, encouraging, accompanying
each tale so it was not isolated, so it could reach us, every one of
the voices that Kerry had collected finding its way into the public space, one by one by one breaking down the solitude and the

despair and the disconnection. Coming out of the darkness, my darkness and that of the world.

Even so, this could not be enough. There was still the need for some sort of dramatic tension, something more than a repeated litany of oppression and atrocity and faith and personal resolve to fight injustice. I had to provide a dramatic antagonist, a figure who would deny this quest for redemption, someone who could give the human-rights defenders and the audience an intimation of who is really in charge, someone who represents those with the very concrete ability to harm and mock our desires for a better world, one ominous voice on stage who would suggest the enormous forces each of us must face in our everyday lives if we are to change the destiny of our species. I needed somebody not that easily defeated. Somebody who did not believe that the play itself—my words, the words of my heroes—would make a difference

And so I proceeded to invent a mythical character, a sort of Evangelist of evil whom I quite blatantly call the Man. At the start of the play, he (or is it He?) embodies the repression of the State that my protagonists have confronted over and over again, the figure who controls the names and movement and emergence of the defenders. But gradually, as his victims find the strength and the solidarity to resist his power, he is transformed into something else: a projection of their deepest fear. Indeed, I eventually turn that Man into the representative of those who do not care, who stand by and watch the terror without doing anything, the many who add to the silence by turning their eyes away, that Man as a demonic inner dimension of the activists themselves, a temptation and enticement to let themselves grow weary as he invites them to cease and desist. In other words, I put the audience itself, my own doubts and uncertainty and puzzlement and guilt, into the cruel core of the play. I made the full force of indifference the true enemy, what really allows all that pain to continue. I had him wait there, in the darkness, the Man, nearby, always there, in the corridor of death, always ready to claim the light and also the shadows.

I am not sure yet whether I have succeeded with this play, whether it will have the intended effect, whether Kerry Kennedy Cuomo's trust last year was warranted. In its world premiere eight months ago, in September 2000, at the Kennedy Center in Washington,

D.C., an all-star, multiethnic cast (Kevin Kline and John Malkovich, Sigourney Weaver and Rita Moreno, Alec Baldwin and Julia Louis-Dreyfuss, Alfre Woodard and Hector Elizondo and Giancarlo Esposito, with music by Jackson Browne and Hugh Masekela) performed the play for a select audience of more than one thousand spectators. They seem to have been moved intensely, particularly when forty of the human-rights defenders themselves appeared from behind the curtain and, in a Pirandello moment that I will always cherish, met and embraced the actors and actresses who were representing them on stage, some of the most recognizable and filmed people in the world telling us that the real celebrities should be these faces and bodies of the unknown. But does the play have any staying power? We will discover the answer to that question in the months to come, as it is performed in other cities around the world, starting tomorrow in London when *Speak Truth to Power: Voices from Beyond the Dark* will have its European premiere with another extraordinary group of actors and actresses and a superb director. Regardless of whether the audience is changed in any way by the words I have transcribed, the words I borrowed from the human-rights activists themselves to tell their story, there will be one way, one very practical way in which this presentation is sure to have some sort of effect, however minimal, on the sorry planet we inhabit: it will be a benefit for *Index on Censorship*, one of the finest and most creative magazines in the English language, the embodiment itself of the struggle against silence across frontiers. Many years ago, it was *Index* that first published my *Death and the Maiden*, before it was even staged. It seems fitting that they should again be the ones to present one of my plays to London spectators, that we should be collaborating one more time to bring to the globe the story of those who defend the Paulinas of the world, who would not abandon her to silence and sorrow, who would try to redeem an Earth that has too often forgotten that if we witness so much pain and do nothing about it, we are in danger of becoming accomplices. It's about time we all knew who Wangari Maathai is, who in hell and heaven Wangari Maathai is.

Writing the Deep South

In order to come here we have had to travel from far away, from a distance that is not merely geographic. Our three nations—Chile, South Africa, and Australia—have coexisted for many years in the same hemisphere and yet have never attempted an intellectual interchange, an exchange of experiences, such as we are initiating now. We cannot blame the gigantic oceans that divide us; the more crucial and real distance derives from the self-fascination we have felt with our own immediate continents, the omphalos of our own world, not to mention our incessant attraction to the immense culture to our North and its languages, which predominate in our speech and writing. Even so, this first meeting of the writers of our countries is only possible because we have in fact (and in fiction) been interconnecting through our imagination over many decades, our books have preceded us to this gathering in Santiago. More than the circumstance that we are global neighbors, that all three nations face Antarctica, the fact that we could even conceive of the term *Deep South*, is due to our having anticipated in our disparate and coincidental literary work the hint of a tentative common identity.

Given the extraordinary emotional and intellectual wealth of our guests, the vast interior worlds they have assembled from the fragments and fractures of the outer countries they inhabit, it is difficult, now that our bodies share this physical space here in Santiago for the first time in history, to forecast the ways in which our interaction will modify the imaginary space of this New South. I

Delivered as the inaugural speech of "Writing the Deep South," a gathering of writers from Chile, Australia, and South Africa in Santiago de Chile, November 1998. First published in Spanish under the title "Escribiendo el Sur Profundo" in *La Jornada* (Mexico City), November 14, 1998.

would like, however, to make a prediction. Our guests, as well as the spectators who have come to listen to us, to question us and themselves, will find themselves pulled between two fundamental human experiences: what in Spanish I would call *extrañeza* on one hand and *familiaridad* on the other. The English equivalent of the latter, familiarity, easily translates the idea that we recognize and discover that which joins us, but *extrañeza*, though literally the act of feeling strange, also contains the notion of estrangement, a process of *extrañamiento*, to become alien to something, to let it surprise us. If I predict that we will plunge into these simultaneous and conflicting processes, it is because that was the dual and contradictory educational adventure that marked my own visits to the two countries whose writers have now come to confer with us in Chile. And I can think of no better way to welcome them than to briefly divulge my own early approximation to South Africa and Australia, voyages of discovery that are culminating in this new encounter cohosted by my friend Antonio Skármeta, greeting you now in my own country.

It was on a recent trip—my first—to South Africa that I was visited by a revelation that grew into this assemblage, this "Writing the Deep South."

It was in June of last year, 1997. The sun was coming down in Pretoria, and I had arrived in South Africa a mere few hours earlier. With my friends and hosts, Jorge Heine, the Chilean ambassador to Nelson Mandela's government, his wife, Norma, and their son, Gunther, I went out for a long walk through the suburban streets of Pretoria, winding this way and that until we passed the high fence of a golf country club. Behind the fence, everything was green splendor, impeccably, immaculately British. Outside the fence, in a no-man's-land overgrown with weeds and wild flowers and rank with floating remnants of garbage, a group of jobless South African men, all black, had improvised a small blaze. They were warming their hands, laughing, passing around a bottle, not looking at the nearby street full of trendy new cars.

This scene, completed by several black women who resolutely walked along, returning to their far-off homes after a day's work as maids in the neighborhood's mansions, seemed to me, all of a sudden, incredibly familiar, almost routinely customary and recognizable. This wasn't South Africa. It was Chile, my Santiago. I have passed the Prince of Wales Country Club in the barrio of La Reina in the same way, I have seen that resplendent green grass and these same men with their knitted caps over their ears and their tattered clothes and this same smoking fire and that same woman walking toward her remote home after caring for children she had not given birth to. All this duplicated a time and a space that I had already lived—that mixture of the native and the European, of poverty and opulence, of those who were included and those who were excluded, two nations in one land divided by centuries of visible and invisible barbed wire.

But immediately, underneath that sensation of a human land-scape being replicated inside me, another sort of certitude swam into my mind: this interlocution with South Africa had been prepared for me during decades, not merely because this country was a mir-ror of my own country, but more crucially because this imaginary place had been loaned to me already by South African literature. Literature had announced with words the split and cracked streets I was now strolling through, the gestures and openings I was recu-perating. I had visited South Africa in *Cry the Beloved Country* and in the works of Nadine Gordimer and André Brink and J. M. Coetzee and Athol Fugard and Wally Serote and Dennis Brutus and Allister Sparks and so many other friends. They had sent me the multiple gifts of Mandela's land that I could now smell, touch, devour with my eyes, and yes, recognize.

During the weeks that followed, this recognition of a society that resonated in me and seemed to belong to me was accentu-ated. In meetings with Bishop Tutu's Truth and Reconciliation Commission, in visits to Soweto and the Market Theatre and to a church in Cape Town, in dialogues with students and writers, in concerts, in endless conversations, in a novel by Zakes Mda that I began to read, I felt that the South Africa that had fought against its own dictatorship and was now making the arduous journey to democracy exhibited an array of resemblances to the Chilean situ-ation that drove me dizzy. I even came to believe that I felt more comfortable and at ease in South Africa than in my own Chile, given that South Africa was exploring in an open, public, almost desperate way its multiple identities, while Chile, in my opinion, was more interested in hiding its wounds and contradictions than revealing them.

In spite of this affinity and attraction to the country I was visiting, I slowly began to realize that, even though the political, social and cultural challenges of our nations are similar, it is dangerous and reductive to proclaim that we are, in effect, identical. It dawned on me that what was most valuable about my stay in South Africa was precisely that which was different and new and startling—the novelties and surprises accentuated by their surfacing from within a reality that I perceived as profoundly parallel.

If my exposure to South Africa was born under the sign of an excessive familiarity and evolved toward a consideration of its mystery, my relationship with Australia developed in a symmetrically opposite way. When I visited Sydney in 1993, my first hallucinatory hours were spent noting how dissimilar this country was from mine. I was, admittedly, influenced by the fact that a Chilean essayist, Joaquín Lavín, who is now the mayor of Las Condes and the right-wing presidential candidate for the presidency, had written an article called "*Adiós, América Latina*" (Goodbye, Latin America), in which he suggested that Chile's economic takeoff allowed our country to abandon its Latino and American destiny and position itself internationally as an equal of the Asian tiger countries as well as of Australia and New Zealand.

Now that I was entering Sydney's bay over that breathtaking bridge and began walking around the modern and vibrant city, a city without beggars or blazes in front of manicured golf resorts, now that I could see a functioning democracy that had not suffered the abuses and crimes of my poor Chile, now that I was surrounded by intriguing and exceptionally strange birds and trees, I confirmed that Lavín did not know what he was talking about, and that is precisely how I spelled it out to the Foreign Correspondents Club when I addressed them a few hours later as their lunch guest. "It ain't so," I told them, using that colloquialism to emphasize that Chile was definitely *not* Australia, despite the prophecies and desires of the enthusiastic entrepreneurs of my country. And yet, as the next two weeks allowed me to explore and accentuate even further these differences, I also gradually started to comprehend that Chile and Australia did echo each other and had deeper analogies than were apparent at first, though the approximation did not rise as much from political or social equivalence as from a series of uncertainties about identity that Australians were posing to themselves, cultural challenges that sistered us, both countries entangled in similar dilemmas of colonization and history.

Beneath Australia's functional and superlative modernity, I registered a swamp of questions that implied that not everything was heavenly in that country. Questions about racial minorities and their millenary contact with the earth. Questions about the solitary connections between men and women on the edge of the planet. Questions about how language and fantasy change at that edge when you confront a dissonant world. Questions about the relationship with remote and seductive Europe and with a nearby threatening Nature. Or was it Nature that seduced and Europe that was a threat? What was sure was that these problems and puzzles had been anticipated by my previous readings of Patrick White and Tom Keneally and Peter Carey. I had also seen them in the films written by Helen Garner and David Williamson and so many more, and I had not yet even come across the work of Roberta Sykes, whom I was to discover thanks to our conference. What was sure was that what Australians were discussing and trying to understand was marvelously close to my own intellectual and emotional predicament, yet I wondered, nevertheless, if this proximity was due to my being a Chilean or if it originated in the simple fact that I belonged to the human species and nothing should be alien to any of us.

It was that sort of wondering in 1993 that resurfaced four years later when I walked on a beach in Cape Town with Jorge Heine. We were arguing passionately about how alike and yet divergent Chile and South Africa were. And during those hours when we doubted whether these similarities, these disparities, were rooted in history or in geography, if racial issues or economic ones could explain these distances and affinities, or if perhaps what was crucial in both cases was the need to copy a faraway Europe in a promised land that resisted easy interpretations and categories, I think it was then that Australia started to smuggle itself timidly into our conversation. We realized that a dialogue between Chileans and South Africans would be infinitely enriched by the triangular presence and singular destiny of that other country of the South. It must have been then, in that South African location equidistant from both Santiago and Sydney, that the need for our gathering to be of all three countries, rather than two, dawned. It must have been then and there that the mystical number three broke upon us.

Our countries have been constituted through *encuentros*, encounters. The encounter of humans with a nature that is turbulent and immeasurable and hard to tame; the encounters with the Europeans and their descendants meeting those who resided in our lands before the arrival of those foreigners; the encounters of our nations over and over with the outer world to the North that influenced and modeled and used and demanded and claimed us; the encounters with frontiers, always with frontiers.

To those encounters, which have been the foundation of what differentiates us from other societies and also what inserts us into the whole of humanity, we now modestly add this new confluence, this new manner of vindicating and imagining a South that belongs to us and alters us and that we are building at this very moment, modifying right now, learning and redefining right now, a South near and far to which we will all return different and identical, ready to continue writing it together and apart, hopefully more *extrañados* and more *familiares*, like the dispersed and distinct brothers and sisters of the same family who gather for the first, but not for the last, time in history.

The Hidden Censors

Somewhere in the world today, a journalist is being beaten. Policemen are beating him, beating her, somewhere in the world today, on the shoulders, on the head, on the hands. Somewhere in the world today, another journalist, yet another, is being thrown in jail, joining so many others who have spent days, months, years in prison. One more journalist somewhere in the world today is answering the phone, and a voice on the other side says, "If you keep writing, you're dead," and then there is a click on the other end and the deafening buzz of silence, and, for a second that seems to last forever, that journalist remembers people just like her who have been killed in the past—for a second, it is as if she were already dead, as if her body had already been discovered in a ditch on the outskirts of town.

Somewhere in the world today, one journalist, two, three, four, any number of journalists—are being asked by their editors to tone down a news report, not to investigate something that would bother powerful people or companies or bureaucracies or religious authorities. They are being asked to erase an adjective, a comment, a quotation; all over the world today, people working in the media are being required to censor themselves, and you can be sure that somewhere in the world today, a journalist is being fired because he will not comply. Right now. At this very moment. I say somewhere in the world today, and yet I could specify each of the instances I have brought up. I could put faces on those who are being repressed, and I could give sad names to each country where that repression is perpetrated.

Delivered as a speech to the United Nations General Assembly on World Press Freedom Day, May 2, 1997. First published in *Index on Censorship* (London), July 1997.

We are here to observe World Press Freedom Day, and yet, ironically, many of the delegates who sit here at this very moment in this wonderful hall dedicated to world peace represent some of the very nations where the freedom of expression established in the UN Declaration of Human Rights has been violated in the last twelve months, according to the London-based magazine, *Index on Censorship*. It would take more time than we have right now to examine, even briefly, each violation or, more crucially, to distinguish the more blatant violators from the less permanent ones, so I will leave with you, Mr. Secretary General, a list of those nations, 142 of them, to be exact.

It is even more urgent, however, that we celebrate today, in this hall, those men and women who, across the globe, are risking at this very moment their lives and their livelihoods in order to connect us through words. Even if their names are not always known, their existence, their persistence, can be felt everywhere. We have a saying in Spanish, in Chile, where I come from: "*Si el río suena, piedras trae.*" If the river makes noise, it must be carrying stones. If there is so much repression it is because there has to be something to repress; it is because all over the planet people in the media are defying silence. If those clubs wielded by policemen are coming down on heads, it is an incontrovertible sign that those heads have been thinking independently and daring to transmit to others what they have witnessed. Censorship is only ferociously necessary because, in spite of all the barriers, stories are incessantly being told. And censorship is not only applied in countries without democracy. A more insidious pressure, because it is more invisible, is exercised by the concentration of the ownership of the production and distribution of stories and opinions in the hands of monopolies and conglomerates. The fact that those who are the guardians of the news do not themselves own the newspapers, television, radios, publishing houses they work in means that they must therefore defend their independence with fortitude, integrity, and cunning, looking for ways to resist the directives from the men who run the business itself and who, in general, tend to place profit ahead of truth.

And yet, the courage of hundreds of thousands of professional men and women who dare to continue to speak out in the face of so many menaces, is not sufficient by itself to guarantee real pluralism and real information. Courage is necessary, of course, but will not ultimately have an effect unless that courage is accompanied by a community, by many others who, in less spectacular ways, join with those who are trying to speak out and prepare multiple spaces where those voices can be heard and understood. A free press, with many dissonant voices, can only exist if it is nurtured by millions of free people who, one by one, also speak out and respond to what is being said, written, and transmitted.

To pursue further our metaphor of a river, if its water flows over stones and tries to drown out their noise and makes believe they do not exist, we must ask, of what use is the sound of stones against the silence if those who drink from the river don't want to attend to the cry of the stones, if those who cross the river are too fearful to listen and are not ready to respond with their own voices to what they hear?

We are all responsible, in our public and our private lives, for the many other freedoms that allow the press itself to be free. Somewhere in the world today, a teacher is tearing up a story that a child has written for the school newspaper or for the school bulletin board, somewhere in the world today, that teacher is tearing up that disturbing story because if somebody else reads it, that teacher could be sacked. That teacher is drilling into that child the lesson that it is better to remain silent.

Somewhere in the world, a marketing executive in a big corporation is canceling sponsorship for a program because it is too controversial, or refusing to place an advertisement because another program is not entertaining enough, is too serious, too offensive. That executive is also teaching fear, cowardice, submissiveness.

Somewhere in the world today, a husband is telling a wife to hush or the neighbors will hear, and a wife is telling a husband not to risk losing his job by telling his colleagues what he really believes. They are teaching each other to hide who they are.

Somewhere in the world today, a book is being burned, an exhibition of paintings has just been forbidden, a film has just been banned, a customs officer at a border is confiscating material he deems to be annoying. Somewhere in the world today, right now, as I speak, a poet is in hiding, a novelist is on the run, a theologian is being excommunicated, an actor is on trial for quoting Kafka.

All, all of them, teaching us to be afraid.

All, all of them, these acts, apparently isolated from one another but constituting, in fact, part of an interlocking web of distrust and dread. Every time we show intolerance toward a fellow human being we are diminishing our own liberty and identity, our chance to grow with those who ask us questions. There will be no press freedom, finally, until we learn to deeply respect those with whom we disagree; respect them, not in spite of how different they seem, but precisely because they are different. There will be no authentic press freedom until we stop suppressing, all of us, what challenges us to be different human beings in our everyday lives.

What to do, then, given the vast, almost devastating, array of problems that freedom of expression must overcome worldwide? How to fight the feeling that an act of celebration such as this one serves no practical purpose, the despairing suspicion that these words of ours do not change anything for the journalist threatened with death, for the photographer beaten with clubs, for the newspaperman whose publication has just been shut down, for the writer who censors himself in order to survive?

I would not be here today if I were not firmly convinced of the value of an observance like this one. Symbols matter. Words *do* matter. Their words and our words. We are congregated today to symbolically alleviate the loneliness of all those who, around the world, struggle against enormous odds to give birth to the weight of those words that are as necessary to our survival as the air we breathe. It is that solitude and the fear that nobody is listening, that nobody cares, that can be the worst enemy of freedom of expression.

I once felt that solitude and that fear; I was once one of those who needed to know that somebody, somewhere, was keeping me company. It was then, back in the times when General Pinochet was misruling my country, that I wrote a poem that I believe still resonates today, particularly in a place like the United Nations, because it explores the dilemmas that writers share with functionaries of an international organization such as this one. It explores our commonality. And because it is not often, I am sure, that this

assembly has the occasion to hear poetry, I would like to end my
intervention by reading that short poem in which I tried to respond
yesterday and try to respond again today to the question of how
we can listen to the stones that bleed, hidden, at the bottom of the
rivers of silence of humanity. The poem is called "Simultaneous
Translation."

I'm not so different from the interpreters
in their glass booths
at endless international conferences
translating what the peasant from Talca
tells about torture
repeating in English that they put him on the cot
stating in the most refined and delicate French
that electric shock produces lasting transmissible effects
finding the exact equivalent for rape by dogs
pau d'arara I insulted the murderers
finding a phrase without emotion
that describes exactly the sensation
—please forgive any rhymes or rhythms you may find—
when the wall is at your back
and the captain begins to say the word fire,
trying to take the melodrama out of the sentences
trying to communicate the essence and the feeling
without giving in to the dark cloying current
of what they are really saying
they were torturing my son in the other room
they brought back our *compañero* unconscious
they put rats inside our *compañera* it's God's truth.
Not so different from them
with their voices their dictionaries their notes their
culture their going back home
in Geneva in New York in the Hague,
an intermediary—not even a bridge,
simultaneous translation for good pay
because we are specialists
and the incredible thing is that in spite of us
in spite of my river of interpretations and turns of phrase

something is communicated
a part of the howl
a thicket of blood
some impossible tears
the human race has heard something
and is moved.

The Children Are Watching

S everal centuries ago, the Italian philosopher Giambattista
Vico became the first thinker in history to propose that the
essential quality that defines human communities, regardless of country or stage of development or religion, is that they all
invariably engage in coming-together ceremonies that mark transitions, those special occasions in our individual and collective existence when we publicly and ritually share with others the moments
of birth and marriage and death and also, though Vico—who is
known as the father of the social sciences—did not mention them
as such, graduation observances as well.

All these rites of initiation, where we say good-bye to one state
of being and are welcomed into another, are primarily celebrations,
and graduation ceremonies are no exception. We are gathered here
today so that the society and family that has fed you and paid your
way can now rejoice in your accomplishments and in your new
maturity and can also declare to the world that you are ready to face
the challenges that await you outside the institution of higher learning that has nurtured you for the past years. But just because these
moments are jubilant does not mean that they should be allowed to
pass without one last attempt to meditate upon their deeper meaning, what new responsibilities accompany your entry—called for
that very reason a Commencement—into a new world.

I believe that the world you graduate into has the means, the
resources, the technology, and certainly the oft-repeated objective of creating a virtual paradise for the six billion citizens alive
on this planet today. There is some cause for optimism that this
goal may be closer than ever before: in the last decade, the international community has taken gigantic steps toward democratic

Commencement address, American University (Washington, D.C.), May 2001.

rule in scores of countries, the quality of life and life expectancy have been steadily rising across the globe, there is an ever stronger belief in the rights of minorities and women and children, and an increased awareness of the need for a different, ecologically sound approach to the natural world that sustains and surrounds us. Even so, there can be no denying that the lives of most members of our common humanity in this new millennium are mired in misery and need—and I include among these hapless many millions of your abject fellow countrymen, as one of every six children in America is trapped in poverty.

The paradox is glaring: never have the ideals of perfection been so lofty and the technology to achieve them so sophisticated, and yet never have so many people been so far from controlling their own everyday destiny.

At this very moment that I speak to you, terrible things are happening. Words like *war* and *famine, plague* and *child prostitution, corruption* and *torture* and *exploitation* should be part of a vocabulary that belongs to the past, whose excesses should be visited in museums or remarked with detached curiosity in the crumbling pages of ancient books. Instead, these words of sorrow are everywhere, overwhelming, degrading, indeed so prevalent that the naming itself has started to lose its capacity to shock or move us, is gradually becoming part of an indifferent landscape. That is why I always prefer to imagine the individual, one plus one plus one: a child in too many places on this planet is so hungry and emaciated that she cannot at this very moment digest food even if it were to be fed to her a morsel of pap at a time; at this moment that I speak, a bomb is tearing apart somebody's father and also destroying the picture of that father's wedding and the quilt he gave his wife for their anniversary and smashing the toy he had just made for his child; that bomb in too many places; yes, in too many places a woman is being raped at this very moment and another woman's throat is being slit because she has dishonored her family by getting pregnant, at this very moment in Africa the heart of a young man with AIDS has stopped beating and now his brain no longer sends messages of conjecture or remembrance to his hands and those hands, which used to be his, cannot ever again soften into another hand in many, too many places; in far too many places at this very moment a blindfold is being strapped onto an old man's eyes so he will not recognize the men who come toward his naked body; in too many places at this very moment someone is bribing an official so a stream can be polluted, so drugs can poison a street, so guns can cross a frontier, so justice can be undone. And though the majority of these bodies that suffer survive outside the fortunate frontiers of the United States, we should not forget that your country is not immune to such distress and violence, such malnutrition and poverty, such discrimination and abuse.

One might suggest that it is offensive to invite such a host of troubles, these unwanted and unwashed guests to a graduation. But if I have introduced these visitors and their innumerably invisible brothers and sisters to this celebration today, it is not to mitigate our joy or dampen your spirits, but rather to lift those spirits. What a privilege it is that you will soon find yourselves in a position to do something about these troubles. How wonderful that you have received from your university, if it has done its job well, the values and the skills and the intellectual instruments with which to understand the world, act upon it, and change it. How thrilling it is to be young and look out at humanity and see there, staring you in the face, so many millions who have desperate need of your dialogue and intervention. How lucky that you belong to a nation that is so powerful and wealthy that it can allow itself the luxury of wondering how it can help mend the world—a question that leads each of you to the possibility of a magnificent struggle for justice and kindness and tolerance ahead. So a complex and interesting life may indeed await us, as long as we wish to do something about the suffering of others.

Two assumptions underlie my last words. The first assumption is that the disasters of the world are made by men and women and that it is therefore up to those same men and women to fix that world. In other words, that we can undo the conditions that created those man-made catastrophes.

But there is a second, more subtle assumption. I used the words *us* and *we*. Yes. *Us* and *we*. Which means that I take for granted that you, the young who are graduating, are part of the collective that must confront the grief of the world, that you are accountable, along with your elders, for our common fate.

Yes. We. Because a graduation is the precise occasion when you, the class of 2001, start to say we, when you are included in the vast plurality of those who must face a major dilemma, the paradox, my friends, that though you did not make the world as it is, you are nevertheless responsible for it, that world now belongs to you.

This coming of age, this coming into the world, then, is no ordinary transition. How unique and unparalleled and enormous an event it will eventually be in your lives can be best illustrated, I believe, through a story that was first imagined by the great Greek writer from the island of Crete, Nikos Kazantzakis, in his novel *The Last Temptation of Christ* and then reimagined some years ago by Martin Scorsese and his screenwriter, Paul Schrader, in a controversial film. In the celluloid version, Scorsese brings to life on the screen a prophet who is being taken to his crucifixion. He is about to be executed for having preached rebellion against the injustices of his age, for having dared to dream of his nation's liberation from outside interference. The prophet turns to the crowd of bystanders who, along with the young Jesus, is passively watching him being dragged to his death and shouts at them: "Fight, fight! Rise up, rise up, the children are watching! The children are watching!" What that man, who is about to die for his ideas, is howling to those who stand by in dread is that, by their inaction and apathy, they are teaching their children to fear, they are educating their children in impotence and despair, closing the eyes of the future. What that prophet, and indeed every prophet, is proclaiming is that whenever somebody stands aside in the struggle between those who repress and those who rebel, there is a child watching, nearby, nearby, there is always a child watching.

And that is why I have brought up the infinite pain of the world at your graduation. Because from this solemn and joyous moment onwards, you will be faced every day with the decision of whether to rise up against that pain or whether to stand by the wayside and let it continue. It would be presumptuous on my part, and perhaps insulting, to suggest that you have not yourselves suffered or witnessed suffering around you, and I am sure and would hope that, in many cases, you have already tried to do something to alleviate that condition. I would never want to accuse any young person of apathy, the young who are so frequently the most damaged victims of history and are also often those who struggle hardest to contain and stop that damage. This happened recently in Belgrade and Jakarta and in my native Chile where, had it not been for the extraordinary sacrifices of students the same age as those assembled here today, we would still be governed by a dictator who is now indicted for murder and whose name I will not mention so as not to ruin our festivities. This sort of activism happened in your own country not so long ago, in the sixties, when youngsters not older than you are now found themselves at the forefront of the movements for civil rights and free speech and against an unjust war, and today, right now, they are at the forefront of the movement against sweatshops and in favor of fair trade merchandise, which is sweeping campuses across the United States. So why should a graduation mean anything different in your lives?

The answer is that a time invariably comes when young people, who have until then been classified by society as the ones who watch, as the children who inherit an earth they have not yet made, a time comes when those young people grow old enough to make fundamental choices that others, younger than them, will now watch.

That time has come for you. You are no longer the children. You are the ones the children will be watching, and soon enough, in fact, your very own children will be the ones watching you. And twenty or thirty years from now, you will be at the graduation of those children and will be handing them a world that you had a real chance to remake.

The essential question then becomes: Will the world you hand them be better than the one you inherited?

I am not suggesting that the only way to answer yes to that question, the only way to guarantee that it will indeed be improved, is to dedicate your lives to repairing the world of its wrongs twenty-four hours a day. Some of you may decide that this is indeed your calling, but most of us are not meant to be prophets or leaders or even activists, most of us do not look forward to the small crucifixion of the daily grind and even less look forward to the possible final sacrifice of a real crucifixion, the real death that at times awaits those who believe deeply in a cause. I am aware that excessive demands on our time or our commitment can often be self-defeating, leaving us with a sense of frustration instead of courage, of skepticism instead of hope, of guilt instead of altruism. You must each decide for yourselves how much you wish to do, how much you can do, to bequeath your children a world where speeches such as the one I am giving today can become obsolete. Your energy can be channeled through your job or it can be channeled outside your job, it can be dedicated to a large and lifelong cause or to a series of smaller ones, it can engage injustice and discrimination in your neighborhood or in your city, or in your country, itself or in lands whose names you can hardly pronounce but whose misfortunes are all too often the result of the policies of your own government or the consequence of the interests of American companies. So the road you take may be a throbbing avenue or a tiny side street, but what you cannot do, what you should not do, what you must not do, is retreat from the need to journey on some sort of road that leads to service to the rest of humanity. Or as Nikos Kazantzakis himself stated in another book: "Be always restless, unsatisfied, unconforming. Whenever a habit becomes convenient, smash it! The greatest sin of all is satisfaction."

The decision to search and care in this way is not as easy as it looks. Soon, you may be asking yourselves if you can afford to feel the outrage you felt as students, you may ask yourselves if you can risk your status or your standing or your salary by being as critical as you were taught to be in college, soon you may ask yourselves if you have the time to worry about faraway others when there are needy ones in your own home and backyard. And the day is near when you may ask yourselves the most dangerous question of all: Can I make a difference, can anyone make a difference? By then you will have heard many telling you unceasingly that the affliction that surrounds us and saturates us in the media is the natural lot of mankind and that it is therefore better not to tamper with the way things are, because tampering only makes it worse. By then you will have heard over and over that it is best to worry about your own children and forget the remote children of the rest of the world.

So let me confer the only true graduation present somebody like myself can offer. Let me bestow upon you these final words: do not believe those who tell you that you do not matter, that you cannot change the world. Hold fast to the dream that a time can come when people will not slaughter each other due to their national or racial or linguistic or religious or ethnic differences, hold fast to the certainty that it is unnatural that street children be murdered or that their mothers die of hunger or that someone should be denied a job because of the color of her skin or the sex she was born into, hold fast to the belief that we can imagine a world where certain sicknesses can be conquered and medicine can be reasonably within the grasp of those who need it, where women are free to go out at night without looking over their shoulders, where information or cooperation is not extracted from others with a whip or a threat.

These words, then, are my only advice to you at this crucial moment of transition: the world does not have to be the way it is. And also: you can make a difference. You can make a difference.

Let us hope that as the nearby and faraway children incessantly watch you, let us pray you do not disappoint them.

Letter to the
Six Billionth World Citizen

I know what you're up to.

Don't try and deny it: ever since you heard through the baby grapevine that you were slated to be the Six Billionth World Citizen, admit it, you've been planning to go on strike and refuse to be born.

As soon as the other unborn children, using their vast and secret network of intercommunicating worldwide wombs, told you the news, you started to make subversive plans for the day of your solitary birth, what would happen on October 12, 1999, when all the leaders of every legitimate and illegitimate government in the world will, according to your sources, be gathered in the vicinity of your mother's swollen tummy, tumultuously awaiting your presence. You have imagined the scene so many times you could film it, maybe someday you will. The media experts and pundits and camera operators lined up by the thousands, creating havoc in your family's neighborhood. Protestors, held back by the police, chant slogans in favor of birth control and lift placards that scream that there are too many of us already, no more babies! But most of the planet is far more welcoming, most people know that if this is yet another mouth to feed, it is also a mouth that, when it grows, will help solve the problems brought by so many of the other mouths, that this mouth that has arrived may be able to sing for its supper. Most of humanity, let's face it, can't resist a newborn baby. So the world populace is getting ready to watch or listen to the event live from every corner of the earth and celebrate your triumphant arrival. And, of course, in your mind's eye you contemplate legions of doctors and nurses vying for the honor to deliver you, giving

First published in the anthology *Letter to the Sixth Billionth World Citizen* (Amsterdam: Uitgeverij Podium, 1999).

interviews and advice. Yes, you're so close to the hue and cry there, inside that maternal shelter, that you can almost look out through the peephole of your mama's belly button to view what's happening outside, the blue ribbons and the banners waving, and even if your view may be obstructed by the placenta, nobody can stop you from hearing the shining trumpets and the drums—above all you love the percussion, there's never been a culture that hasn't had people banging away with rhythmic relish, rejoicing at the renewal of the universe that accompanies each new child.

And then the great moment arrives and there's your marvelous mom sweating you out as best she can, and we're all cheering you on, and then . . . And then, well, nothing, you don't appear, my little one, my six billionth. Instead, you send this message, resolute, defiant and not at all what one would expect from an exemplary future citizen, a representative of the whole of humanity, someone chosen to make us all look good on this day of all days, you're not behaving according to the script laid out for you, you're not posing for photos and gurgling agoo, agoo, as every obedient baby should. And to make matters worse, it seems that no more babies are being born; rules stipulate that they all have to wait for you, the designated nativity child. And now, in lieu of your presence, what we harvest are these remarkable words mysteriously transmitted straight onto our television screens: "First Message to Humanity: I'm not making my appearance until you people out there, the five billon nine hundred ninety-nine thousand nine hundred ninety-nine, in other words, until the whole gang of the living have fixed the world. Go ahead, get to work!"

Great consternation. Pie on everybody's face. Naturally, they all blame your mother who is not taking your insurrection against birth all that well herself, who is, in fact, in quite a bit of pain, which is something you didn't think of. Well, you've sure managed to disconcert her along with the rest of the world. A murmur of resentment swells up from many quarters: What sort of a baby spoils its own reception in this way?

Let me admit that I'm alternately sympathetic and skeptical regarding this planned rebellion of yours. One part of my mind urges me to join the increasing ranks of your critics. After all, you've been in there for nine months and too much security is not good for anyone, so why don't you just open the door into the world and risk the fabulous adventure of life, like a reasonable child. While another part of me is scandalized by the word *reasonable*. Look at where reason has led us, look at this century, which is ending with over sixty million civilians dead in wars committed in the name of superior reason. Whose reason? Who decides what's reasonable? And this anarchic and playful side of my existence is delighted with this madcap idea of ceasing and desisting from any birth until your babyhood can receive ironclad assurances that the journey upon which you are about to embark is worth the heavy fare you are going to pay at the end of it. And yet, even while both my sides discuss the pros and cons, I am aware that, in the final analysis, this revolt of yours is not going to work. Before the merits of your fetal insurrection can even be submitted to a popular referendum (which is the secret democratic scheme you're hatching in there), I'm afraid the confrontation will be over, and you'll be squealing into the very air that you have been denouncing as toxic and that must be thoroughly cleaned up before you will deign to breathe it. You are aligned, my boy, my girl, against very powerful forces.

They will try to save face. At first, of course, they won't use violence to force you out of the womb. They'll make your stomach rumble with offers of candy and your hands itch with visions of toys and teddy bears, they'll try to flood your mind with all manner of documents and investigations proving how much things have improved. And that's true, things have improved for a few people all of the time and for lots of people part of the time, but not for all of the people all of the time, and that's what you're demanding, right, freedom for everybody. Freedom? The people who want you to be born will point to all the freedoms you are entitled to solely by virtue of your humanity, freedoms guaranteed by innumerable international covenants and treaties and charters that everybody loves to sign (great photo ops, like your birth itself) but which then turn out to be so difficult to enforce back home. So watch out, they'll try to lure you out of your mother's safe haven with a plethora of promises: "We'll study your petition, child, we'll set up a committee to issue a recommendation (some are even implemented, once in a long while, let's not be too cynical here), we'll fix all that soon." The people in charge have been proclaiming similar vows for a good while, just ask the fifth billionth world citizen who was born twelve years ago, or the fourth billionth baby who was born twenty-five years ago. Those infants also threatened, though less vocally and publicly than you have, to decline birth, and they were lured out by the solemn pledge that before the millennium ended, poverty and war would be abolished and men and women would be treated equally and there'd be no more child labor or slavery anywhere and . . . Just ask those former babies if those promises were kept.

But it's clear that you don't need to consult them or, in fact, yours truly either, that you have a strategy of your own, because now, from deep inside the refuge of the other world, comes your enigmatic answer: "Second Message to Humanity: This baby is not convinced. I'm not taking one little push into that planet of yours, not dipping my pinky in the polluted waters of that planet, unless you have created a place where I am not measured by the color of my skin, nor by how much money my parents have accumulated, nor by the country I happen to land in, where my sex or my religion do not determine my freedom as guaranteed in all those charters that everybody quotes so much. There. My nonnegotiable condition for risking life: Deliver unto me a world where every birth gives every child the same wings of opportunity. Level that damn playing field."

Are you aware how dangerous those last words are, particularly that word *damn*? Have you heard of censorship, my dear? Or is that word itself censored in the world of the unborn, so they will not be scared to leap into this earth so full of words and so ripe as well with silence?

What I'm getting at is that if your obstinate diatribes are being carried straight into every residence and conscience on the face of the earth—"And the underbelly of the earth," you add from that deep interior you inhabit, "let's not forget umbilical cords and bellies, after all I am still in here. On strike against a world where some are scarred by knives and excessive malnutrition and others are scarred by indifference and excessive consumption. Neither privileges nor poverty: that's my motto."

Would you please listen to me, child? I'm trying to point out that your actions will make *thousands* of Very Important Folks

Extremely Uncomfortable, and they are by now eagerly looking for a pretext to shut that mouth of yours and intercept any new messages. So watch your language. That's enough—an uncouth word, a slightly off-color joke, anything that some individuals or organizations will take as an obscenity or a blasphemy—that's all they need to cut you off. "Oh, did you hear that? He said damn, she said damn, wash his mouth, her mouth, with soap, and such a young child too, at that early age already using expletives, what is the world coming to, they begin swearing before they're even in the nursery! Sorry. We really have to pull the plug."

And if you dare to lodge a protest with the United Nations—using that word you just unfortunately learned, *censorship*, and invoking all those covenants that supposedly warrant your freedom of speech—the people in charge would answer no, we're not trying to silence this silly baby, not at all. It's simply too expensive to translate those infantile words into all the languages of the world, that's why we've decided to stop transmissions. Financial reasons, you know, restrictions, IMF adjustments, that sort of bottom-line thing.

But all this talk about economics doesn't interest you. It should, as it will determine your life. What really fascinates you is that there are so many languages in the world, thousands of them, something you just realized. Babies speak to each other from their separate wombs through prenatal utterances, they babble in a tongue that is before Babel, they articulate across birth canals and classes and races, they are the first to be surprised that those of us who are already born do not have a common universal code with which to interconnect. "No wonder you're in such trouble," the Six Billionth World Citizen tries to shake that small head in astonishment. "You should have only one language. One, and you'd all understand each other."

And here, perhaps, there is a parting of ways with you, little baby who refuses to be born, because I, for one, believe that all these languages, such a gluttony of them, are the summit of our glory and diversity as a species, the multiple bridges of nuance with which we reach out to one another and domesticate the demons of death. That's the good news. The bad news is that by the time you're my age, by the middle of the next century, many of those languages will have disappeared, and with them entire cultures will be swallowed, even at this very moment somewhere on this Earth of ours one of our ancient brothers and sisters is growing toward death, their individual death that is also the death of the language they bear as its last representative, and when he or she is gone never again will anybody ever pronounce those syllables that contain the memories of the universe, never ever until the end of time and beyond the end of time will two humans make love or make a child in that tongue.

"What!" you exclaim. Your sudden rage makes your mother complain, rub her tummy, wish you wouldn't take this long to crawl out. But you exclaim the same "What!" again. "Extinct!" you say, and you note this atrocity down indignantly, and you decide, then and there, right now, in fact, to add another demand to your already long list of nonnegotiable conditions for birth. "Here," you say, "right after the stipulation that *The Poorest Baby Will Have the Same Chances As the Richest One* and just before the condition that *No Future Child Shall Be Forced to Become a Target of Bombs or the Worse Fate of Being the One Who Bombs That Human Target from Afar*, right there, in between, we'll squeeze these words in: *This Baby Decrees That All Languages Are Created Equal, and Those Now in Existence Will Be Preserved and Encouraged to Expand by Offering Resources to the Communities in Which That Language, Just Like a Child, Has Been Born and Nurtured.*

"There," you say to the lawmakers of the world who have not exactly been anxious to enact such directives in the past, who think there are more crucial things to be done with scarce funds, such as pay back loans to banks. "There! Take that. This baby will not tolerate any form of linguistic extermination or genocide."

And all of a sudden, I am filled with sadness and dread for the first time since your strike started. That you should have used that word, that you should know exactly and minutely what it means, a word that should be a stranger to us both and to every other breathing human and animal and plant on this earth, so strange to us that if it ever came up, as it has just now, we humans would gaze at each other in bewilderment, wondering what those sounds could possible allude to. Genocide? Genocide? It deserves to be incarcerated in archaic dictionaries instead of defining the century that is ending, this century you are just managing to enter by a squeak.

And you *are* going to enter this century and this humanity. Adults tend to be patient with children, but you may have crossed the line. At this very moment you are denying your elders their drinks! By now, they presumed, they would be uncorking the champagne bottles. No, not for you, little one, you're underage, you're not supposed to guzzle booze until you're old enough. But what I was trying to get at when you so rudely interrupted your own self and got us off track is that if the temptations and the sweet talk falter, if the friendly catalog of longer lives and better health and less illiteracy worldwide (all true, my little one, all true) is not met by your instant and obsequious birth, I'm afraid the people in charge will be forced to resort to more extreme methods. It's against their will, you understand, they're reluctant to apply violence. According to the men (mostly men, my little one) who have all those weapons at their disposal, it's always a last resort, only to be used when all else has failed, but use it they have and use it they will. You're *expected*, my dear, you've been *announced*. My God, you R S V P'd that you could make it, and your hosts won't allow you to irresponsibly back down at the last moment—you'll simply have to join the party for the Six Billionth World Citizen.

"But that's the point," you spout out excitedly, in one of your last messages. Time is running out, my tiny mutineer. "That's exactly the point I want to make. My strike against birth is to protest the fact that there are far too many places where that word *citizen* is empty, a dream of what we'd like people to be rather than a description of what people really are. And that word *world* designates a globe shattered with shrapnel and so fragmented and divided that it can't really be said to belong to those of us who live on it, let alone those who are about to arrive. And as to the word *billionth*, it's outrageous that there are so many of us and that we still haven't been able to figure out something as simple and obvious as the need for not one of those billions to go to bed hungry at night, how can it be? So I'm not withdrawing from the celebration; it's the celebration that is withdrawing from me. I'm merely trying to impose a true meaning on this name that you living beings have plopped on me like a diaper, plunged into me like a nice bottle of mildly heated milk. All I want is to be greeted by one beautiful world instead of twenty beautiful letters."

One beautiful world.

There are voices that repeat those three words to themselves, One Beautiful World.

They are pondering an offer, those voices. A real temptation. Not a few succulent slurps of food or some glossy toys or the evaporating promises of mere mortals. This offer is being made by the gods and godfathers of dark energy of the universe, the forces above and beyond and below who control the ebb and flow of time. These are powers that deliver. Or don't deliver, if you piss them off. And they happen to be exasperated by what they call the Dilemma of the Stubborn Fetus. They've been getting irate calls from their allies, powerful people on Earth. And have decided to take the matter in hand and bring it to a close. You want a beautiful world? They have one for you.

The Lords of Life and Death begin by waving a thick set of statistics in your face.

But you insolently—and imprudently, I might add—correct them right off the bat. "In my face? Hold it," you pipe up. "In fact, those statistics are being waved outside my mama's round bulging breadbasket, right? I don't have a real face yet."

"Quiet! You will remain quiet!" Because your visitors do not like jokes. "What sort of face you'll have, whether that face will be slapped repeatedly, that's the question you should be attending to. Whether you'll even have a face or if it will be eaten by dogs and what horrors or joys that face might see as soon as it is born. That's what should worry you. Now. Statistics. A science that calculates your probable future. Prognosticating that you will probably land somewhere in Asia or Africa or Latin America, and that, furthermore, you will be born poor. This victorious reception you're conjuring up, all those parades in your honor and Heads of State—it's all an illusion, fed to you by the other babies because they feel sorry for you. You'll be lucky if you get so much as a midwife."

There is a moment of silence. You tremble and wait for their next gambit. Here it comes: "However," those voices continue, "in view of the fact that you have indeed been selected to represent humanity, we could come to . . . let us call it, an arrangement. Because there is also a chance—a very slight one—that you might see the light of day among the opulent few, and if you care to cooperate, we could make it worth your while. We could guarantee, for instance, that you wouldn't be born a woman in one of those areas of the world that we prefer not to name in order to avoid hurting any national feelings, but if you were born there, well, your freedom to choose a spouse, for one, would be severely limited. Or we could orchestrate things so you don't wind up in a village where your female genitalia might be mutilated. We'd make sure that you were placed elsewhere, well placed and in an area that is technologically primed. With a chance of getting cloned in half a century. Immortality," they say, "is not something to be sniffed at. All you need to do is let yourself be born without a fuss. You pose for some baby-food ads, appear in a couple of cheery news items, and we'll take care of the rest. A mutually beneficial solution. We'd look good and you'd look good. In fact, you'd look like a million dollars."

I know your answer almost before I hear it: "This rebellion," you say, my little six billionth utopian and heroic and unrealistic citizen, "is not on my behalf. This transitory abstinence from the pleasures and music of life is not to make things better for little me-myself-and-I. I didn't ask for this job. Maybe worse than being that woman your lordships were describing is to be born to a family in a society so wealthy that it is able to shut its children off from the pain of others. I wouldn't want to turn into a young man who doesn't care that on the other side of the planet (or the other side of his city) someone who could have been him, who might be me, is about to be damaged beyond repair. Damn it, just let me be a human being! Isn't that what I'm supposed to be?"

That's a great little final speech, but it is a final one. Your egalitarian curtain call. The last straw. You have sealed your fate. And now, the show must go on, the ceremony can't be postponed, the millennial clock is ticking, your mother is having a dreadful time, you're her hostage and she's a hostage of the world, and your dad is beginning to get all sorts of sneaky looks from the community. What sort of a tiny troublemaker are we bringing into this world supermarket? And no, please don't get started on markets and market economics—they're not going to let another word of yours get through. Now's when you're going to be pressured into birth; there are all sorts of drugs and machines and massages and methods and herbs and incantations and surgeons and who knows what

else, and you will not be able to resist for long, even if you are the
lucky six billionth, even if the whole world is watching. Not even
that can ultimately save you: think of all the horrible things that
we humans have quite blatantly and madly done to each other and
to ourselves while the whole world was watching. Though I don't
want this little exchange of ours to end on an overly negative note,
my little one: things of wonder also materialize when the world
watches in its entirety. Wait until you're old enough to look at the
World Soccer Cup, and that's only one of the bizarre rituals of global
bonding that awaits you. I don't want you to get the impression
that everything out here's gloomy and depressing.

So prepare yourself for what lies ahead, good and bad, because
you'd better believe me that you won't be able to hold out much
longer.

We've all tried. You're not the first one. Every baby in the world
makes the attempt and does not manage it. Unborn children are a
fractious, squabbling bunch who know that they had better stick
out their tiny tongues in the nest, where nobody can see them,
before they find themselves at the mercy of a pair of hands and a
pair of eyes and a hovering face, before they are classified, you over
here to this mansion, you over there to the mud outside that hut.
The unborn know that once they've left the warmth of the womb,
they can be punished, you could and will be punished, my boy,
my girl, for sticking your tongue out really far, spanked and sent
to bed for not accepting Orders from Above. It's been tried before,
every one of us alive has tried it before we were born at least six
billion times. So it's you against the six billion others, and you're
just going to have to take your chances like the rest of us and try
to change things from this side of reality, where conditions and
dreams are less utopian and more messy, those are the cards that
have been dealt to us.

"It doesn't matter," you sing to me, always the optimist. "I'll be
born and I'll go on strike right away, we'll change the world, all
of us, as soon as I arrive."

Should I tell you the truth?

You'll forget. You'll forget you ever rebelled as an unborn child,
and you'll forget these words you said and the words I am murmuring back to you now, as we say good-bye.

That's the price we all pay for being born.

And now, as the day, the night, the dawn, the minute, the second before your birth approaches, just before you become the six billionth world citizen, I visualize you there at the dream frontier that has always existed between the unborn and the living.

You are in line, waiting your turn. In front of you and to the sides and behind are vast stretches of others, just like you, awaiting inspection. We have all been there, passed this scan and scrutiny and scrubbing that happens on the way to existence—every man, every woman, each philosopher and each idiot, the few kings and the many peasants—they have all watched, as you do now, the other babies being searched by the border guards, stripped down to the bone of memory and then even the bone is gone, slashed away. Everything except your nakedness will be taken from you and the blurred promise of future hands that are about to receive you, the hands that chance will make warm or cold, loving or distant, black or white or yellow or brown. On your way to life you must give up even the stories that the deep dead told you as they passed through the womb on their way to extinction, their last chance to leave a memory with someone, anyone, all gone.

Now you step up, the part of you that remembers, that will be left behind and that has to be purged, erased like a slate in order to accompany the body, you step up and there is a lull, the hesitation of an interlude, and in its hollow you are suddenly beset by fear, the fangs of a white fear worse than anything you have felt before or anything you will ever feel again, the knowledge that the life that awaits you is no more than a flicker of light between the void you are about to leave and the pit of nothingness that already haunts the light and devours it at the end. Suddenly, all your bravado and ingenuity and defiance are gone, and you are no more than a baby.

And even though you may be the Six Billionth World Citizen, there is no dispensation for you. The Head Guard, angel or demon, who commands that boundary is not authorized to relieve that panic. And he's not very sympathetic anyway. He's impatient, behind in his quota, the souls are piling up, you've held everybody up for hours, you rejected the Upper Offer of a Better Existence, if you don't take that leap forward on your own, they're going to slingshot you over so fast you won't know what hit you, they're going to have to—

You look across the border, you call into the womb of the lonely world for a word, for something to take with you, one little thing that the rest of us, the almost six billion others, can send you as a gift of farewell or a gift of greeting.

And if we have failed, in spite of all our efforts, to change the world and make it perfect for you, little one, and for all your brothers and sisters, if in that we have fallen short, in this, at least, we can offer help.

Here is our voice, here is the First Message from Humanity to the Six Billionth World Citizen, here it is:

Don't be afraid. We are waiting for you.

What more can I say, can we say, to your shadow as you are finally born?

Conclusion As Manifesto

Imagining a Possible Peace

The world does not have to be the way it is.

Each moment softly taken into captivity by each photographer for peace, each storyteller for peace, is precarious. It can cease to be. It has, in a way, already ceased to be the very moment we look at it—a few hours, a few days, a few decades later. And yet, there is a hushed victory in the image that still tells us, if even for an instant, that everything could be different, the prayer that everything could be different, that possibility.

The world does not have to be the way it is.

The same technology that brings us war can also bring us images of peace. The same click that sounds when a trigger goes off and a missile is guided to its target can also sound so that the lenses of a camera may capture trees, elephants, cathedrals, old couples at rest who cry out for an armistice.

The world does not have to be the way it is.

We have created a planet where what matters most, what sells most, what entertains most is the spectacular. And violence has become the spectacle to end and outsell all spectacles. To watch that violence leaves us sullied and is an inevitably obscene act. Because we either can do nothing about it and are contaminated by our impotence. Or we enjoy what we are seeing and are turned into accomplices. Peace, on the other hand, can never be a spectacle. For peace to exist, to really exist, we have to become part of the pact between the eye that sees and the object that reveals itself, between the object that sees and the eye that begs for revelation. Peace is impossible without dialogue, without giving as

---

Commissioned for the book of photos *Pictures of Peace* (New York: Alfred A. Knopf, 1991).

you take, without understanding that the other truly exists and is open to pain.

The world does not have to be the way it is.

The history of war has been the history of a failure to see. Distance has become necessary to kill comfortably, to erase that killing before it happened and after it happened. So it can happen again. Get near enough, get inside the person who is to die, and killing (how I hope what I say is true) would be, should be, unthinkable. Killing is a matter of distance.

The world does not have to be the way it is.

These pictures invite you in. They demand that, for the instant they last, during the island that they are in a world gone mad, we share the vision of hope at the edge of disaster, we share the bodies that have not been mothered so that they might damage one another irreparably. And for the enduring flash of their existence, these controlled recollections wonder whether we could not invade the world with that vision, if we could not spread it from the pictures out into the universe that threatens these images with extinction, if we could not make beauty as contagious as anger and make the world over and over and over as if on the eighth day of creation.

The world does not have to be the way it is.

Each image insists: This is how it could have been. This is how it might be. If we saw it like this, even if only for that vulnerable instant that perseveres in the crack between the violence that comes before and the violence that stretches out afterward, if we build it with our eyes, if we imagine it as possible and necessary, how can we not be able to build it in the reality that awaits us outside the pictures for peace?

Please believe me. Let it be so.

The world does not have to be the way it is.

Acknowledgments

IT WOULD TAKE another book to thank those who helped me write these multiple provocations, and it would take far too many pages to explain why and how this support arrived.

This book covers, after all, almost a quarter of a century of exile and wanderings through the world, returns home to Chile, and my ensuing voluntary expatriation—difficult years that my family and I could not have survived, nor could have my writings, without the enthusiasm and assistance of hundreds of friends, colleagues, and *compañeros*.

I will, therefore, simply state here—with hardly an adjective or an adverb—those who were directly responsible for the works anthologized here. Starting with my wife, Angélica, my first reader, and the other readers in my immediate family: Rodrigo, Joaquín, and Melissa. And going on to my agent, Jin Auh, at the Wylie Agency, my agent for Spanish, Raquel de la Concha, and my editor at Seven Stories Press, Dan Simon—all of whom are also dear friends. And my assistant, Jennifer Prather, who laboriously recuperated and typed out so many of these versions and subversions and rescued some from the purgatory of the Internet. Tom Englehardt, you know what I owe you. Thanks to India Amos and Anna Lui at Seven Stories, M. Mark at the *Village Voice*, my many editors at *El País* (Joaquín Estefanía, María Cordón, Carlos Tasitano, Lluis Bassets), Bob Berger at the *Los Angeles Times*, Kathleen Cahill at the *Washington Post* Outlook section, Becky Sinkler at the *New York Times Book Review*, Marie Arana Ward at the *Washington Post Book World*, Annalena McAfee at the *London Guardian*, Adrian Hamilton at the *London Independent*, Mike Holland at the *London Observer*, Anthony Barnett at Open Democracy, Howard Goldberg at the *New York Times* op-ed section, Ian Jack at *Granta*, Ron Weber and Peter Hakim and Pat Breslin at the Inter American Foundation, Nick Hern at Nick Hern Books, Paul Slovak and Nan Graham at Penguin, Susan Gray (editor of *Writers on Directors*), Kofi Annan for inviting me to address the United Nations General Assembly on World Press Freedom Day, Howard Chua-Eoan, George Russell and Alberto Vourvoulias at *Time* magazine, Lou Goodman of American University, Ursula Owen at *Index on Censorship*, Liz McMillen at the *Chronicle of Higher Education*, and Anne Fadiman at *American Scholar*.

To one and all, it is my hope that this book you helped me write is worthy of the relief you gave me through years that were difficult both for me and for the world.